JOYCE EFFECTS
On Language, Theory, and .

Joyce Effects is a series of connected essays by one of today's leading commentators on James Joyce. Joyce's books, Derek Attridge argues, go off like fireworks, and one of this book's aims is to enhance the reader's enjoyment of these special effects. He also examines another sort of effect: the way Joyce's writing challenges and transforms our understanding of language, theory, and history. Attridge's exploration of these transforming effects represents fifteen years of close engagement with Joyce, and reflects the changing course of Joyce criticism during this period. Each of Joyce's four major books is addressed in depth, while several shorter chapters take up particular theoretical topics such as character, chance and coincidence, historical writing and narrative, as they are staged and scrutinized in Joyce's writing. Through lively and accessible discussion, this book advances a mode of reading open to both the pleasures and the surprises of the literary work.

Derek Attridge is Leverhulme Research Professor at the University of York and Distinguished Visiting Professor at Rutgers University.

JOYCE EFFECTS

ON LANGUAGE, THEORY, AND HISTORY

DEREK ATTRIDGE

CAMBRIDGE
UNIVERSITY PRESS

PUBLISHED BY THE PRESS SYNDICATE OF THE UNIVERSITY OF CAMBRIDGE
The Pitt Building, Trumpington Street, Cambridge, United Kingdom

CAMBRIDGE UNIVERSITY PRESS
The Edinburgh Building, Cambridge, CB2 2RU, UK   http://www.cup.cam.ac.uk
40 West 20th Street, New York, NY 10011–4211, USA   http://www.cup.org
10 Stamford Road, Oakleigh, Melbourne 3166, Australia

First published 2000

Printed in the United Kingdom at the University Press, Cambridge

Typeset in Baskerville 11/12.5pt [VN]

A catalogue record for this book is available from the British Library

Library of Congress Cataloguing in Publication data
Attridge, Derek
Joyce effects: on language, theory, and history / Derek Attridge.
p.   cm.
Includes bibliographical references and index.
ISBN 0 521 66112 9 (hardback)
1. Joyce, James, 1882–1941 – Criticism and interpretation.
2. Literature and history – Ireland – History – 20th century.
3. Joyce, James, 1882–1941 – Language.   I. Title.
PR6019.09Z525647   2000
823'.912–dc21   99–30727   CIP

ISBN 0 521 66112 9 hardback
ISBN 0 521 77788 7 paperback

For Laura and Eva
avant la lettre

Contents

vii

Acknowledgements

Earlier versions of the named chapters appeared in the following publications (sometimes under different titles), and the original editors and publishers are gratefully acknowledged:

'Introduction: On Being a Joycean' in *A Collideorscape of Joyce: Festschrift for Fritz Senn*, ed. Ruth Frehner and Ursula Zeller (Lilliput Press, 1998; reprinted with the permission of the Lilliput Press); 'Deconstructive Criticism of Joyce' and 'Joyce and the Ideology of Character' in *James Joyce: The Augmented Ninth. Papers from the Ninth International James Joyce Symposium*, ed. Bernard Benstock (Syracuse University Press, 1988; reprinted with the permission of Syracuse University Press); 'Popular Joyce?' in *Joyce and Popular Culture*, ed. R. B. Kershner (University Press of Florida, 1996; reprinted with the permission of the University Press of Florida); 'Touching "Clay": Reference and Reality in *Dubliners*' in *Le dit et le non-dit* (*Tropismes* 6), ed. Jean-Jacques Lecercle (Université de Paris X – Nanterre, 1993); 'Joyce, Jameson, and the Text of History' in *'Scribble' 1: genèse des textes*, Revue des Lettres Modernes, Série James Joyce, 1, ed. Claude Jacquet (Minard, 1988); 'Molly's Flow: The Writing of "Penelope" and the Question of Women's Language' in *Modern Fiction Studies* 35 (1989), special issue *Feminist Readings of Joyce*, ed. Ellen Carol Jones; 'The Postmodernity of Joyce: Chance, Coincidence, and the Reader' in *Joyce Studies Annual 1995* (©1995 by the University of Texas Press; reprinted with the permission of the University of Texas Press); 'Countlessness of Livestories: Narrativity in *Finnegans Wake*' in *Joyce in the Hibernian Metropolis: Essays*, ed. Morris Beja and David Norris (University of Ohio Press, 1996; reprinted with the permission of the University of Ohio Press); 'Finnegans Awake, or the Dream of Interpretation' in *James Joyce Quarterly* 27 (1989; University of Tulsa); 'The *Wake*'s Confounded Language' in *Coping with Joyce: Essays from the Copenhagen Symposium*, ed.

Morris Beja and Shari Benstock (Ohio State University Press, 1989; reprinted with the permission of the Ohio State University Press).

References and abbreviations

The following abbreviations, editions, and methods of reference have been used:

D   James Joyce, *Dubliners*, ed. Robert Scholes and A. Walton Litz (New York: Viking, 1969). References to page number.

FW   James Joyce, *Finnegans Wake* (London: Faber & Faber, 1939). References in the form page number.line number (e.g., *FW* 318.24). (Only the first line number of the passage given.) All editions have the same pagination.

Letters James Joyce, *Letters*, ed. Stuart Gilbert and Richard Ellmann, 3 vols. (New York: Viking, 1957–66). References to volume and page number.

P   James Joyce, *A Portrait of the Artist as a Young Man*. Ed. Hans Walter Gabler with Walter Hettche. New York: Garland/Viking, 1993. References in the form section number.line number (e.g. *P* IV.796). (Only the first line number of the passage given.)

SH   James Joyce, *Stephen Hero*. Ed. Theodore Spencer, revised John J. Slocum and Herbert Cahoon. London: Jonathan Cape, 1956. References to page numbers in this edition.

U   James Joyce, *Ulysses: The Corrected Text*. Ed. Hans Walter Gabler with Wolfhard Steppe and Claus Melchior. London: Bodley Head and Penguin, 1986. References in the form episode number.line number (e.g., *U* 13.950).

Critical Heritage Robert H. Deming, ed., *James Joyce: The Critical Heritage*. 2 vols. London: Routledge & Kegan Paul, 1970. References to volume and page number.

JJ   Richard Ellmann, *James Joyce*. Revised edition. Oxford and New York: Oxford University Press, 1982.

Preface

A lambskip for the marines! Paronama! The
entire horizon cloth! All effects in their joints caused
ways. Raindrum, windmachine, snowbox.

(FW 502.36)

Joyce's four major books, *Dubliners*, *A Portrait of the Artist as a Young Man*, *Ulysses*, and *Finnegans Wake*, all go off like inventive and spectacular fireworks, and one response is to sit back and enjoy them – enjoy their intricate construction, their subtle phrasings, their play with conventions and expectations, their engagement with the twists and turns of history, their often hilarious exposure of prejudice and pomposity. Joyce effects are dazzling, funny, sometimes disconcerting, occasionally astringent or even lethal. Like the special effects of the pantomime tradition, or those of which Hollywood is currently so enamoured, Joyce effects, while they amaze or entrance the audience, openly invite admiration for the skill of the artificer. Whatever argument I pursue in the different parts of this book, I try always to reflect my own pleasure in these effects and to do them some kind of critical justice. Although I have been able to touch on only a few textual moments in Joyce's writing, examined in the light of wider concerns, my hope is that the reader's enjoyment of his *œuvre* as a whole will be enhanced and some of the characteristic effects of each of the four works given renewed power to awe and entertain.

The Joyce effects that form the main focus of my attention, however, are of a different kind. These are the effects *produced* by his work, when it is read with the attention and commitment it demands – effects upon the way we think about a number of significant topics, and upon our involvement in other cultural (and more than cultural) activities. Readers of all sorts have testified to the transformative power of Joyce's writing; perhaps more than any other twentieth-century author he has

xiii

changed the way we conceive of literature and a variety of other institutions and practices, including language, history and historiography, sex and sexuality, and modes of interpretation. *Joyce Effects* examines a number of these incitements to reconsider our attitudes and concepts, not as a matter of past cultural history but as continuing challenges to thought. I make no claim that this book demonstrates what Joyce's writing is *really* about; my aim is simply to bring alive for the reader certain issues that it raises (or better, that it powerfully and pleasurably dramatizes) as the twentieth century gives way to the twenty-first. For the most important effects of literature are not mechanical consequences of the text; they are the products of readings that are simultaneously faithful responses and fresh inventions, rediscovering the literary work in its original time and place while making it anew for the reader's time and place.

Critical essays, like works of literature, belong to their moment of production at the same time as they lay claim to a future effectiveness. The chapters of this book present a history of changing responses to Joyce (both personal responses and those of a wider body of readers and critics) over the period 1984 to 1999; at the same time they elaborate a continuing intellectual project which I believe to be still valid. Indeed, in some ways it seems to me more urgent now than when I wrote the earliest of these pieces. That project – which started with the four chapters on Joyce in my *Peculiar Language* (published in 1988) – involves an attempt to do justice to the literary not as some timeless and absolute realm, but as a concrete cultural space produced by, but not reducible to, the social, economic, and political forces at work at any given moment. Literary works have effects precisely because they do not float free from the material and intellectual conditions of their time – and 'their time' should be understood both as the time of writing and the time of reading – but perform a kind of staging of those conditions, whether in a spirit of interrogation or celebration or (as often with Joyce) both. They do so not from a political, moral, or religious platform raised above the terrain they survey (though they can function in all of these non-literary ways as well) but out of their own semi-submerged situation, half in and half out of the determining circumstances of the time.

My various endeavours to register the effects of reading Joyce over the past fifteen years have all been motivated by this interest in the peculiar capacity of literature to engage with crucial intellectual, ethical, and political issues without attempting to resolve them, and by a fascination with the specific ways in which Joyce, through an extraordinary linguistic and generic inventiveness, was able to make the most of this potential. From one point of view, this book is a reading of some central features of Joyce's works that aims to bring out the contribution they make to an understanding of the literary, such as its complicated relation to referentiality and to historiography, its linking of the linguistic and the erotic, and its capacity to both tempt and frustrate the hermeneutic drive. From another point of view, it is a discussion of some central features of the literary using Joyce's writing as a kind of testing ground, chosen for this purpose because those features are both heightened and troubled in it. From either point of view, of course, it is possible to ask: why this particular set of choices? Construed as primarily a book on Joyce, it prompts the question, 'Why concentrate on these particular literary issues and not others that are also operative in important ways in his writing?' Construed as a book on the nature of the literary, it prompts the question, 'Why choose Joyce as an exemplar and not other writers who also address and work through these issues?'

The obvious answer is that I believe the issues I have chosen to be particularly important ones in the current state of our understanding of literature and the literary, and that I believe Joyce to be a particularly important figure in the twentieth-century's investigation of, and exploitation of, these issues. Joyce's version of modernism, that is to say, by producing heightened attention to *both* language in its multiplicity of forms and functions *and* the concrete world of sensation, emotion, drive, and desire, situates the literary precisely in the conjunction or crossover of the cultural and the material – hence his curiously double notoriety, as exceptionally difficult in his handling of language and exceptionally direct in his handling of the body and the world it encounters. At the same time, it would be absurd to claim that there are not many other significant issues that his work addresses or that there are not many other writers who address the issues I have chosen to concentrate on. There is, however, a further answer to the question of choice, which relates to a third way of viewing the book: as the representation of a particular fifteen-year history, both mine as a reader of and commentator on Joyce and that of literary criticism, especially Joyce criticism, more generally. There is, that is to say, an element of historical contingency about the scope and targets of these essays, begun as they were in response to a variety of invitations and opportunities and first published in a variety of places, but it is a historical contingency which I hope is itself illuminating for anyone interested in the situation of the literary critic, and the place of the literary, in the late twentieth century.

In order to bring out this aspect of the book, the introductory chapter provides an autobiographical framework for the pieces that follow (in the context of the changing climate of Joyce criticism), as well as pursuing some of the theoretical implications of the critical trajectory depicted in this chronological account. After the introduction, the main spine of the book consists of four long essays – chapters 3, 5, 8, and 11 – that take up in turn *Dubliners, A Portrait of the Artist as a Young Man, Ulysses*, and *Finnegans Wake*. Each of these chapters focuses on a particular topic (or set of related topics) that lies at the heart of the work in question. My claim in each case is that the work effects a revaluation of many of the habits of thought that underpin conventional assumptions about the particular subject addressed in the chapter. *Dubliners* is known for its tight embrace of the real; my essay, starting from one paragraph in 'Clay', asks what Joyce's method in the collection suggests about the process whereby a literary work – or language more generally – *refers* to what we think of as the real world. The topic explored in the chapter on *A Portrait* is the relation between language and sex, two of the most powerful forces in the novel, an exploration that leads to a consideration of the wider issue of the peculiar potency of literary language in its relation to bodily experience. The essay on *Ulysses* concentrates on the final episode of the book, Molly Bloom's nocturnal monologue, examining Joyce's challenge to our thinking about the representation of gender in language and by language. Finally, I broach the issue that *Finnegans Wake* raises for every one of its readers – interpretation – by taking a hard look, historically and theoretically, at the notion that the book represents a single long dream. These essays all attempt to start afresh in approaching these works and these subjects (a project which can have only limited success, of course, since we are able to rid ourselves of only so much of our inherited web of prejudices and mental habits), and treat the dominant critical assumptions about Joyce's books as products of historical processes that bear careful examination. Thus, for example, I question the well-entrenched notions that *Dubliners* is an exercise in careful realism, that Molly's style is the embodiment of a feminine fluidity, that *Finnegans Wake* is so strange because it portrays a dream. My purpose is not to dismiss these critical commonplaces, or the large body of fine exegetical work they have made possible, but to create space for alternative approaches that may bring with them new ways of enjoying, and experiencing the vivid and lasting effects of, Joyce's writing. The book ends with a chapter that I believe is in the spirit of that writing: a self-questioning which is at the same time a questioning of the state of Joyce criticism as the new millennium begins.

Interspersed among these longer chapters are shorter pieces, tracing a number of other Joyce effects, in both senses of the word. Each was written for a specific occasion, usually a talk that formed part of a panel about some particular aspect of Joyce's work, and marks a moment in the fifteen-year history which the book represents. In a couple of cases, where this seemed particularly relevant, I have indicated precisely the nature of that original occasion. The subjects that these pieces address (or rather that they show Joyce ingeniously addressing) include character, chance and coincidence, history and historical writing, and – through the *Wake*'s evident challenge to these notions – narrative and linguistic transparency. I have resisted the temptation to expand these pieces to the length of the other chapters, believing that their brevity is part of their suggestiveness, and that the reader will have no difficulty in locating further relevant examples or in imagining how a fuller discussion could be developed.

Language is a constant concern throughout the book, as it surely must be in a full response to a writer like Joyce, but not in isolation from those processes that give rise to it and upon which it impinges: the physical body, the literary institution, the movements of history, and the network of power relations that entails, among other things, political authority, gender, education, and class. Joyce understood as well as anybody that language is not one thing with one origin or one function; the challenge to his readers is, in every sense, to live up to that comprehensive awareness.

In the course of fifteen years of writing on an author, and the numerous conferences, visits, collaborative projects, communications via e-mail and snail mail, and other opportunities for interchange that writing on an author like Joyce encourages, the number of debts one accumulates are such that to acknowledge all of them (or even all of which one is conscious) would produce something like one of the monstrous lists in *Finnegans Wake*, and detract from the very genuine gratitude motivating the gesture. I shall therefore run the opposite risk and avoid names, hoping that no one feels unappreciated in consequence, and simply express my thanks to all those whose conversation and writing have spurred and enriched my thinking on Joyce. I also thank those who invited me to give the talks out of which most of these chapters arose, all those who listened, all those who asked questions or made comments. My thanks, too, to those who asked me to contribute to collections and journal issues, and those whose editorial work improved many of these texts on their first publication. I am indebted to the book's anonymous readers, and the editors, copy-editors, designers, and many others at Cambridge University Press who have, not for the first time, made me the author of a better book for their patient and expert labours. I was able to complete *Joyce Effects*, in spite of the distraction of a change of institution and country, thanks to the award of a Research Professorship by the Leverhulme Trust. I am grateful to Laura and Eva Attridge for putting up with my writing of yet another book for grown-ups, and to Suzanne Hall for more than I can say here, or anywhere.

Glasgow–New Brunswick–Cambridge–York

INTRODUCTION

On being a Joycean

MAINLY AUTOBIOGRAPHICAL

I was taught not to like Joyce. The semicolonial experience I shared with him did not count for anything in the literary education I received during the 1950s at an all-white English-medium South African high school, which – in spite of being in the state education system – modelled itself on a certain idea of the Victorian public school. I remember being taught Shakespeare and Shaw, George Eliot and the Georgian poets, but little that could be called 'modernist'. (However, I used school prize money to buy anthologies of recent poetry, and discovered in the work of a writer named Dylan Thomas a linguistic exuberance that at once baffled and excited me.) The English department at the university to which I proceeded in the early 1960s, also in South Africa, broadened my horizons considerably, but still within strict bounds. As was the case with many colonial English departments, its guiding spirit was the English critic F. R. Leavis, and the curriculum was based, for poetry, on the winnowed canon he presented in *Revaluation* and *New Bearings*, for fiction, on the equally circumscribed list of writers celebrated in *The Great Tradition*, and, for methodology, on 'close reading' or 'practical criticism' (for behind Leavis was the influential figure of I. A. Richards). (Not that this methodology was ever offered *as* a methodology; it was just what we did when we did English.) D. H. Lawrence was the presiding genius of twentieth-century literature and cultural criticism, followed at some distance by T. S. Eliot; Conrad and James were their most illustrious forebears. (However, I picked up e. e. cummings's *Eimi* in a book sale, and went through it with a mixture of relish and consternation.)

I don't remember any extended engagement with Joyce, and no doubt many of my teachers shared Lawrence's hostile reaction to his fellow-writer. The following characteristic Lawrentian comments presumably had a strong effect, the first, from 1923, on *Ulysses* (and Dorothy

Richardson's *Pilgrimage*), the second, from 1928, on *Work in Progress*, as it was appearing in the Paris-based magazine *transition* before publication as *Finnegans Wake*:

Through thousands and thousands of pages Mr Joyce and Miss Richardson tear themselves to pieces, strip their smallest emotions to the finest threads, till you feel you are sewed inside a wool mattress that is being slowly shaken up, and you are turning to wool along with the rest of the woolliness. (*Selected Literary Criticism*, 115)

James Joyce bores me stiff – too terribly would-be and done-on-purpose, utterly without spontaneity or real life. (*Selected Literary Criticism*, 149)

Leavis, in his notoriously dismissive review of *Work in Progress*, 'James Joyce and the "Revolution of the Word"', quoted the best known of Lawrence's fulminations against Joyce: 'Nothing but old fags and cabbage-stumps of quotations from the Bible and the rest, stewed in the juice of deliberate, journalistic dirty-mindedness' (Lawrence, *Selected Literary Criticism*, 148).[1] It was a view with which Leavis clearly had much sympathy. Although he felt some admiration for *Ulysses*, he detected in it 'a certain vicious bent manifested . . . in the inorganic elaborations and pedantries', and the chapters of *Finnegans Wake* appearing in *transition* he found to be pervaded by 'spuriousness' and 'mechanical manipulation' ('James Joyce and the "Revolution of the Word"', 107, 198). That Joyce did not loom large in my English classes is hardly to be wondered at.

My experience in a South African English department was probably very similar to that of many others at institutions of higher learning throughout the English-speaking world in the early sixties.[2] The powerful Lawrentian/Leavisian model, premised on a moral earnestness and an attachment to organicism that left little room for playful ingenuity or the foregrounding of linguistic and literary conventions, for effects of the Joycean kind, fostered in students an appreciation of strenuous verbal engagements with perennial human dilemmas but did so at the cost of rendering them impervious to the pleasures and insights of a large body of literary writing. This was not just a matter of being taught to prefer one type of writing to another; the enjoyment of the favoured authors

---

[1] Joyce was almost as unflattering about Lawrence: 'That man really writes very badly', he advised Nino Frank, and he wrote to Harriet Shaw Weaver about *Lady Chatterley's Lover*: 'I read the first 2 pages of the usual sloppy English and [Stuart Gilbert] read me a lyrical bit about nudism in a wood and the end which is a piece of propaganda in favour of something which, outside of D. H. L.'s country at any rate, makes all the propaganda for itself' (*JJ* 615n).

[2] South African universities were not, at that time, distinguished from British universities by a special interest in South African or African literature; as students we were led to believe that not very much of value had been written close to home.

depended upon the rejection, as wanting in maturity, of the disesteemed writers such as Joyce or Auden. And one of the prime functions of the literature that was deemed valuable (and of the teaching which promoted it) was to forge in students a sensitivity that would react to such work with the appropriate repugnance. In small quantities, Joyce's writing could be used to demonstrate the local felicities produced by the skilful deployment of literary language,[3] but the larger-scale enterprises demanded too much 'surface' decipherment for too little yield of imaginative, psychological, and moral 'depth'. And, of course, Joyce demonstrated his commitment to false gods quite clearly by increasing the surface-to-depth ratio with each work that he wrote.

There were those, of course, who did their best to save Joyce for the Great Tradition, stressing the humanity and precision of his portrayals of human life and minimizing his games with the medium of representation – which usually meant dismissing *Finnegans Wake* and giving short shrift to *Ulysses* from 'Sirens' on.[4] Richard Ellmann's comprehensive biography (published in 1959) gave some support to this enterprise, investing the known outline of Joyce's life and personality with meticulously and elegantly presented detail, and overthrowing the cartoon-character versions that had made condemnation an easy matter. The massive labour to which the weighty volume testified, coupled with the evident seriousness and decency of Ellmann's own approach, had a considerable impact, quite apart from the picture of Joyce he painted. And the picture itself, of the artist who sacrifices all for his art, who battles like a new Milton with his own blindness and like a new Blake with incomprehension all around, and whose work may be read as the faithful representation (give or take some artistic licence) of his own experience – Ellmann's essay on 'The Dead' is the classic instance[5] – this picture no doubt made it possible for many who had thought of Joyce as an insubstantial trickster to recategorize him as a weighty author. The later chapters of *Ulysses* and all of *Finnegans Wake*, even when held to be

---

[3] One of my teachers used the description in 'Proteus' of Stephen's progress across Sandymount Strand – 'His boots trod again a damp crackling mast, razorshells, squeaking pebbles' (*U* 3.147 *et seq.*) – for an exercise in 'practical criticism'. Only later did I discover that Leavis had singled out this passage in his review of *Work in Progress*: 'There is prose in *Ulysses*, the description, for instance, of Stephen Dedalus walking over the beach, of a Shakespearian concreteness; the rich complexity it offers to analysis derives from the intensely imagined experience realized in the words' ('James Joyce and the "Revolution of the Word"', 194).

[4] See, for instance, S. L. Goldberg's *The Classical Temper* and *Joyce*; and John Gross's *Joyce*. Fritz Senn has called Goldberg's earlier book, with a characteristic mixture of praise and blame, 'the best book ever written against *Ulysses*' (*Joyce's Dislocutions*, 159).

[5] This essay, 'Backgrounds of "The Dead"', became a chapter of Ellmann's biography (*JJ*, ch. 15).

regrettable in comparison with what Joyce might have done, could be accorded some value in the light of the familiar narrative of artistic innovation in an unappreciative world.

It might be thought, then, that when I started reading Joyce for myself, and finding the experience hugely enjoyable, my Leavisian training would have led me to value the early work most, and to feel some discomfort in engaging with the writing after 'Wandering Rocks'. But the pleasure I took in Joyce's works (like my earlier pleasure in Dylan Thomas and e. e. cummings) stemmed in large part from their *resistance* to the model of literary appreciation I had been schooled in. It was precisely Joyce's refusal to treat literature as a moral tonic, his comic scepticism about the novel's claims to faithful representation, his exorbitance and excessiveness, his predilection for extravagant effects, that appealed to me. The result was, of course, that I was drawn most strongly to Joyce's later writing, and that I tended to interpret the earlier work in the light of what came after. How I first came to Joyce I cannot now remember, but I do recall reading *Ulysses* – the plump green Bodley Head edition, which of all the editions still gives me most pleasure as a printed text to hold in the hand – on the *Windsor Castle* in 1966 as we steamed towards Southampton and my new life as a student at Cambridge. I tackled *Finnegans Wake* a few years later, armed with whatever guides and reference books I could get hold of in the Cambridge University Library, and, although in due course I was to discover that the best way to read Joyce's last book is as part of a group, the experience of reading – or rather 'reading' – from cover to cover was absorbing and exhilarating. I was at the time writing a Ph.D. thesis on Elizabethan attempts to create quantitative verse in English, and no doubt my fascination with those strange deformations of the language was related to my fascination with the linguistic extravagances of the *Wake*.

The criticism of Joyce which I found most helpful, therefore, was not criticism which tried to save Joyce for the 'English' tradition of moral healthiness and organic wholeness, but criticism which put a high value on his preoccupation with verbal craft, his encyclopedic ambitions, and his tendency to puncture the illusion of immediate representation. These features, after all, were exactly what made his work so energizing and enjoyable for me. The critics I valued were for the most part Americans – among them William York Tindall, Harry Levin, Joseph Campbell and Henry Morton Robinson, Adaline Glasheen, Louis O. Mink, and Hugh Kenner – who had a certain no-nonsense briskness about their engagement with Joyce's difficulties, often characterized by an unashamedly 'technical' approach which was a great relief after a style of reading governed by the need to identify subtle enactments of human values and to pronounce judgement accordingly. At the same time, no doubt as another component of my reaction against the way I had been taught, I was turning to linguistics as a useful tool in analyzing literary texts, and drawing on various intellectual movements of the time that gave linguistics a central role, whether as a set of techniques, a body of knowledge, or a model: stylistics, semiotics, and structuralism. Linked with this was an interest in aesthetic theory, both as a historical and as a philosophical issue, which had always lurked around the questions I asked of literary texts.

During my first years of teaching at Oxford and Southampton Universities in the mid-1970s, Joyce remained no more than a hobby, while I concentrated on periods before the twentieth century, and on poetry, in my classes and in my writing. I first began to appreciate the pleasures and rewards of working on Joyce in a more committed fashion while on an exchange in the USA in 1979, where I participated at the University of Illinois in a *Finnegans Wake* reading group run by Berni Benstock, one of the originators and presiding spirits of the James Joyce Foundation.[6] But it was a more far-reaching change in my thinking that precipitated a professional interest in Joyce: in the early 1980s, thanks largely to the commitment and patience of younger colleagues at Southampton, I began to understand the importance of the various intellectual developments, especially in France, that in English-speaking countries were being called 'post-structuralism' or just 'theory'. My reading of this work fed into and complicated my existing interests in literary language and in philosophical aesthetics, and at the same time I found Joyce becoming more central to my thinking. I didn't realize at the time just how important Joyce's work had been to the leading figures in the French movements I was becoming interested in, but there was clearly an affinity between them, and I felt that to teach a course on *Finnegans Wake* – a year-long seminar with a small group of senior undergraduates – would be a way of developing my own, and encouraging my students', interest in the intellectual opportunities offered by the new modes of thought.

I was right: the *Wake* turned out to be the perfect instrument by means of which to shake inherited assumptions about literature and

---

[6] I reflected on the importance of this reading group in 'Remembering Berni Benstock' and 'The Postmodernity of Joyce', 10–11.

criticism. Because the Leavisian model was also highly influential upon the teaching of literature in English secondary schools, most of my students had come to university with broadly the same assumptions that I had acquired in South Africa, and the great virtue of the *Wake* was that it simply did not respond to them. Our work in the classroom was not a matter of 'applying' theories derived from philosophers or psycho-analysts, however; it was a process of trying to develop ways of reading that seemed to do justice to Joyce's writing, and thus to enhance our pleasure in it. It was certainly helpful to be reading Derrida, Kristeva, and Barthes at the same time; but *this* reading also required the breaking of old habits, and the *Wake* in turn proved helpful in making headway with the peculiar difficulties of the French writers with whom we were grappling.

Teaching Joyce soon led me to the discovery that there was a body of continental writing on Joyce that was very different from the bulk of what I had read in the English language. What I had valued most up to now was explication: the meticulous, ingenious, and sometimes inspired deciphering of parallels, allusions, deformations, and parodies. What I found now were ways of thinking of Joyce's texts not as extremely complicated puzzles with no final answers (for I had always found myself resisting conclusions) but as stagings of some of the most fascinating and important properties of language, culture, and the psyche. Hélène Cixous in Paris, Jacques Aubert in Lyon, and Fritz Senn in Zürich were among the more senior members of this group, and although their approaches to Joyce were very different, they each represented a way of responding to the extremity and excess of the Joycean text that offered something different from what I have elsewhere termed the 'transcendentalist' and 'empiricist' approaches dominant in Anglophone criticism.[7] Younger critics working in the same vein whose work I came to know included Jean-Michel Rabaté, Daniel Ferrer, and André Topia; and two influential English voices with strong connections to Paris whom I had already encountered were Stephen Heath and Colin MacCabe. Around this time I also read some trail-blazing North Americans who were swimming against the prevailing currents in Joyce criticism, notably Jennifer Levine, Margot Norris, and David Hayman.

Aided by two Southampton colleagues with strong French connections – Robert Young and Maud Ellmann – I found myself becoming involved personally in the scene I had hitherto encountered only in books and journals. In 1982 I was persuaded to join a group of young

---

[7] Derek Attridge and Daniel Ferrer, 'Introduction: Highly Continental Evenements', *Post-structuralist Joyce*, 5.

critics who were preparing for a session at the Centenary Joyce Symposium in Dublin, and as a preliminary venture to give a paper – a first version of the symposium paper – at a Joyce colloquium in Paris some months prior. There I met several of the people who were to become collaborators and friends in the years ahead, including Rabaté, Ferrer, Topia, Aubert, and Senn. Fritz Senn, in particular, responded warmly to my talk – my first attempt to speak publicly about Joyce, or about any twentieth-century topic, for that matter – and gave me the kind of encouragement that counts for a great deal at the uncertain beginning of a new project. (Not that I had any inkling how large a project it was to become; it seemed at the time like a brief digression from my main scholarly interests, which at this time were focused on the forms of English poetry.) If there was a moment at which I became a Joycean, perhaps it was then, in response to the generosity and openness of what I began to think of as the 'Joyce community', a foretaste of which I'd experienced a few years earlier at the Benstocks' house. 'Joycean' is not a term I very willingly acknowledge, with its connotations of single-minded and uncritical adulation, but it has become hard to deny its applicability to me, given the repeated returns to Joyce which I have made since 1982, of which this book gives some evidence. I have written elsewhere that – in the sense in which I am willing to accept it – the word betokens 'not an academic interest in the writing and life of James Joyce, but a certain attitude to literature and to experience, a certain capacity to relish, without feeling threatened or becoming defensive, the imperfect world in all its multiplicity and messiness' ('Remembering Berni Benstock'). I would add that it involves not just an intellectual or an institutional commitment, but an oddly personal commitment to a vast, in many places absurd, in a few places highly impressive, assembly of individuals and their endeavours and productions, all in some way energized and stimulated by the writings of James Joyce.

If Paris was my baptism, the other pre-eminent Joycean city, Dublin, was my first communion. The 1982 symposium (one of the international symposia held every two years in a different European city) seemed huge after the intimate Paris affair, and our session just a drop in its teeming ocean. There were eight of us on the panel, four from France and four from Britain, so our papers had to be extremely brief.[8] Our intention was far from programmatic: this was not to be an exposition of a body of

---

[8] The other participants were Michael Beausang, Maud Ellmann, Robert Young, Colin Mac-Cabe, Jean-Michel Rabaté, André Topia, and Daniel Ferrer. Six of the papers read were published in the conference volume (Beja *et al.*, *James Joyce: The Centennial Symposium*, 57–92). I later expanded my contribution, 'Lipspeech', for my 1988 book *Peculiar Language*.

'theory' and a demonstration of its 'relevance' to Joyce (a genre of critical discourse that has unfortunately become common in Joyce studies as it has elsewhere), but an engagement with a single chapter of *Ulysses* from our individual perspectives, enriched as they had been by our reading of new theoretical work. Literature, for us, was not the merely passive object of theorizing, but a discourse preempting and exceeding all theories. The title, 'Sirens Without Music', was a signal that we would start with no preconceptions about the interpretation of *Ulysses* of the kind installed by Stuart Gilbert's pioneering and 'authorized' – and still highly influential – account of the book (Gilbert, *James Joyce's 'Ulysses'*).

In retrospect, the panel does seem to mark something of a turning point: a thin wedge of 'French theory' in the Joycean critical discourse that by the time of the next International James Joyce Symposium, held two years later in Frankfurt, had apparently become the dominant approach to Joyce's writing.[9] (Although the 1975 Paris symposium had included a good deal of French theoretical discussion – Jacques Lacan gave a major address, and other contributors included Philippe Sollers, Jacques Aubert, and Hélène Cixous – one gets the impression that it left the divide between Francophone and Anglophone approaches as great as ever, or perhaps even greater.[10]) What I didn't realize at the time was that this panel would turn out to be a turning-point in my own career as well, and that I would go on to attend one International Joyce Symposium after another, finding that, whatever else I was working on at that moment, I had something to say on a Joycean topic. It was not so much that the task of understanding and explicating Joyce proved endless – though this was certainly the case – but that I repeatedly found my reading of Joyce puncturing any settled complacency about theoretical issues, provoking questions about the way we read and employ literature, and throwing fresh light on many of the areas I was interested in, including literary language, issues of interpretation, and the relation of text and history. I also found that each time I was getting to grips with a new theoretical discourse, Joyce's work provided an apt testing ground and whetstone.

[9] See Bernard Benstock, ed., *James Joyce: The Augmented Ninth*. It must be said that the conference programme itself was less markedly influenced by 'theory' than the volume of proceedings published four years later; though this is in itself of some historical and sociological significance.

[10] See the collection of papers from the conference, *Joyce & Paris*, edited by Jacques Aubert and Maria Jolas. In a tangible reflection of the dichotomized conference, the proceedings are presented in two volumes, one featuring the contributions from French speakers, the other the contributions from English speakers.

Most of my writing about Joyce for the following fifteen years bene-fited from the stimulus and provocation of French post-structuralism, and more particularly the work of Jacques Derrida. Derrida gave a memorable lecture at the 1984 Frankfurt symposium (memorable, among other things, for its brilliance, its humour, its extreme length, and for the fact that a large part of the audience could not follow it, since it was in French with only brief English summaries interpolated by a heroic translator), and it was during the same symposium that he and I had the conversation which began what was to be a long and rewarding collaboration.[11] The earliest of the essays in this volume were written for that symposium: the essay I here call 'Deconstructive Criticism of Joyce' (which was actually the title of the panel, organized by Ellen Carol Jones, in which I spoke), and chapter 4, 'Joyce and the Ideology of Character' (given as part of a panel on 'Character and Contemporary Theory', organized by Bonnie Kime Scott). These essays, published in the conference volume (see note 9 above), clearly reflect my early enthusiasm for the work of Derrida, as well as that of Jean-François Lyotard and Hélène Cixous. The year 1984 also saw the publication of the collection which Daniel Ferrer and I co-edited with the aim of bringing French writing on Joyce to the attention of the English-speaking world, called, at the publisher's urging, *Post-structuralist Joyce* ('un peu "marketing"' was the wry comment from Derrida, whose first essay on Joyce, 'Two Words for Joyce', we were glad to include).

Although the early 1980s can be seen as the watershed (or in some mythologies, the Deluge) after which Joyce criticism – and literary studies more generally – would never be the same, new critical trends did not cease to arise, sometimes in competition with one another, sometimes complementing one another. In the mid 1980s, the text-based criticism that predominated in post-structuralist approaches to literature was being enriched by an increasing concern with historical contexts and changes. One reflection of this critical mutation was a panel organized by Morris Beja for the 1986 International James Joyce Symposium in Copenhagen on the topic 'James Joyce and the Concept of History', to which I contributed 'History is to Blame' – revised here as chapter 7, 'Wakean History: Not Yet'. This talk was not a consideration of historical detail (the panel was not on history, but the concept of history); rather, it addressed the ways in which Joyce – particularly in

[11] See, in particular, *Acts of Literature*, the selection of essays by Derrida on literary topics which I edited. I was pleased to be able to include a revised translation of the Frankfurt lecture, 'Ulysses Gramophone: Hear Say Yes in Joyce'.

Finnegans Wake – 'undoes history'. I also wrote 'The *Wake*'s Confounded Language', included here as the final chapter, for a panel on '*Finnegans Wake* and the Language of Babel' at the same symposium, chaired by Berni Benstock. In both these pieces, the second of which was published in the conference volume, the influence of deconstruction is again strong, but the main source of the 'theoretical' thinking in these pieces is Joyce's own writings, and *Finnegans Wake* in particular.

History continued to be a pressing question for anyone interested in literature and theory, and it was again the topic I chose to focus on for an MLA panel at the end of 1986 on 'The Ideology of Form in the Works of James Joyce', in a paper entitled 'Joyce, Jameson, and the Text of History', first published in *Scribble* and also included here, as chapter 6. The new interest in historical contextualization was once more evident at a 1987 conference on '*Finnegans Wake*: Contexts' held at the University of Leeds; my contribution, 'Finnegans Awake: The Dream of Interpretation', published in a special issue of the *James Joyce Quarterly* featuring European critics (ironically enough, as I had just moved to the USA), and reprinted as chapter 11, is an attempt to historicize the major critical trope used in the reading of the *Wake*.[12] At the same time I was finishing a book, published in 1988 under the title *Peculiar Language*, whose purpose was to trace discussions and literary manifestations of the vexed relation between literary and non-literary language from George Puttenham in the sixteenth century to Joyce in the twentieth, and which included revised versions of some of my earliest writings on Joyce.

Along with the influence of historical approaches on Joyce studies during the eighties, and the continuing importance of deconstruction and psychoanalysis, the influence of feminism increased.[13] One of the feminist panels at the 1988 symposium in Venice, 'Textual Mater: Women, Language, Joyce', was organized by Shari Benstock and Ellen Carol Jones, and it was for this panel that I wrote a short paper called 'Molly's Flow', expanded for a special issue of *Modern Fiction Studies* on feminist readings of Joyce and included here in a rewritten version as

---

[12] A historical impetus has continued to motivate much Joyce criticism, and the mid-1990s have witnessed a real flowering; see, for instance, James Fairhall, *James Joyce and the Question of History*; Robert Spoo, *James Joyce and the Language of History: Dedalus's Nightmare*; Thomas C. Hofheinz, *Joyce and the Invention of Irish History*; and Mark Wollaeger, Victor Luftig, and Robert Spoo, eds., *Joyce and the Subject of History*.

[13] See, for example, Bonnie Kime Scott, *Joyce and Feminism*, and Christine van Boheemen, *The Novel as Family Romance*. Feminist criticism remains one of the strongest areas of Joyce studies, often in combination with other approaches: among the notable books of the 1990s have been Kimberly Devlin, *Wandering and Return in 'Finnegans Wake'*; Margot Norris, *Joyce's Web*; and Christine Froula, *Modernism's Body*. The considerable influence of Lacanian psychoanalysis on Joyce criticism has most often been exerted in conjunction with feminist approaches.

chapter 8. 'Postmodernism' had also become a much-discussed topic,[14] and in 1990 John Paul Riquelme asked me to contribute to a panel at the Monaco symposium on Joyce's relation to modernism and postmodernism. A version of this talk, published in the 1995 *Joyce Studies Annual*, is included here under the title 'The Postmodernity of Joyce: Chance, Coincidence, and the Reader' (chapter 9). In the same year I wrote 'Touching "Clay"' (chapter 3 of this volume) for a seminar at the University of Paris–Nanterre on 'Le dit et le non-dit', and delivered versions of it at a number of other places, always with helpful comments from my auditors. (And here I should add that virtually every chapter in this book has gained from the responses I received when giving it as a talk.)

By the early 1990s the most rapidly growing research area in English departments was cultural studies, and if many working in this field regarded Joyce – and Joyce readers – as an example of cultural elitism at its most pronounced, there were many others who found a fertile new terrain in Joyce's relation to popular and consumer culture (the overlap between the two being one of the vexed issues requiring examination).[15] I was asked to introduce a panel on 'Theories of Popular Culture' at the 1992 'Miami J'yce' conference (an annual meeting held at the University of Miami), which had as its topic 'Joyce and Popular Culture'. This short talk was published in the conference volume edited by Brandon Kershner, and appears here in a revised version as chapter 2, 'Popular Joyce?' The International James Joyce Symposium for that year was back in Dublin, for which I was persuaded by Berni Benstock to address one of the perennial questions about *Finnegans Wake*, which ten years of 'theory' had not resolved: the question of the narrative, if any, of *Finnegans Wake*. The result was the brief essay, 'Countlessness of Livestories: Narrativity in *Finnegans Wake*', included in the symposium volume and reprinted here as chapter 10.

A relatively new field, gay and lesbian studies, was now making an impact on Joyce criticism, registered most impressively in the spring 1994 special issue of the *James Joyce Quarterly* on 'Joyce and Homosexuality', edited by Joseph Valente.[16] Having missed the 1994 Symposium in Seville for family reasons, I was drawn back to Zürich in 1996, where,

---

[14] Joyce features importantly in many studies of postmodernism and fiction, such as Brian McHale's *Postmodernist Fiction* and *Constructing Postmodernism*.

[15] See, for example, Cheryl Herr, *Joyce's Anatomy of Culture*; R. B. Kershner, *Joyce, Bakhtin, and Popular Culture*; the special issue of the *James Joyce Quarterly* on 'Joyce and Advertising', guest-edited by Garry Leonard with Jennifer Wicke; and R. B. Kershner, ed., *Joyce and Popular Culture*.

[16] Four of the essays in this issue have been reprinted, with a number of others, in *Quare Joyce*, also edited by Joseph Valente.

invited by Laurent Milesi to contribute to a symposium panel on Joyce's language(s), I gave a shorter version of the essay included here as chapter 5, '"Suck was a Queer Word": Language, Sexuality, and the Remainder in *A Portrait of the Artist as a Young Man*'. Although my focus in this essay is not on homosexuality *per se*, I could not have written it without the work of scholars like Valente, Jennifer Levine, and Colleen Lamos, who have shown that the homosocial and the homosexual are woven throughout Joyce's writing in ways that up to now have largely been occluded.

The other strikingly vigorous critical domain of the mid-1990s has been colonial and postcolonial studies, and once again Joyce turns out to be a figure of immense interest when a fresh theoretical light is shone on his work.[17] Like New Historicism, feminism, postmodernism, cultural studies, and gay and lesbian studies, 'postcolonial theory' (to give it its common, if not strictly accurate, label) is a post-poststructuralist approach, including among its influences the work of such writers as Derrida, Lacan, Foucault, Levinas, Cixous, Kristeva, Barthes, Deleuze, and their English-language followers and interpreters (though of course it has other sources as well); questions of marginalization, alterity, and difference have been crucial to these discourses since the 1960s. In addition to my familiarity with the theoretical underpinnings of the new work, my South African background and my interest in the literatures of the former British colonies – which I had hitherto never thought of as connected to my interest in Joyce – quite suddenly became a resource for new kinds of thinking about Ireland and Irish writers, with their complex relation to English metropolitan culture.[18] It was probably inevitable, then, that I should find myself drawn to this growing body of criticism, and it was as much with the aim of learning more about it as with any other purpose that I co-organized, also at the Zürich symposium, with Marjorie Howes, a panel entitled 'Semicolonial Joyce', which examined some of the complexities of Joyce's relation to Irish nationalism and British hegemony. The fruits of this new enterprise will appear under different covers.[19]

[17] See, for instance, David Lloyd, *Anomalous States*; Enda Duffy, *The Subaltern 'Ulysses'*; Emer Nolan, *James Joyce and Nationalism*; Vincent J. Cheng, *Joyce, Race, and Empire*; Joseph Valente, *James Joyce and the Problem of Justice*. Important contributions have also been made by Seamus Deane, Luke Gibbons, Terry Eagleton, Declan Kiberd, and Joep Leerssen. One notable, and pleasing, feature of this most recent wave of criticism is that critics based in Ireland have, for the first time, played a significant part in the development of new ways of reading Joyce.

[18] There is no mention of Joyce in the book I co-edited with Rosemary Jolly, *Writing South Africa*, but it would have been possible to make numerous connections.

[19] See Marjorie Howes and Derek Attridge, eds., *Semicolonial Joyce*.

MAINLY THEORETICAL

The question I wish to raise by means of this potted autobiography of a Joycean – which of course has left out many conferences, lectures, reviews, reading groups, classes, internet sessions, public readings, and other events and publications – is this: what are we to make of the changing course of Joyce criticism, to which my own trajectory in the past fifteen years bears clear witness? One view would be that it reveals the intellectual vacuity of a great deal of what goes on under the name 'literary criticism': much-vaunted 'new approaches' succeed one another, each proclaiming their superiority to earlier approaches, each destined to give way to the next wave of intellectual fashion. The academic marketplace, like any other marketplace, it is pointed out, thrives on rapid obsolescence: scholars who wish to make names (and more material profits) for themselves, publishers who wish to sell their books, institutions of learning that wish to increase their visibility – all these stand to gain from a cycle of critical fads, each rendering last year's ideas, books, and courses out of date as it stakes its own (equally short-lived) claims. The realm of Joyce studies – not inaccurately known as the 'Joyce industry' – is merely one part of this process, perhaps a particularly striking instance because of its massiveness and because of the leading place that North American criticism plays in it. And my own career, it would be observed, reflects a typical eagerness to be up to date with the latest fashion.

There is a great deal of accuracy in this picture, and the critical history of the fifteen years I have been concerned with suggests that the process of rise and fall, flowering and displacement, is undergoing a remorseless acceleration. The conclusions to be drawn from this set of facts are not obvious, however. Those who complain most loudly about it usually imply that obscured by the frenetic musical chairs of critical fashion is some solid, abiding, dependable approach to literature, and that readers of real intelligence, sensitivity, and taste will ignore the razzmatazz of competing *isms* and *posts* while going about their self-evident, and self-evidently valuable, business. From this point of view, my fifteen years as a Joycean would be an example of how not to do it.

The problem with this position is that the approach it favours is necessarily itself historical, the product of specific social, economic, and cultural forces. It usually turns out to be a version of what I learned in South Africa: a cultivation of individual sensibility which claims to be free from the pressures of class and politics, but which in fact has clear

class and political allegiances.[20] (In North America, the nearest equivalent to the Leavisian conception of literary study in terms of influence
and ideology is New Criticism, though there are important differences
as well – including a more favourable view of Joyce.[21] Another tradition
with many similarities is that descended from Reuben Brower's teaching at Harvard.) Of course, the approach one has absorbed at a
formative stage of one's life, especially if it is also the approach that most
satisfies other needs, will appear to be 'natural', and it takes considerable
effort to distance oneself from it. (To some degree, in spite of everything
I have noted above, the style of reading and commentary I inherited at
second hand from Richards, Eliot, and Leavis still presents itself to me
with a certain feeling of naturalness – and the appeal of Derrida's work
for me could be related to the affinities that exist, along with huge
differences, between these approaches.[22]) But one of the ways in which
the Leavisian–New Critical approach differs from most later critical
schools is that it actually obscures, as a significant element in its view of
literary practices, the fundamentally historical constitution of all processes of reading and judgement: it thus reinforces the tendency to rely
on an experience of 'naturalness' where later approaches contest this
tendency, analyzing it under such names as 'ideology', 'literary competence', 'logocentrism', and 'the Imaginary'.

It remains true that much that has been written in a deconstructive,
feminist, Marxist, or New Historicist vein – to take a few labelled
approaches of recent decades – is derivative and limited in its interest
(both as to the audience it reaches and as to the length of time it will hold
its value), and there is no doubt that the marketplace's increasing
demands for up-to-dateness bear some of the responsibility for this state
of affairs. The pressure to be 'on the cutting edge' has never been
greater. However, it is also the case that a great deal of Leavisian–New
Critical writing (or, for that matter, Arnoldian or Bradleian writing) is
derivative and not particularly interesting, except as historical docu-
mentation. Any powerfully articulated approach that exposes weaknesses in a previous mode of thought and provides a blueprint for new

[20] In *Peculiar Language* I argued that from the Renaissance onward, attempts to define literature as a
separate realm of discourse have relied on such allegiances, necessarily disguised in the language
of autonomy and universalism. For studies of the social and political stakes in modern literary
studies in Britain, see Francis Mulhern, *The Moment of 'Scrutiny'*, and Chris Baldick, *The Social
Mission of English Criticism*.
[21] Jeffrey Segall gives a valuable account of New Criticism's dealings with Joyce in *Joyce in America*.
[22] Stephen Heath has argued for the similarities between Leavis's and Derrida's approaches: see
'Modern Literary Theory'.

kinds of critical writing will bring in its train a host of quite mechanically produced texts. New Critical Joyce, deconstructive Joyce, feminist Joyce, New Historicist Joyce, cultural Joyce, and now homosexual and postcolonial Joyce all necessarily entail easily parodiable, formulaic applications of what at their best are insightful and rigorous ways of reading.[23] Indeed, it is the overproduction of such applications that in part spurs the development of new approaches.

Fifteen years on, it is clear to me that my early enthusiasm for post-structuralism – and for the *Wake* as its exemplar – involved a degree of exclusivity. What I experienced was an approach to literature which did a great deal more justice to the complexity and internal disjunctions of the works I read than the habits of interpretation and evaluation to which I had become accustomed, an approach which held up for question (as I believed Joyce's works did) many of the central assumptions of more traditional conceptions of the literary work, including authorship, historical origin, thematic focus, moral force, psychological truth, and formal unity; an approach which invited a reconsideration of the place and purpose of literature itself. I still find all these virtues in deconstructive writing, but I now see that my strong endorsement of them was not simply a faithful response to some kind of inherent value in the theoretical work I was reading. I was responding, too, to the conditions of a specific time and place, to a perceived exhaustion of critical methods in a changing world, to an excitement and glamour attached to what was new (and perhaps also, especially after 1968, to what was French), to the challenge of difficulty (and the satisfaction of learning how to deal with it); and I was reacting against my own early training (and thus against the culture of white South Africa, which I had done my best to put behind me), and against powerful individuals under whose authority I was restive. All this was, I believe, perfectly normal, since no one embraces a new intellectual method for purely intellectual reasons. In retrospect, I see more value in some of the critical methods I then regarded as entirely superseded, and I see limitations in the new thinking I endorsed that were then invisible to me but which I am attempting to overcome in my current work. While it is not for me to judge, it is my hope that in the various talks I gave and pieces I wrote during this period, many of which are collected in this volume, the blinkering effect of a historical moment and cultural situation is outweighed by more lasting positive qualities.

[23] Derrida has written illuminatingly on the constitutive reproducibility of inventiveness in 'Psyche: Invention of the Other' (*Acts of Literature*, 310–43).

In answer to the wider question about the changes in styles of Joyce criticism, then, I would argue that these changes provide evidence that modes of literary criticism, and more generally the ways in which books get read and talked about, are historical through and through. Not only are the normative judgements that are made about literary works dependent on time and place, but so are the very meanings that readers find in them; in a quite real sense, therefore, the works themselves keep changing. The values that underlie critical assessments inevitably change with changes in broader cultural preferences and social mores, and the specific aims and methods of literary commentary are constantly shifting as well. But this does not mean that criticism is weightless or worthless: such a claim could be based only on a belief in the attainability of absolute, unchanging, and eternal critical truths. It is precisely its historicity, its absorption of and into the currents of its time, that gives criticism its purchase, allowing it to speak not only to its immediate audiences but very often (though there is a certain amount of chance involved here) to those of the future as well.

To say that critical values are historical is not to say that they all change as rapidly as critical fashions, however; there are some fundamental values which have been widely acknowledged for a very long time, and are likely to retain their importance for the foreseeable future. Among the names we give to these enduring values are rigour, accuracy, honesty, originality, and responsibility. Even in these instances, however, there is no universal agreement about exact meaning or applicability; every value one might propose as possessing a lasting and consensual status could be the subject of a lengthy and polemical book, and many have been. (One of the problems in discussing such long-term values is that the continued employment of the same word may conceal quite marked shifts in its meaning.) But this is not a reason for dismissing the notion of enduring critical values; on the contrary, it is a reason for continuing to argue about such values, and continuing to try to live up to those that we can agree on. This debate and this attempt will be never-ending, because history will continue to effect its changes, but the struggle to identify, articulate, and honour a set of lasting obligations will itself remain a constant value.[24]

Other values and assumptions change much more quickly, and their historical status is to that degree more evident. Often, a strong and influential set of attitudes and practices provokes a necessary reaction,

---

[24] Steven Connor has eloquently argued for this value – the value of value – in *Theory and Cultural Value*.

because its strength has relied on the occlusion of significant aspects of readers' experience; I have tried in this essay to demonstrate how my own critical preferences arose in part as a recoil from my early training. Our reading and criticism are also importantly influenced by place, and the kinds of criticism current in English departments in, say, the USA are bound to be different from those current in India or Sweden or Tanzania – although one evident historical change in the past fifteen years is that these differences have been steadily diminishing. It is important to recognize that there is no intrinsic limit to what can be said about a text, even the simplest one, and to appreciate the consequences of this fact. It means that what we choose to say or write about a given text cannot be determined by any concept of 'inherent importance', as if what *really* matters is to focus on this, not that – on, say, thematic explication, or stylistic commentary, or biographical discussion, or historical analysis, or genetic study. Each of these ways of talking about a work, and many others, contributes to some wider discourse, and its value depends on the status of that discourse, a status which will vary across times and places. If I were to carry out a detailed examination of the quality of the paper on which different editions of *Ulysses* were printed, this would not be *inherently* absurd: just absurd in view of the absence of any larger discussion to which it would contribute (as far as I know). The international Joyce community is anything but a united body of scholars; in fact, the common focus on James Joyce is in many ways a spurious one, since it conceals huge differences in what people value Joyce *for*.

Even what we might think of as a single mode of criticism will always serve many different purposes, and its value will be correspondingly complex. To take a currently thriving field of Joyce studies, the patient examination of Joyce's drafts and notebooks achieves a number of things: among others, it illuminates Joyce's working methods, and thus contributes to discussions of Joycean biography and of human creativity more generally; it prolongs and enriches the debate about the appropriate texts to enshrine in print; it influences interpretations of Joyce's works (whether, on the one hand, by providing evidence to those who believe in the achievability of a correct interpretation, or, on the other, by entirely exploding the notion of a 'final' text and meaning); it authorizes a certain 'historical' or 'materialist' approach to the literary text; and it provides new opportunities for research, teaching, and publication (and hence for reputations and advancement). At different times and in different places, these wider goals and activities will have more or less prestige, something which will depend in part on the success of the practitioners in the field itself, but to a greater extent on broader social and intellectual currents. It is not a matter of 'advances' in criticism, though at any given historical moment, certain ways of writing about literature will possess more of these different kinds of value than others.

So the fact that at a given moment a large proportion of talks and publications on Joyce draw on the methods and findings of feminism, or stylistics, or deconstruction, and that at a different moment none of these is particularly prominent is not a cause for dismay or dismissiveness; it is a reflection of the historical character of our reading. There is, however, an obligation on every critic to deploy the resources he or she chooses in accordance with the kind of long-term values I mentioned earlier, such as originality, responsibility, and precision (even though these values are themselves the subject of debate); and there is an obligation on everyone who reads criticism to judge it on similar grounds. One asset in attempting to fulfil these obligations is familiarity with a variety of approaches; thus it is possible that my early Leavisian training and my work on stylistics strengthens the deconstructive criticism included in this book – even though (or perhaps because) there are significant discrepancies between these approaches. Different kinds of adverse judgement can be passed on a critical text, therefore (though these judgements can never be absolute, since they themselves are always made by means of the lens of a place and time): it can be uninteresting or impotent because it fails to contribute to any discourses or practices of its time, or it can be lacking in one or more of the enduring qualities we value, or it can, of course, be both. A critical work that fails here and now for the first reason may in some other time and place succeed – by which I mean both find approving readers and influence the way literature is read, and perhaps written. A critical work that is weak in the latter sense, though it may also succeed in the short run (since there is no guarantee that the virtues I have listed will gain more attention than such characteristics as topicality or stylistic self-advertisement), will presumably have a minimal long-term effect, at least if the cardinal values I have enumerated continue to be held in esteem.

What, then, would be the qualities of good Joyce criticism at this moment in history? Posed like this, the question is obviously unanswerable. 'Good' could mean a host of different things, given the variety of purposes which criticism serves. To avoid this problem by rehearsing what I have called 'long-term' or 'cardinal' values would be to ignore the point of the question, which is concerned with changing demands and trends in our responses to literature. All I can do is identify the kinds of criticism that seem particularly valuable *to me, here and now*, because they answer to what I perceive as the needs of our time, because they take account of other discourses engaged with those needs, and because they do these things in ways which are genuinely new. Anyone who conducts such an examination is, of course, subject to the same blind spots as everyone else, so any judgements that are made are necessarily provisional (and, in a sense, essentially so, since the verdict that posterity passes will itself be a limited and revisable one). Nor is it possible to identify the hidden determinants of one's judgements: genetic predispositions towards certain kinds of work, the effects of early training, unconscious influences, ideological refractions, and so on. It is important to acknowledge that these factors exist, for it is all too easy to take one's limited perspective as universal comprehension – and this is just as true for one's preference for, say, Joyce over Lawrence as it is for certain styles of criticism.

With all these caveats, I would single out the pressing need today to reassess the system of assumptions and values that have dominated – I use this word as unavoidable shorthand for a complicated history of tensions, shifts, and revolutions – Western thought, Western politics, Western ethics, and Western culture since its inception in classical Greece (at least as this origin has been retroactively constructed). The word *Western* is the give-away here. Until quite recently it was possible for those whose identities were formed in a Western mould to use the term as a mere honorific; but the historical process whereby Western control of the globe, achieved and maintained through one form or other of colonialism, yielded to a more complex interrelation of nation-states and cultures was a process that has culminated in a profound relativization, exposing the term *Western* to a vigorous questioning.[25] Of course, under such scrutiny it turns out to be a far from unitary concept, and its internal systems of domination (based on class, gender, region, sexuality, etc.) have thus also become much more evident. Many still refuse to acknowledge the relativization that has occurred, and the power of the West (and within the West the power of the traditional strongholds) remains vigorous enough to permit such refusal. However, for those who have acknowledged – whether from a Western or non-

---

[25] See Robert Young, *White Mythologies*, especially chapter 1.

Western perspective – that there is no set of values which can be taken as
merely given, the task of refashioning social, philosophical, cultural,
economic, and ethical tools is an urgent one. Accompanying and inter-
relating with the processes of decolonization (to use another oversimple
label for a complex process) has been the technological revolution which
has broken down many of the barriers that insulated the West for so
long; these changes, too, demand new practices and new modes of
thinking.

Among the most important examples of Joyce criticism of the present,
then, are those which attempt to reread Joyce in this historically
changed (and still changing) context, and at the same time to rethink
what reading, criticism, and the whole institution of literary production
and reception, are. At its best, it seems to me – and this points to the
good fortune or good planning of those who work on Joyce – this
criticism, while it brings a great deal to Joyce, also learns from Joyce, not
by way of absorbing overt lessons but by way of attending scrupulously
to what goes on in his writing as he engages with his own environment
and history. So it is not just a matter of identifying Joyce's racism or
anti-racism, his logocentric or deconstructive tendencies, his gender
politics, his views on homosexuality or imperialism, but of responding to
the way such concerns are staged, are transformed by literary language
(with its strangely non-referential references), are reinvented, parodied,
juxtaposed, grafted, inverted. Because the shaping forces of Western
culture and politics operate unevenly and contradictorily, any writer in
English is likely to have some purchase on the fault lines of class, race,
and gender, and the possibilities they offer for a challenge to the givens
of Western thought and 'common sense'. Joyce, however, was better
placed than most, given the particular status of Ireland as a metropolitan colony struggling for and gaining its independence (as yet another
turbulent stage in its long history of conflict), and his own situation in
Ireland, as an urban Catholic intellectual in a family on a downward
class-slide, and in a divided Europe, as a self-exiled artist.

This view of the imperatives of Joyce criticism, though it claims to be
current, is – like any such view – necessarily retrospective. I have no way
of knowing if there is a critic, or a number of critics, now writing the
words – not necessarily on Joyce – which will reveal the blinkers we have
been wearing in our deconstructive, historical, postcolonial, feminist,
queer, or culturalist approaches, and will point out to us what we have
not been seeing; nor if there is a historical event brewing that will help to
produce a burst of innovative and influential writing after which the

entire scene will look different once more. Even what I called cardinal or long-term values may, at any moment, be on the brink of a thoroughgoing revision. In this process, literary works will play, as they always have played, a central role. The publication of *Ulysses* not only brought about a revolution in modes of reading and interpretation, but also initiated a fresh consideration of what a responsible or accurate reading might be. For although all the texts that have been written are products of their time and place, it is only hindsight that allows us to understand how this happened; for the future, our best guesses are bound to be wrong. That unpredictability is at the heart of artistic production is widely accepted, but what is not always appreciated is that it is at the heart of critical production too.[26] The responsible reading of a literary work, if it is to be more than a mechanical consequence of the work and of the prevailing discourses through which the work is approached, has to be original too. There is no knowing what kinds of response to Joyce's works will be compelling our interest in fifteen years' time, but we can be certain – and it is on this certainty that the practices of both literature and criticism depend – that they will be significantly different from the ones that command our attention as the millennium ends.

[26] I have discussed this imperative more fully in 'Innovation, Literature, Ethics'.

CHAPTER I

Deconstructive criticism of Joyce

This talk was given at the 1984 James Joyce Symposium in Frankfurt, as part of a panel following Jacques Derrida's address, 'Ulysses Gramophone'. The paper was originally entitled 'Of', but I have here appropriated the title of the whole panel. The references to that occasion are integral to the talk and have not been removed.

'*Amor matris*: subjective and objective genitive', thinks Stephen Dedalus in the role of part-time teacher in the 'Nestor' episode of *Ulysses*, contemplating his graceless pupil Cyril Sargent as the boy wrestles with his arithmetic problems and wondering at the mutual bond summed up in the ambiguity (which survives translation) of the phrase 'the love of a mother' (*U* 2.165–6). Later in the day, during his rhapsodic lecture on Shakespeare to a select audience in the National Library, the whole phrase surfaces again in Stephen's mind (*U* 9.842–3).

Thanks to the same ambiguity of 'of', the title *A Portrait of the Artist as a Young Man*, instead of designating a young man as he appears in a painting that is the work of his older self, might just refer to a painting *by* a youthful artist (a possibility not without critical consequences).

The title of Joyce's last book has, among its many meanings, a genitive that also works in two ways: the wake, or waking, of Finnegan may be that which he does as (reviving) subject or that which is done to him as (dead) object.

'The whole of this essay', writes Jacques Derrida in a footnote to his long essay 'Plato's Pharmacy', is 'itself nothing but a reading of *Finnegans Wake*' (*Dissemination*, 88 n20; translation slightly modified); and in 'Two Words for Joyce' he comments on this earlier footnote: 'This double genitive ["reading of *Finnegans Wake*"] implied that this modest essay was read in advance by *Finnegans Wake*, in its wake or its lineage, at the very moment that "Plato's Pharmacy" was itself presenting itself as a reading-head or principle of decipherment . . . for a possible under-standing of *Finnegans Wake*' (150).

How, then, are we to read the genitive in my title – 'Deconstructive Criticism of Joyce' – if both Joyce and Derrida warn us of its duplicity? Do Joyce's texts allow us to read the phrase as referring simply to a set of procedures performed on, or over, a body of writing? Equally, does the practice of deconstruction (as we encounter it in Derrida's writing) allow us to read it in such a way, implying the application of a critical technique which remains unaffected by the object to which it is applied? What if the body at the wake, splashed by some hermeneutic whiskey, should wake, to the embarrassment of the mourners? What if the critical text should find itself addressed by the writing on which it comments, perhaps even given life and sustained by it, as the 'squashed boneless snail' of a schoolboy is by a mother's love?

As we move into the 1980s, British and North American Joyce criticism is, as one might put it, waking up to deconstruction and post-structuralism, as movements, or tremors, in the critical space around it. Better late than never, some might say, but perhaps better never than in the shape of a new set of rituals to perform around the coffin, with not a drop of whiskey going astray. It is worth pausing, therefore, to ask what 'deconstructive criticism of Joyce' must mean if it is to do justice to what is distinctive both in deconstruction and in Joyce, and in their possible relationship. It will have become evident that 'of' must be a double genitive: deconstructive criticism of Joyce would have to be that which Joyce practises upon us as much as that which we practise upon Joyce. Derrida draws attention to the two-way relation-ship in a discussion of the problem posed for the critic by the scope and power of Joyce's writing, using the ambivalent genitive once more: 'You have only one way out: *being in memory of him* . . . : not necessarily to remember him, no, but to be in his memory, to inhabit his memory' ('Two Words for Joyce', 147). Joyce remembers us as we remember him.

Most criticism offers itself to be read in a manner that can be called *epitaphic*, keeping the literary work alive in memory while reasserting and ensuring its death as text; a deconstructive criticism, on the other hand, would be a critical practice acknowledging that *its* life is dependent on the continued life of the text it helps to keep alive, and which attempts to work through, or at least with, that enigma. In a different sense, all criticism comes into existence as the wake of the text it reads, marking the eddies thrown up by its powerful surge through the cultural matrix, yet all criticism tries to escape this condition of secondariness and belatedness that points ineluctably towards death. This usually entails an assumption that it is the *work* that is dead, and in need of being both waked and woken (but only into a life foreseen and constrained by the critic); but a deconstructive criticism would advertise its secondariness, its existence as the text's wake, waked and woken by it, while at the same time demonstrating that that which is 'secondary' may predetermine or generate that which is 'primary'. Deconstruction also functions as the wake of *criticism*, at once thrown up by it, celebrating its death, and arousing its deconstructive potential as mode of attentive reading that attempts to do justice to the text with which it engages.

The criticism of Joyce with which we are most familiar – objective genitive, unidirectional, and epitaphic – operates according to the model of testable hypotheses (offered to the community of scholars for its verdict) and the accumulation of ever more precise and detailed knowledge: the model, that is, of science.[1] So we scan each new essay or book on Joyce for its contribution to the growing body of increasingly accurate information, coming ever closer to the truth as errors are corrected and new insights added. Just as knowledge of the facts of Joyce's life grows until a 'definitive biography' can be produced, and knowledge of the words Joyce wrote culminates in a 'definitive edition', so knowledge of the meanings of Joyce's writing moves towards a 'definitive interpretation'. Of course, we are prepared to acknowledge that these goals are fictions, and may even be willing to admit that there is no 'life' as such, only stories that create one, no 'text' as such, only editions that legitimate one, no 'meaning' as such, only interpretations that generate one; but every time we claim to add to or correct the existing biographies, texts, or interpretations of Joyce, or make a judgement on someone else's addition or correction, we confirm the belief in an accessible truth independent of our commentary, which it is our goal to approximate as closely and fully as possible.[2] Literary theory is constituted according to the same assumptions: it takes Joyce's writing

---

[1] My argument in what follows owes a great deal to Jean-François Lyotard's *The Postmodern Condition*. Lyotard discusses the distinction between 'scientific knowledge' and 'narrative knowledge', which use completely different criteria; the former judges the latter as 'primitive' and composed of 'opinions, customs, authority, prejudice, ignorance, ideology', but depends upon it to legitimize its truths in the public domain (see especially pages 18–31). We may recognize Shem and Shaun in yet another guise.

[2] These three enterprises do not work in isolation, of course. For instance, a new fact in the biography, or a new word in the text, is adduced as 'evidence' for a 'correction' to the current interpretation, or confirmation of a previously disputed one.

as a sample or example, and operates upon it in order to add to or correct the body of knowledge relating to literature, determined again by the ultimate goal of a definitive and final account. The procedures of literary history or stylistics or the sociology of literature are no different.

I do not wish to suggest that we could do without these assumptions and practices, or that there is a position from which one could simply challenge or overturn them if one wanted to. Their internal inconsistencies – like the fact that the actual histories of criticism, biography, editing, and theory belie the assumptions that enable them to operate – do not render them meaningless or useless, except, perhaps, from the perspective of their own fictions of self-consistency, testability, and productivity. Since literary commentary of any kind is constituted by and within institutions and societies, and their discourses and power systems, and since we live at a time and in a society in which the scientific model is deeply ingrained and politically effective, its dislodgement – supposing this were deemed desirable – would not be a straightforward or localized matter. The ease with which deconstruction – or something bearing its name – has been pressed into service in the academic sphere to provide 'improved' readings or theories in accordance with the scientific model is testimony to the power of the dominant discourse and its politico-institutional underpinning. (One could expatiate here on the structures of competition and 'objective' evaluation in the academic profession, the economic and ideological forces at work in the publishing industry, the glamorization of technology as an aesthetic category, the role of gender in the science/arts division, the educational practices of post-industrial society, and so on, but the analysis of such factors would not in itself loosen the hold of the discourse upon the academy – indeed, it might strengthen it, if the analysis itself were undertaken according to 'scientific' principles.)

Let us try to imagine, instead, how a 'deconstructive criticism' might operate within this context, accepting that the word *deconstruction* has taken on a wider meaning than that sanctioned by Derrida's first use of it, but still understanding it to refer to Derrida's practice as a reader of texts.[3] Where and how could it take effect? What would it be able to achieve? What would be the importance of deconstructive criticism of Joyce?

First, we have to imagine it seeding itself within the crannies and

---

[3] This brief discussion has been supplemented by longer considerations of deconstruction and criticism in my essay 'Singularities, Responsibilities' and in my introduction to Derrida's *Acts of Literature*.

along the fault lines of institutionalized criticism (including, perhaps, much of what is today called 'deconstruction'), and functioning only within an initial moment, before the inevitable appropriation by the institution made necessary a new locale and a new strategy. Deconstructive criticism would weave itself through the text being read, and weave that text through itself, and thread other texts through both, in a patient and careful movement of displacement and dissemination, at once exposing and destabilizing, however momentarily, the boundaries and hierarchies that have enabled the text to be pinned into (and to serve as a reinforcement of) an ideology or a metaphysic that denies it its specificity, its inexhaustibility, its unrecuperable otherness. It would in the process yield useful material for the literary critic, theorist, and historian (perhaps even the biographer and textual editor), the value of which is not to be underestimated, but which would not be among its effects as *deconstructive* criticism. (And to the extent that it did *not* furnish such material, it would be accused – from the point of view of scientific knowledge – of being useless or frivolous, of contributing nothing to our understanding of the text or our understanding of literature; as if the interest of, and justification for, a careful reading, deconstructive or otherwise, lay solely in the nugget of truth it added to the pile.)

A deconstructive criticism, or the deconstructive as it might be read in *any* criticism (for there are no generic or historical boundaries to be observed here, and no doubt there could never be such a thing as 'pure' deconstructive criticism), would offer no insights, conclusions, or detachable propositions, but would instead have the character of an *event* (and it must be remembered that there is nothing immediate or self-sufficient about the structure of events: they are constituted, like texts, by a changing and unsaturable context).[4] It would not contribute a brick to the growing edifice of knowledge, nor even mark a step on the road to the Last Deconstruction, but, in place of teleology or eschatology, would offer a unique conjunction or coincidence (I shall come back to this word)[5] of cultural traces, existing only by virtue of, and in anticipation of, an answering event, destined to repeat it and to change it with every occurrence: its reading.

This is why 'deconstructive criticism of Joyce' must be understood as *Joyce*'s deconstruction of the critic's text as much as the critic's decon-

---

[4] See, for instance, Derrida's essay 'Signature Event Context' (*Margins of Philosophy*, 309–30). The event plays an important part in Lyotard's thinking, too, as is well brought out by both Bennington, *Lyotard*, and Readings, *Introducing Lyotard*. For a discussion of the importance of the event in Foucault, see Young, *White Mythologies*, 81–5.   [5] And see also chapter 9 below.

struction of Joyce's text: the critical text would have been made possible by Joyce's text, by the specificity, the uniqueness, of Joyce's writing, as an event calling forth, and being called forth by, another event, equally specific, equally unique. In neither case is the specificity in question originary or self-determined, the transcendent uniqueness of a 'free subject' mastering the culture and the language; it is the specificity of a particular knot in the cultural, linguistic, political, ideological fabric of a place and a time. To read Joyce's text is to read a vast number of texts, radiating out as a network through Western culture and beyond, to read them through it and it through them, texts which the reader knows and doesn't know. (But what is it to 'know' or 'not know' a text? It is not the same as having 'read' or 'not read' a text, which is itself not a straightforward distinction.) Any criticism of Joyce's text will itself be already situated in that network, deriving terms, positions, modes of argument from it (more or less silently and compliantly, according to the degree of its deconstructive self-scrutiny), and will therefore offer itself to be read by the Joycean text, which constitutes a far more comprehensive and tightly bunched gathering of cultural threads than any foreseeable criticism.

To gain a sense of the network in which every text and every reading (and reader) is situated, as in a large telephone system, is also to appreciate the role of *coincidence* in culture, in history, in language. The more complex the network, and the more overdetermined every node within it, the more likely is it that 'coincidences' will occur – and the less they will conform to the character of what we usually understand by that word, since they will be not purely random convergences but the necessary products of a system of certain complexity, the outcome of a law which links, by a longer or shorter route, everything with everything else. And here we can take up the question that has been hovering in the background since the beginning of this essay: what has Joyce, *specifically*, to do with deconstruction?[6] Could this name, as it has occurred in this discussion, be replaced by that of *any* writer of literary texts? To a certain extent, the answer must be 'yes': the literary (which is not confined to literature) is that which refuses and resists the scientific model of knowledge, that which makes deconstruction possible (and necessary) by being itself an event and not an argument or truth-claim. To that extent,

---

[6] One could, of course, give a purely historical answer, pointing to Derrida's long familiarity with Joyce and his recurrent appeals to Joyce's work (a history which he himself has begun to document in 'Two Words for Joyce'), and to the importance of Joyce's texts to the new ground broken in Parisian journals in the 1960s, but this would still leave the question, why *Joyce*?

Joyce's texts are paradigmatic. But the particularity of Joyce (and I am using the name to stand for the group of texts bearing that signature), the place of Joyce within cultural, philosophical, and political history, and the conditions under which Joyce is read today, cannot be generalized to other writers in any simple way. Derrida's reading of *Ulysses* and *Finnegans Wake* point up – by detailed involvement with the text and its interrelations with other texts he has commented on – the peculiar aptness of Joyce's writing for anyone embarked upon a deconstructive engagement with the governing ideological system of our time (and its political, institutional, and cultural manifestations). In particular, Joyce's simulacrum, or parody, of the scientific model of cumulative knowledge – the encyclopedic inflation of *Ulysses* and *Finnegans Wake*, the concern with precise factual information, the interconnecting networks that run through each text, and that reach from text to text, and from text to history and biography (Joyce's, our own), to produce an endless series of coincidental effects that are not at all random (or whose randomness is programmed in advance by the laws of the text) – produces an unparalleled field in which the ruling principles of scientific knowledge can be tested against themselves, can be made to reveal their dependence on the aleatory, the excluded, the counter-rational, and the contingent, and, perhaps most important of all, and most specific to Joyce, can be exposed to a laughter which overruns all enclosures, penetrates all boundaries, and travesties all laws – not the irreverent laughter of the carnival (although that is a part of it), but the laughter that pre-exists, and presupposes, all the efforts of the scientific or analytic tradition to erect laws that protect the territory of the 'serious'.

This work – this play – of deconstruction within the writing of Joyce (and bequeathed by Joyce to us, if we will accept the gift) operates first at the level of the literary establishment, since the preordained consequence of Joyce's encyclopedic, overdetermined, texts (and I do not mean to exclude the earlier works), coinciding, but not coincidentally, with the growth of literary criticism as an academic subject, was the institution of a massive enterprise of exegesis and explication on the scientific model, the model of the international computerized data bank, ever more comprehensive and accurate. But we may regard the Joyce industry itself as nothing more than a vast extension of the Joycean text, equally a simulacrum or parody, producing its own irruptive laughter, testing and travestying the scientific model of knowledge at work in society at large, where the issues are of greater scope and significance. Joyce, and the 'Joyce industry', are important today not just because they parody the dominant post-Renaissance model of knowledge, but because of their relation to its more recent, and more totalitarian, complement: the drive towards (and hence the discourse of) technological efficiency and the maximization of profit (as wealth, knowledge, and power).[7] What is urgently needed is a criticism which is able to turn this discourse against itself, to tease out the wastefulness and internal differences of its own premises and procedures, in a gesture – a unique event that cannot be appropriated or pinned down – of parody, of laughter, of excess; not a criticism made in defiance of, or in retreat from, the discourse of efficient production and technological gain, but a criticism which finds itself already inhabiting the structures and practices of the postmodern machine. The deconstructive criticism of Joyce, perhaps.

[7] See Lyotard, *The Postmodern Condition*, 44–7. This drive is even more evident in 1999 than it was in 1984.

CHAPTER 2

Popular Joyce?

In many minds, the name 'James Joyce' stands for a kind of writing that is arcane, obscure, and of interest only to students of English literature – indeed, for some it may stand for literature itself, understood as an impenetrable and elitist manipulation of words that is best left well alone. Most academic studies of Joyce, were they to fall into the hands of those who hold such views, would do nothing to diminish these connotations. Even scholarly investigations of 'Joyce and popular culture', important though they have been within the critical tradition, tend to reinforce this attitude to Joyce, since what they often document is the process whereby the dross of second-rate material is transmuted into the gold of high art by a supremely sophisticated author catering only for a minority audience.

I am not about to argue that this perception of Joyce is, in some simple sense, wrong; my purpose is just to point out how the development of new ways of talking about the issues involved in the notions of 'popular' and 'elite' culture complicate the picture. The current theoretical debate about popular culture has been going on for a long time, beginning perhaps with Max Horkheimer and Theodor Adorno in *Dialectic of Enlightenment*, with its famous and much-discussed chapter on 'The Culture Industry: Enlightenment as Mass Deception'. More recently, however, the conversation has become increasingly intense and many-sided, with important contributions by, among others, Andreas Huyssen, Fredric Jameson, Tania Modleski, and Slavoj Žižek.[1] (Perhaps the most vivid manifestation of the clamour and disputatiousness that have characterized the discussion in the final decade of the twentieth century is the massive volume entitled *Cultural Studies*, edited by Lawrence Grossberg, Cary Nelson, and Paula Treichler, the consummation

---

[1] See the essays by Michael Walsh and David Glover in Kershner, ed., *Joyce and Popular Culture* for accounts of the theoretical debates over popular culture.

of a 1990 conference published in 1992.) Although the focus in this debate is for the most part on the productions and practices of mass culture, Joyce is far from an irrelevance: discussions of popular culture have often entailed discussions of modernism, which appears both to set its face against and yet to be dependent upon the cultural productions that give pleasure to the majority of the population.

A danger in such discussions, however, is that the notion of a homogeneous 'modernism' can come to be used without careful scrutiny, and one of the tasks that lie ahead in this area is the careful discrimination among those artists who have been obliged by our taxonomic insistence to share that reductive label. Joyce's frequent invocation of *Ruby, the Pride of the Ring* in *Ulysses* may have little in common with Eliot's 'Shakespeherian Rag' in *The Waste Land* or Pound's use of popular locutions in *The Cantos*. Woolf's distaste for much of working-class culture is complicated by her position as a woman, subject herself to many of the exclusions implicit in notions of 'high culture'. For too long modernism has been cast as a reaction against or refuge from mass culture, and we are beginning to understand just how much of a positive engagement it can be at the same time. But it would be a mistake to go from one extreme to the other, and to see all the writers we call 'modernists' as occupying the same relation to popular artefacts and practices.

It is clearly true that some writing has a built-in resistance to wide appeal; it *depends* on the detection of learned references and esoteric allusions, the ability to process highly complex syntax and unusual vocabulary, the possession of an extraordinary verbal memory. Literary texts of this kind have been produced in all periods, but the period 1910–1940 was particularly marked by them. It is also obvious that in time much writing that is accessible on its first appearance becomes difficult, requiring special expertise in order to understand and enjoy it. Joyce's work, at first blush, might appear to fall solidly (and increasingly) in both these categories; a glance at the multitude of reference books aimed at enhancing the reader's comprehension of his writing seems sufficient evidence that only those with special skills and the free time for patient scholarship can appreciate it.

What I would wish to argue, however, is that the distinguishing feature of Joyce's use of recherché material is that it does not constitute the key or the core of the work; it is only taken to be such by those who assume that the more learned or 'high-cultural' the reference the more central its place in the work's scheme and value. In *Ulysses* and the *Wake*, the shards of elite culture mingle with the orts of popular culture, and there is no principle of hierarchy to govern them. The reader of *Finnegans Wake* who is unfamiliar with 'Humpty Dumpty' loses as much as the reader unfamiliar with the *Scienza Nuova*. And if you don't know either, there is still much else to get your teeth into. By refusing the cultural hierarchies that most of his readers take for granted, Joyce builds a principle of accessibility into his work; or, to put it another way, there is a whole series of minority audiences, each of which has access to special knowledge that will illuminate one aspect of his writing, but no one of which occupies a privileged position *vis-à-vis* the text's meaning. There is a sense, then, in which it can be said that with each successive work Joyce increased the openness of his writing, until he created in *Finnegans Wake* a richness of texture and reference that allows any reader to recognize familiar items and begin to construct a narrative chain or a thematic network out of them. (This openness gives a special role to chance and contingency in the reading process, as I argue in chapter 9 below.)

Needless to say, this delightful proposition is hardly borne out in the world of real readers in front of real books. The reason is that it assumes the ability of readers to shed a number of ingrained preconceptions about what it is to *read* – expectations and assumptions about linearity, transparency, directness of plot, singularity of meaning, and so on. Above all, readers would have to give up the fundamental presupposition that reading is an attempt at *textual mastery*; that is, that the words on the page possess a meaning which can be obtained from them by the appropriate process of translation, a process which, if successful, entirely exhausts the text's potential for meaning.[2] This assumption also entails the belief that different readers' responses to a given text should in principle be the same, however diverse they may be in practice. A preconception of this kind is not, of course, something that is held consciously, but it colours the twists and turns of the reading mind from its first encounter with the text.

To imagine reading without this presupposition is not to imagine giving up the attempt at scrupulous and thorough interpretation, but it is to raise the possibility of altering the basis on which such interpretative activity is carried out. Acknowledging that texts are always in contexts,

---

[2] It is only an apparent paradox that the same assumption could be depicted by a contrary metaphor, that of passivity: 'mastery' of the text in this sense, though it might necessitate a certain wrestling with the language to force it to give up its secrets, is also submission to the text, which has only one, pre-existing, meaning, to which absolute faithfulness is demanded.

that contexts are always themselves contextualized and contextualiz-able, that contexts are never exhaustible or predictable, is one way of recognizing the inadequacy of the notion of reading as mastery. Every reader of *Ulysses* or *Finnegans Wake* contextualizes the work differently, producing a different text and a different reading experience. The reader who does not have access to, or any interest in, the learned tomes produced by the Joyce industry and has not internalized the cultural encyclopedia constantly raided by Joyce is not thereby an inferior interpreter, failing in the face of an elite cultural product, but one reader among millions, just as capable as any other – in principle – of careful and responsive attention to the words, and the understanding and enjoyment that follows, though always differently, from such attention.

It may in fact be impossible to shake ourselves free of the assumption that reading is a process of mastery and totalization, so closely im-bricated is it with our usual understanding of meaning itself, but Joyce's *œuvre* might be seen as one attempt (growing increasingly ambitious with each work) to give us the means to do so to the extent that it *is* possible. His version of modernism is certainly a far more effective means of achieving some degree of freedom from totalizing interpretative as-sumptions than abstract theorizing about the reading process, even if what we learn as we plunge into the *Wake* may not always carry over to the other texts we encounter. (Though many of those who have spent some time wrestling with – and laughing at – Joyce's last book will testify that this experience can have a powerful effect on the reading of other books.) And my further point is that it is open to *any* reader to undergo the training that Joyce offers in non-masterful reading; it is not an experience available only to an elite, whether this be construed as an elite of class, of education, or of intelligence. This is not to deny that there is a widespread preference for texts that offer themselves up immediately to consumption and gratification, but this is itself a cultural product, a reflex of, among other things, consumer capitalism's de-mands for instant profit and the anti-intellectualism which it fosters. There is no *intrinsic* reason why the pleasurable labour of the 'difficult' text should not be open to the majority of the population.

This is, of course, utopian thinking; the cultural forces that insist on transparency, immediacy, totality, and so on, are not going to be shifted overnight. But history may be on Joyce's side. The techniques that he, above all, introduced into Western verbal 'high art' have now per-meated much wider reaches of the cultural domain – along with the iconoclastic approach and the destabilizing humour which they serve. It is not too far-fetched to claim that the most interesting and innovative productions of popular culture are, in the very specific sense I have been arguing for, 'Joycean'. So it may be that the generation growing up with postmodern music and video will find Joyce more accessible than their parents did – at least if the aura of impenetrability that surrounds his work can be punctured by readings that manifest the kind of irreverence and exuberance which he himself displayed so brilliantly.

In any case, I believe that one of our goals as scholars and teachers of Joyce should be to dispel the idea that you have to be a specialist to understand and enjoy his work. This is one of the risks at stake in the excellent work being done on the archive material, on the appropriateness of different editorial procedures, on biographical data and historical references. While it is perfectly possible for such work to be part of a project of opening up the Joycean text in just the way I have been describing, it can in some manifestations seem to imply that only those who have internalized a mass of esoteric knowledge can have a 'true' understanding of Joyce – rather than simply a different one. There is a crucial difference between, on the one hand, presenting a method of analysis and its resulting insights as an illumination of one facet of Joyce's work and, on the other, claiming that all other approaches are secondary or invalid.

Joyce, in other words, is *already* part of popular culture – perhaps, though this would demand a longer and even more tendentious argument, part of what is most valuable in popular culture. Professional critics and teachers of Joyce should not deny or smother that congruence, but learn from it and build on it. And above all, enjoy it.

CHAPTER 3

Touching 'Clay': reference and reality in Dubliners

Halloween games are being played at the Donnelly's, and it is the family's guest, their one-time employee, Maria, whose turn it is to be blindfolded and to bring her hand down on one of the three saucers, containing a ring, a prayer book, and some water, each with its prediction for the coming year. The paragraph that describes her moment of choice seems to me one of the most strangely potent in *Dubliners* – indeed, in all Joyce's work:

> They led her up to the table amid laughing and joking and she put her hand out in the air as she was told to do. She moved her hand about here and there in the air and descended on one of the saucers. She felt a soft wet substance with her fingers and was surprised that nobody spoke or took off her bandage. There was a pause for a few seconds; and then a great deal of scuffling and whispering. Somebody said something about the garden, and at last Mrs Donnelly said something very cross to one of the next-door girls and told her to throw it out at once: that was no play. Maria understood that it was wrong that time and so she had to do it over again: and this time she got the prayer-book. (*D* 105)

Responding to 'Clay' – answering to what is unique in the text, and doing so both responsively and responsibly – entails, for me, attending with as much care as possible to the resonances and refractions of this passage. That doing so raises the question of this particular text's relationship to the general laws of representation and reference should come as no surprise; the uniqueness of a literary text is not that of some unrepeatable essence, but precisely that of its singular relation to the general, its endlessly reiterable staging of the once-for-all-time.

As part of an endeavour to respond adequately, we can try to recreate or imagine a first reading of this passage, without commentaries at our elbows or notes at the foot of the page. In such a reading, Maria's experience is briefly our own; character and reader share this moment of contact with a substance which is both real and somehow unreal, a substance whose physical qualities of softness and wetness impinge more directly than those of any other object in the story, yet one which remains nameless, resistant to any attempt to pull it into the reassuring grid of language. A substance which is both substantial and insubstantial, densely present yet strangely absent, an existence without essence. The games, and the narrative, falter, as if for an instant the usually hidden sources of their functioning had been exposed, thus unsettling their confident and unselfconscious progress.

In terms of standard narrative analysis, of course, the absence of any name for the substance Maria touches is explained by the point of view that has been adopted throughout the story. Although the narration is in the third person, we recognize in this paragraph a style that we have associated with Maria from the beginning (whether her own way of speaking or thinking, or one that she would in some way endorse[1]): the simple paratactic syntax, the non-literary diction, the slightly awkward repetitions – 'she put her hand out in the air', 'She moved her hand about here and there in the air'; 'Somebody said something', 'Mrs Donnelly said something'. Knowledge of the world possessed by this narrator goes no further than Maria's;[2] and since Maria never discovers the true nature of the substance she touches, we are not informed either. But this is not a full explanation of the strange absence of identification: Joyce may utilize narrative conventions, but he is never wholly bound by them. There are moments throughout the story when a distinctly different style breaks through the jejune, repetitive language that we associate with Maria's consciousness, providing a sudden external view couched in a conventional 'literary' rhetoric: 'her grey-green eyes sparkled with disappointed shyness' (101), 'her minute body nearly shook itself asunder' (101), '[she] ferreted her way' (102).[3] Even more strikingly,

---

[1] This second possibility would be a version of what Hugh Kenner, in *Joyce's Voices*, famously named 'The Uncle Charles' principle, after the sentence in the opening passage of Part II of *A Portrait* which informs us that 'uncle Charles repaired to his outhouse' (II.12–13). The word *repaired*, as Kenner points out, is not simply one that the character would use (and thus a type of 'free indirect discourse' or *style indirect libre*), but one that he would choose to have used of him by someone describing his action. The style we associate with Maria is not, however, a literary style of the kind Uncle Charles favours. For further discussion, see notes 3 and 11 below.

[2] The assumption that we can identify a 'narrator' or 'narrative voice' – which implies a persona responsible for the telling of the story – is one whose untenability will become evident; however, it serves as convenient shorthand for a more theoretically laden phrase, such as 'narrative instance' or 'discourse', which would bring its own problems.

[3] These rather self-conscious literary phrases are not easy to interpret: one might expect them all to offer glamorized images of Maria, but this is not so – 'ferreted' is a case in point, and the 'witch' image may be another. We certainly cannot posit a single consciousness which sometimes presents Maria through her 'own' style and sometimes through a consistent narrative style, nor can we securely identify a voice we could call 'authorial' (a point made of *Dubliners* more generally by Colin MacCabe in his chapter 'The End of a Meta-Language: From George Eliot to *Dubliners*'

a deliberate inconsistency in the technique of limited point of view follows soon after the passage I have quoted, when Maria sings the first verse of *I Dreamt that I Dwelt* twice but, we are told, 'no one tried to show her her mistake' (106). Not only is the narrative here pointing out something which Maria fails to perceive, but our attention is being drawn to that failure and thus to the literary strategy being used: the limitations of Maria's awareness are the very reason for the step which the narrative takes outside her consciousness. Joyce could have found a way of doing something similar for the 'soft wet substance' had he wished to, and therefore we are aware that the name is being withheld from us by the author as well as by the narrator; that the disjunction being enforced here between language and the material world is not to be passed over as a mere side effect of a technique that, once chosen, cannot be varied.

It might be claimed that Joyce *did* provide the missing external comment when he entitled the story 'Clay', and no doubt our first-time reader, after a moment of bafflement, makes this connection. The reader is then in a position to reconstruct the events of which Maria remains ignorant: the saucers with ring, water, and prayer book have been replaced, with mischievous intent, by one containing garden clay, pushed surreptitiously under Maria's descending hand.[4] Although such an appeal to the title seems satisfactorily to fill the void threatening to open at this moment in the story, we will find it useful to interrogate a little more closely the interpretative operations involved in such a solution to the puzzle.

Firstly, in order to make this move, we have to give the title an authority that the text clearly lacks, setting the utterance 'Clay' outside the narrative as the emanation of a transcendent consciousness with access to a full truth. This is how we frequently treat titles, forgetting that our reading of this element of the text is in part determined by our reading of the very text it names: if 'Clay' had turned out to be a story

(*James Joyce and the Revolution of the Word*, ch. 2); it is, of course, applicable to all Joyce's fiction).
[4] Not all readers will want to ascribe this much malice to the children; thus Warren Beck states, 'It is scarcely possible to assume, as one critic does, that the children trick blindfolded Maria into choosing the clay; she is merely told "to put her hand out in the air"; she then "moved her hand about here and there" and it "descended on one of the saucers"' (*Joyce's 'Dubliners'*, 213). But the fact that the critic in question, William T. Noon, does assume it shows that it *is* possible to do so; and it is central to my argument that such an assumption is impossible to disprove. Beck, in citing the words that reflect *Maria*'s sense of what is happening, simply reproduces the text's doubleness at this point. Cóilín Owens, in the first part of a three-part article on 'Clay' and Irish folk traditions, also assumes that these words provide objective 'information' about what is happening ('"Clay" (1)', 344). It is equally possible to assume, as Noon does, that the Donnelly parents arrange things so that Maria, on her second attempt, gets the prayer book, though here I find it easier to imagine a free choice being allowed (see Noon, 'Joyce's "Clay"').

about a sculptor the title would, at least in retrospect and in further readings, be interpreted rather differently. On a first reading of any work, we have to suspend full interpretation of the title until we have reached the end of the work, and it is only the inclusion of the passage about the saucer that enables us to interpret the word *clay* in the title literally. Secondly, and rather more unusually, we have to make the primary function of the title the revelation of the name of an object which appears unnamed in the text, as if the story were a bizarre kind of riddle where the answer appears before the question – a sort of gargantuan 'Jeopardy' game. And thirdly, we have to relegate any figurative interpretations of the title, including the obvious implications of malleability, frailty, and mortality, to a secondary place; or if we do not, we have to reverse our normal hierarchies and regard 'Clay' as a general, symbolic title which *also* happens to have a literal meaning in reference to one specific paragraph – a rather difficult feat.[5]

I don't intend to mount a challenge to the view that the title names the substance which Maria, and the narrator, fail to identify, but merely to stress that in order to reach this conclusion we have to pass through a number of interpretative mechanisms and negotiate a number of literary conventions, and that this is not a perfectly smooth process. Our knowledge of the clay under Maria's fingers is not direct; it comes only *after* our moment of bafflement, and our hermeneutic activity is impelled by that initial sense of resistance to understanding. However secure may be our eventual certainty that the title names the substance, it is a certainty always haunted by the knowledge that it depends on a prior uncertainty, and on a mechanics of deduction following in its wake. The transparent relation that we expect between title and text is permanently shadowed; and we cannot *simply* say that the words 'soft wet substance' refer to clay.

A comparison with earlier titles Joyce used for the story in progress will clarify the point further. The first completed version was called 'Hallow Eve', a name which embraces the entire narrative rather than focusing on one object in one paragraph, and demands much less interpretative work in relating title to text. (Of course, it would also leave us much closer to Maria in our uncertainty about the contents of the saucer.) In a letter to Stanislaus some months later, Joyce refers to the

---

[5] Jean-Jacques Lecercle has pointed out to me that the passage signals the missing term to us in another way, but by a logic that is even less acceptable within the norms of a philosophical reading: in the phrase 'that was no play' the text comes as close as it ever does to repeating the title of the story.

story as 'The Clay',[6] a title which has the opposite effect: its function as an explanation of the substance that Maria touches is more secure, since the definite article signals more clearly its literal operation and keeps the metaphoric associations – malleability, frailty, and so on – at bay.

There remains, then, something in the description of Maria's hand reaching the saucer that resists the well-oiled machinery of our cognitive apparatus, and that recourse to the title 'Clay' does not quite remove; a sense that the gears which smoothly connect language to the physical world have slipped out of their normal mode of efficient and unnoticeable operation. And my argument is that it is just this slippage, this hesitation, that makes the passage so powerful and its power so hard to account for.

A WOMAN OF NO IMPORTANCE

I want now to broaden the discussion to the whole of 'Clay' (and by implication to Joyce's method throughout *Dubliners*). After all, if this passage is a crucial one, as the title suggests, we should be able to read it in a way that sheds light on the entire story. At first, it is not easy to see why this particular episode should be singled out. It does not appear to have narrative centrality: it is not the most acute of Maria's petty humiliations on this Hallow Eve (in fact, her hosts are more discomfited by it than she is, a point to which I shall return). If the title were to reflect a passage with this kind of thematic centrality, it would have to be called something like 'Plum Cake'. (It is interesting to speculate whether, with this title, we would come to a different conclusion about the identity of the 'soft wet substance' in the saucer.) Nor does this passage constitute the culmination of the narrative; for a title that would reflect the final phase of the story, with its revealing mistake by Maria, one might suggest 'I Dreamt that I Dwelt'.

The most common way of dealing with this problem is, no doubt, to rely on the title's general, symbolic overtones to give the passage extra weight; a number of the stories of *Dubliners* have titles which refer in a literal sense to something specific in the text, and then in a more general way delineate the story as a whole. 'A Painful Case' is a case in point, where these words form part of the newspaper report quoted in the story but clearly allude to Mr Duffy's personal history; and so, in different ways, are 'Araby' (the name of the bazaar, but also a pointer to the

---

[6] About 24 September 1905; *Letters* II, 109.

young boy's yearnings and fantasies) and 'The Dead', where we experience a complex interrelation among Gretta Conroy's revelation of
Michael Furey's death, Gabriel Conroy's reverie following it, and a
certain view of the characters at the party as a group. But in none of
these is there a disjunction between the specific and the general significance as there is in 'Clay'; in these stories the specific reference within
the text is itself a crucial moment in the unfolding of the narrative, and
already functions both literally and figuratively. Maria's failure to recognize the substance she is touching does not seem immediately to radiate
significance through the story in the same way as do the report of Mrs
Sinico's death (another example of a story which covers up a grim
female existence), the romantic Eastern name of the bazaar which the
boy longs to visit, or the desperate act of love which Gretta describes.[7]

In the case of 'Clay', the wider meaning that immediately springs to
the interpreting mind is 'death'.[8] If Maria had recognized the substance,
and read into it a prophecy along the lines of the other items in the
saucers, she would no doubt have concluded that she was being warned
of an early demise. Some versions of the game include clay with just this
meaning, and it seems likely that the next-door girls have reintroduced a
choice banished from many family parlours.[9] But what remains unsatis-

[7] Several of the stories of *Dubliners* have titles whose relation to the story is open to various interpretations; 'The Sisters' and 'An Encounter' seem to focus on only one section of the text, though a much more prominent section than is the case in 'Clay'; there is no obvious eponym within the text of 'A Little Cloud', though a number of alternatives are available; and the title 'Grace' presumably exists in some kind of ironic relation to the story it names.

[8] Examples of this interpretation in studies of 'Clay' abound; I note only three instances, all collected in Garrett, ed., *Twentieth-century Interpretations of 'Dubliners'*. Hugh Kenner: 'Maria as "Clay" as humanity itself, as susceptible to moulding, and as death in life' (47); Brewster Ghiselin: 'She is ready for death, as her touching the clay in the Hallow Eve games intimates' (77); Florence Walzl: 'Her hidden fortune, the clay, prophetic of death, suggests all that the ultimate future holds for her' (109). It is perhaps the influence of this interpretation of the title which leads so many commentators to refer to Maria as 'old'; thus Beck, who is generally scrupulous in avoiding symbolic readings, uses the phrase 'little old Maria' four times in his chapter on 'Clay' (201, 203, 206, 207). She is old enough to have looked after (perhaps as a young girl) two boys who are now old enough to have small children of their own, and she admires her body in the mirror 'in spite of its years': but neither of these things *necessarily* makes her a little old woman. Once again, what is significant is that there is nothing in the text to indicate *unquestionably* Maria's stage of life.

[9] Cóilín Owens cites the 1943 Irish Folklore Commission survey of Halloween customs as indicating that the most widely reported version of the game at that date was the one including clay, though he also notes that the clay was 'sometimes suppressed by parents' ('"Clay" [1]', 344). François Laroque, in 'Hallowe'en Customs in "Clay"', cites from the *Journal of the Kildare Archaeological Society* of 1908 (as quoted in Kevin Danaher's *The Year in Ireland*) a description of the game with four saucers, including one containing clay as a foretelling of death. Jacques Aubert, in his notes to *Dubliners* in the Pléiade edition of Joyce's *Oeuvres*, 1, mentions this fourth possibility (1522), but then suggests that in the transformation of a folk ritual to a family game the clay would have been omitted – except that the next-door girls don't play the game . . .

factory about this interpretative jump, inevitable though it is, is its complete lack of any relation to the rest of the narrative; death does not figure at all among the many human predicaments with which the story deals. A quite different interpretation of the title in its wider function is an appeal to the notion of malleability: Maria exemplifies the human tendency to be moulded by situation, by desire, by anxieties, by the responses of others; and the text itself, with its multiple and shifting meanings, shows that language, too, lacks fixed identities. The problem with *this* interpretation is that it seems to have no relation to the passage in question; malleability is not likely to have been in anybody's mind during the Halloween game.[10]

Though these meanings hover suggestively in the reader's mind, they do not account for the importance accorded to the passage by the title. However, I believe that we *can* fruitfully move from the episode of the saucer to the story as a whole – not in a way that will lessen the title's slight oddness, but one that will justify its underscoring of the passage. To do so, we need to follow through the question that it raises, at the moment when Maria touches something in the saucer and we strain to know what it is: how do words (in fiction, but also in other types of discourse) relate to the world to which they refer? How does referring happen? If the title and its curious relation to this passage raise the question of Maria's capacity – or incapacity – to name what she experiences, then we have in small compass the issue that every reader is caught up in, knowingly or unknowingly, from the beginning of the story.

For in that beginning, from the opening words 'The matron had given her leave to go out as soon as the women's tea was over', we sense a strong pull towards the referent they claim to designate: Joyce uses the traditional techniques of realist narrative to create the illusion of an already existing world, and to release information about this world with a calculated miserliness that has readers eager for each morsel they are allotted. The first paragraph accomplishes a great deal, in spite of its apparent simplicity (let us again assume a first reading):

The matron had given her leave to go out as soon as the women's tea was over and Maria looked forward to her evening out. The kitchen was spick and span: the cook said you could see yourself in the big copper boilers. The fire was nice

[10] These two possibilities do not exhaust the significance that has been found in the title; others include 'an ironic reminder of [Maria's] earth mother archetype' (Hana Wirth-Nesher, 'Reading Joyce's City', 287) and a 'polite circumlocution that eradicates the dirt and squalor of Maria's life' (Norris, *Joyce's Web*, 134).

and bright and on one of the side-tables were four very big barmbracks. These
barmbracks seemed uncut; but if you went closer you would see that they had
been cut into long thick even slices and were ready to be handed round at tea.
Maria had cut them herself.

'The matron had given her leave': already we are assumed to know who
'the matron' is; we are placed in a present that presupposes a past ('had
given'); and, as if we already knew the character being spoken of, we are
told only of 'her'. The use of the pronoun where we might expect a noun
is typical of free indirect style, since one does not commonly use one's
own name in one's own thoughts, and although the second half of the
sentence provides the name that we require, this early sense that we are
getting Maria's own thoughts mediated via another voice keeps reasserting itself.[11]

As accomplished readers of fiction, we process this exiguous material
with ease, and recognize that our task will be, as it has so often been, to
reconstruct the context from the account of someone who gives only
sparse details precisely because of their familiarity with it – and at the
same time to take pleasure in the skilled writer's ability to establish the
detail of this context with the utmost economy of effort. That the
narrative voice is non-literary is quickly evident – largely paratactic, it
deals in cliché ('spick and span') and banal phrasing ('nice and bright'),
and it makes no attempt to avoid random repetition ('go out', 'evening
out'; 'big copper boilers', 'very big barmbracks'; 'they had been cut',
'Maria had cut them'). The point of view is quickly localized as Maria's:
not only does the non-literary language suggest a particular consciousness within the narrative, but the admiration for the apparently uncut
barmbracks assumes a particular station in the room, which appears to
be occupied by no-one other than Maria and the cook ('if you went
closer you would see'). The formally external and neutral statement with
which the paragraph ends – 'Maria had cut them herself' – implies, in
its context, a self-reflective moment of justified pride. The limited point
of view and commonplace style appear designed to achieve the fullest
possible involvement with the main character, Maria, whose view of her
environment we have no reason to mistrust.

[11] Norris argues that 'the narrative voice probably does not speak in the language of Maria's class –
whose diction can't be verified from the text – but in the idiom of someone mimicking the
accents of respectable bourgeois folks' (*Joyce's Web*, 126). The crucial term here is presumably
'mimicking' – and Norris goes on to refer to 'Maria's notion of . . . the phrasing of proper
middle-class speech' (126) – since much of the language is impoverished and repetitive. But the
problem of the unverifiable 'real' diction of Maria's class, like the problem of Maria's class itself,
will not go away.

For many readers, no doubt, this remains true to the end of 'Clay'. Frank O'Connor is one such reader, summing it up as a story which 'describes an old maid who works in a laundry and the succession of utterly minor disasters that threatens to ruin her celebration of Halloween in the home of her married nephew' ('Work in Progress', 307). (I will return to this apparently mistaken description of Maria's relation to Joe.) For others, the insignificance of the story means – according to a strategy frequently applied to the stories of *Dubliners* – that it has to be interpreted on a symbolic level: a reasonable response to a narrative that, interpreted literally, seems to have little to offer to the reader expecting large meanings. The title, as we have noted, suggests one such extension of significance. Another detail crying out for symbolic interpretation is Maria's three times described long nose and long chin, almost meeting when she laughs – this peculiar physiognomy, together with the Halloween setting, seems to imply that she may be understood as a witch; while for some readers her name and her presumed virginity indicate an association with the Virgin Mary. It is undeniable that Joyce scatters tempting clues to large symbolic structures throughout the stories of *Dubliners*, as he does throughout his other works; the question is whether any of these works can be *reduced* to a symbolic system, or whether, instead, what is being offered is the temptation itself, a demonstration of the desire to invest quotidian reality with deeper significance. If this is so, then what is equally important is the inevitable failure of such symbolic reductions, since quotidian reality – and the openness of the text to interpretation – will always exceed them.

I would suggest, however, that most readers accustomed to Joyce's methods, alert to the nuances of his styles, and sceptical of grand symbolic gestures, find that what becomes of absorbing interest in 'Clay' is the growing sense of a gap between the version of Maria's experience being presented by the narrative and an alternative, but obscured, reality. No doubt the point at which this sense is born varies from reader to reader; for many it may come with the delayed information that the 'colonel-looking gentleman' who makes room for her in the tram is – or rather was – in fact drunk, or perhaps a little later when Maria, deciding that she must have left the plum cake on the tram, remembers how 'confused' the gentleman had made her: a confusion of which there was no discursive trace when the event was related. Or the suspicion that the narrative is not presenting reality in a completely straightforward manner may arise with the contrast between, on the one hand, the narrator's repeated insistence on the success of the party at the Donnelly's – how

Joe is 'very nice to her' (104) and 'never . . . so nice to her as he was that night' (105), how 'everything was merry again' (104) and 'they were all quite merry again' (105), how Joe and his wife are 'in such good spirits' – and, on the other, the narrated events, including the children's resentment at Maria's accusation about the plum cake, Joe's anger over the lost (or hidden?) nutcracker, the violent argument about Joe's estranged brother, the failed trick with the clay, the mistake in Maria's song, and the culmination of Joe's drunkenness in maudlin nostalgia and helplessness as he gropes, in the story's final sentence, for the missing corkscrew.

However the reader's suspicions are aroused, they prove a potent interpretative engine, as indeed my somewhat overstated previous sentence might suggest. They make possible the construction of a different version of Maria's situation and experiences from the very beginning of the story: the first sentence reveals that she regularly has to work in the evenings, the second that it is her duty to clean the kitchen and scour the boilers, and that she is on an equal footing with the cook, whose praise she values. The expression of pride in the neatly cut barmbracks is seen as a diversion of the reader's attention away from Maria's other responsibilities to the only one consonant with a genteel lifestyle. The vigilant reader can find alternative meanings of this sort in virtually every sentence.[12] The most forceful summary of this obscured reality that I know is Margot Norris's, in a brilliant essay on 'Clay' from which I have already quoted, entitled 'Narration Under a Blindfold' (*Joyce's Web*, ch. 6):

Maria works long hours for meager pay as a scullion in a laundry for reformed prostitutes who make her the butt of their jokes. She is ignored and patronized by everyone, including the family whose slavey she once was, and from whom she succeeds in extorting only a minimal and ritualized tolerance by manipulating their guilt and pity. (124)[13]

[12] It is somewhat ironic that Chris Hutchinson, in 'The Act of Narration', an article with the admirable aim of criticizing speech-act theories of narrative for their idealizing tendencies, should use the opening sentence of 'Clay' as his example, since he argues that this sentence 'makes no claims for the truth of the expressed proposition and, taken in the null context as a sentence in the language, requires no act of trust on the part of the hearer', and that such propositions 'do not involve criteria of truth or the hearer's trust that the speaker is telling the truth, i.e., not misleading him' (18–19). In the narrative context of 'Clay', the question of trust, of the possibility of the reader's being misled, is precisely the issue; it might be said that Hutchinson has still not sufficiently de-idealized his account of narrative discourse, and that the always possible unreliability of the narrator should be taken into account, and distinguished from the authorial (or, to use a Barthesian coinage, scriptorial) function.

[13] A less extreme account of the occulted reality of Maria's life is given by Warren Beck; thus he regards the praise which is heaped on Maria for her peacemaking at the laundry as a jest which

As Norris argues, the text of 'Clay' that we read, presented by a narrator who embodies Maria's desires, consists of a series of attempts to promote her importance in the face of abundant evidence to the contrary. Since Maria's insignificance is not an inherent quality of the person she is but the product of a social judgement on unattractive old maids, it is by transforming the neutral or hostile responses she receives from those she encounters into positive valuations that she escapes the ever-threatening sense of worthlessness – and, as Norris rightly points out, the reader who cleverly 'sees through' the wishful thinking to the 'real' Maria is implicated as one of those who bring into being the need for wishful thinking. The 'real' Maria – ugly, easily flustered, interfering, unsuccessful, thick-skinned – is as much a social product as the fantasized Maria, who is attractive, popular, respected, admired, influential.[14] The words we read refer twice, both to a reality they name – the reality of Maria's constructed world – and to the reality which that construction is designed to obliterate.

ON REFERRING

There is bound to be some resistance to this negative reading of Maria's experience, since it entails going against the explicit word of the text; and many discussions of the story in print testify to the compelling force of the glamorized version. Thus Maria's exact relation to the Donnellys is not stated, and it is easy to find oneself assuming, on the basis of her claims to an intimate connection, that she is a member of the family – Frank O'Connor, we have already seen, assumes that she is the boys' aunt, and Robert Scholes, in an essay included in his own critical edition of *Dubliners*, regards her as their sister ('"Counterparts" and the Method of *Dubliners*', 381). (To think that two brothers would obtain for their own elder sister a menial job in an institution for ex-prostitutes suggests a

---

she fails to see; he refers to Maria's 'barely suppressed sense of her extraneousness' to the family gathering; and he mentions points in the narrative (including the saucer game) at which 'the truth about Maria is too closely approached for that slim comfort maintained by her modest persistence and by others' connivance in sustaining the fiction of her importance' (*Joyce's 'Dubliners'*, 204, 213). He makes the assumption that the stylistically contrasted sequences that interrupt Maria's perspective are comments by 'Joyce', which is to give them unwarranted authority.

14 By choosing a woman to exemplify the effects of social judgement, Joyce was obviously highlighting gender differences; an unmarried man getting on in years would scarcely need the same machinery of self-delusion to survive in Dublin. But self-construction of this type occurs across gender lines; we might consider what kind of self-image a 'colonel-looking gentleman' given to drink has to sustain in order to combat the negative responses he would receive.

rather grim view of Dublin family life – unless Scholes has also been
taken in by the nature of Maria's employment.) On the other hand,
Norris's reference to her as the Donnellys' 'slavey' can be challenged,
too: would someone who held the position of a maid-of-all-work be
invited to the family Halloween party and treated like an honoured
guest (however patronizingly)?

Once we start scrutinizing details of interpretation like this, however,
the question of where reality lies becomes highly problematic. Put
baldly, the problem is this: if the words of the text that we read are all
devoted to the establishment of the favourable version of Maria's life, by
what interpretative authority can we deduce the version that lies behind
them, and how can we set limits to the sceptical drive that would treat
every overt statement, potentially at least, as the concealment of an
unpalatable truth? If the narrative is capable of distorting, displacing,
and occluding, how do we know of any 'fact' that it is not a fantasy?
Norris writes of 'discrepancies . . . between what is said and what is
shown' (*Joyce's Web*, 125) – but how, in a verbal text, is anything shown
except by being said? It is easy enough to demonstrate inconsistencies
that lead us to suspect the accuracy of the version we are given – I have
already mentioned the different accounts of the gentleman on the tram.
But if the real story cannot be put into words – if the function of the
words is precisely to conceal that story – we can never securely identify
it.[15] This, of course, is the problem raised by the phrase 'soft wet
substance', which succeeds in drawing our attention to the existence of
an object without immediately granting it identifiability; the phrase
appears to refer, but as long as there is even the slightest hesitation about
what it refers to, it cannot be said to do so in the normal sense of the
word.

How can we know *what* Maria's relationship to the Donnelly family is,
since anything the text says about it is likely to reflect her desires on this

[15] It is surely not the case, as Norris claims, that deceptive narratives of this kind *necessarily* give
themselves away. It is only the ones that give themselves away that we can be reasonably sure of.
Although she rightly avoids using the personifying term 'narrator', Norris ascribes to the
narrative voice an extraordinary degree of self-conscious agency; thus she refers to 'its skill in
keeping the true nature of the laundry a secret, and its cunning in remarking, but disguising,
Maria's discomfort with it' (*Joyce's Web*, 128); it 'blurt[s] out a series of damaging revelations'
(131); it – possibly – uses 'an uncharacteristically unflattering image of Maria . . . to divert our
attention from much more painful revelations' (214). In a complementary essay in *Joyce's Web*,
'Who Killed Julia Morkan?', Norris once more finds a narration with an emotional life of its
own, capable of responding directly to the events it describes, and liable to ruin its dissimulatory
project by its honest emotions: 'The narration, caught off guard and surprised by Julia's singing,
blurts out its honestly thrilled appraisal' (114).

score rather than the plain fact of the matter? If she holds a lowly status in the family, this is the one thing that the text *cannot* tell us. If the response to Maria's arrival at the Donnelly's – '*O, here's Maria!*' – really means, as Norris suggests, 'O god, here's Maria already' (*Joyce's Web*, 132), the text will take advantage of the tonelessness of print in order to avoid revealing this. So we are in the curious situation of interpreting words on the basis of their *not* referring to reality, or rather their referring to it by not referring to it; though we cannot make this an interpretative algorithm, since we have no way of knowing when what we are being told *is* the unvarnished truth. We have already noted that the narrative is not consistent in its style and its range of vision; at any point, therefore, it could refer to the unglamorized world. When we first read the sentence 'Everyone was so fond of Maria' we may treat it as an objective comment from the narrator; on a second reading we may decide that it is a reflection of Maria's wishful thinking. But because the narrative is not in a position to say something like 'Everyone found Maria rather an embarrassment, but fortunately she missed most of their mocking irony and patronizing condescension', we can never *know* if this is indeed the case. When the narrative refers to Maria's hand descending on 'one of the saucers', we cannot know whether there are more than one; her blindfold has rendered this knowledge forever impossible, for her, the narrator, and every reader.

The blindfold that Maria wears all the time – the bandage that protects her from the knowledge that would crush her spirit – has exactly the same effect. Had the narrative been presented in the *first* person, we would at least have been able to develop a sense of the typical workings of Maria's mind, but Joyce takes even this degree of calculability away. We could, in fact, gradually increase the distance between the reality which the words actually name and the one they conceal until the latter bears no obvious relation to the former: once a wedge of suspicion has been inserted between the two, we have no grounds for stopping at any particular point. It is not even a question of irony, a difficult enough rhetorical manœuvre to pin down, since the first level of meaning, when it is dominant, completely fails to acknowledge the second. Nor can we draw a parallel with Gerty MacDowell's romantic rendering of her experience in the 'Nausicaa' episode of *Ulysses*, or with HCE's defences of his innocence and worth in *Finnegans Wake*, since in both these instances the language itself is constantly giving its speakers away.

The 'reality' which lies 'behind' the story has a very peculiar status, therefore: it shifts like a kaleidoscope image, depending on the degree of scepticism with which we treat the narrative. There is an array of alternative stories lurking beyond the text, one of which we may choose to fix as the real referent, but whose reality is quite clearly the product of an interpretative decision on our part. And our interpretative decisions are, like Maria's, to some degree the products of our fears and desires; if we substitute a tawdry reality for the images that the narrator offers – like Norris's rewriting of the text's 'elderly gentleman' with a 'square red face' who turns out to have 'a drop taken' as 'a fat flushed old drunk' given to 'intemperate swilling' (130)[16] – we should investigate (as Norris begins to do) what needs of our own are being satisfied.

It may be objected that there *is* a possible reference point against which to check at least some of the text's assertions: actuality, recorded in history. Thus we know – from Joyce's letter to Stanislaus of 13 November 1906 if not from some other historical source, such as Thom's Directory[17] – that there was in Dublin at this time a Protestant-run laundry called *Dublin by Lamplight* whose mission was to rehabilitate reformed prostitutes. Since Maria's laundry has the same name, and a number of puzzles in the text are cleared up when this is assumed to be its function – one which the narrative voice could not possibly admit, of course – it is legitimate to equate the two institutions; and because the knowledge comes from outside the text we feel, for once, a satisfying certainty about the 'real' world which the narrator is (mis)representing. But we have to be careful here: the text does not *refer* to the *Dublin by Lamplight Laundry* that existed historically in Dublin (if we can trust the other texts that tell us it did); it brings into being a laundry with this name, just as *Ulysses* brings into being an Ormond Hotel and an Eccles Street, and at any point it has the power of rupturing the historical illusion – as when a historically vacant property is given fictional tenants called Leopold and Molly Bloom. This permanent possibility of rupture radically transforms all the 'historical references' of fiction, making them pseudo-references, hollowed out from within.

Does this uncertain narrative, which forces us into interpretative acts that we can never fully justify, both leading us towards a hidden referent and denying its possibility, set 'Clay' apart from the rest of Joyce's *œuvre*? On the contrary, it seems to me; not only do we find a similar staging of language's impossible acts of reference throughout *Dubliners*, but the story is a remarkable foreshadowing of the way in which *Ulysses*, with its

---

[16] Norris, it should be recalled, qualifies her own endorsement of this interpretation by associating such readings with the social judgements that make the text's deceptions necessary.

[17] Quoted by Aubert in Joyce, *Oeuvres*, I, 1521.

equal insistence on the reality of historical Dublin life and on the constitutive powers of language and style, both heightens and undermines referentiality. It could even be said to establish the method of *Finnegans Wake*, which allows language to realize all its potential as an instituting rather than a referential force. I would go further: 'Clay' dramatizes, with extraordinary brevity and concentration, the peculiar status of referentiality in all literary texts. The question, 'What do the words in a literary text refer to?' is an impossible one, even if it is one we have to keep asking. Not simply because they refer to imaginary people, places, and events, but because in literature the activity of referring is itself put in question. It is staged, simulated, played at, mimed. Nowhere is referentiality more strongly felt than in some works of literature, Joyce's included, at the very moment when the traditional notion of reference is being most thoroughly undermined. And this staging of reference is not a game which can be confined within the harmless arena of the literary text; it is a demonstration of the limitations of a conventional, or philosophical, understanding of reference; one which attempts to cleanse language of its literary bent, its penchant for storytelling, its ceaseless invitation to interpretation, and all the self-justifications and self-defences that interpretation involves.

MARIA VICTRIX

I want to return now to the Halloween game, because there remains something in it that resists these explanations and theorizations. 'She felt a soft wet substance with her fingers and was surprised that nobody spoke or took off her bandage. There was a pause for a few seconds; and then a great deal of scuffling and whispering. Somebody said something about the garden, and at last Mrs Donnelly said something very cross to one of the next-door girls and told her to throw it out at once: that was no play.' There is no sign that Maria is surprised by the fact that her fingers encounter something not among the expected alternatives in this version of the game, which Joyce has already taken care to specify. The clause that begins, 'and she was surprised' does not, surprisingly, turn out to refer to her reaction to the unexpected physical sensation. What she is surprised by is the silence and inaction that *follow* her touching of the substance – and it is clearly her *lack* of initial surprise that causes the silence and inaction, and the scuffling and whispering that ensue. The trick was designed, presumably, to provoke a vigorous response from Maria: she would be expected to imagine something far more disgusting than clay (Norris suggests that it is a version of the common trick of getting someone to believe they are touching excrement) or, if she did accurately identify the substance, to recoil from it as a known possibility in the game predicting an early death.

However, the trick fails, and it fails because Maria refrains from interpreting conceptually what she experiences by touch alone; she resists any temptation to transform the substance she knows through the most unverbal of the senses into that curious thing that only language can bring into existence, a 'referent'. Instead, she waits for the game to go on, for the blindfold to be removed, and the meaning of her experience to be explained to her. The result of this non-response – or non-epiphany, if you like – is an uncomfortable silence, then restlessness, then adult intervention. The reader is given a hint to confirm the interpretation that links this passage with the title – 'something about the garden' – but although the next sentence begins 'Maria understood', it turns out that all she understands is 'that it was wrong that time'. Even at this stage she has no awareness that she has been the target of a practical joke. The episode casts a general gloom on the party, and not until Mrs Donnelly has played a reel for the children and Maria has been plied with wine are we told that 'they were all quite merry again'; and only, then, interestingly, does Maria get an interpretation of her second attempt at the game. Even in the case of a legitimate object, Maria has to have its significance explained to her.

By failing to introduce language, conceptuality, reference,[18] Maria protects herself from the cruelty of the children's trick – Norris proposes that it is motivated by revenge for Maria's accusation that they are responsible for the disappearance of the plum cake – and she is able to persist in her favourable self-representation as honoured and loved guest of the family, warding off the recognition that she is not a welcome member of the group but an outsider, a target of derision and hostility.[19] To acknowledge that a trick has been played on her would be to destroy her carefully constructed self-image; and for once she – or the resourceful narrative agency that represents her wishes – has no device to turn negative into positive. But her non-conceptualizing actually produces

[18] One might debate whether the words 'soft wet substance' are a reflection of Maria's thought at this moment, or a purely narrative description of a wholly physical experience. If they are to be regarded as a verbalization, they still represent only a minimal step from the physical experience.

[19] There seems to be general complicity in the trick, even though 'one of the next-door girls' is eventually blamed: the adults make no attempt to prevent the substitution from being effected, and are presumably watching Maria during the pause and the scuffling, until 'at last' – when it is evident that Maria is not going to respond – Mrs Donnelly raises her voice.

for her a small victory, perhaps her only triumph over the many people she interacts with during this evening. The pause, the scuffling, the whispering, the anger: though these remain uninterpreted by Maria (except as an indication that 'it was wrong that time'), we can construct out of them a picture of the discomfiture and embarrassment destined for her rebounding on the trick's perpetrators. And we, as secure and superior readers, are *also* subject to a moment of discomfort at this non-naming, before we regain (thanks to our recollection of the story's title) our interpretative composure; like the adults at the party, we reassert our rational control over a situation that for a moment seemed to endanger our authority. But while we process the language of the story with the machinery of reference and representation to deduce what the substance is, Maria touches, and waits. Though her non-entanglement with language is more psychic defence, we may feel, than some kind of pure relation to being, the effect of the passage on us as readers might be to remind us of the need, in acts of responsible interpretation, to respect the other as other. Although 'Clay' demands, more insistently than most stories, intense interpretative activity, it also reminds us that there is sometimes a virtue in not interpreting, that responding fully to a text can mean allowing its otherness to remain other, unassimilable, unconceptualizable, irreducible, resistant. We perhaps shouldn't be too quick to fill Maria's saucer with common-or-garden clay.

CHAPTER 4

Joyce and the ideology of character

There are in a way no characters.
Joyce to Ole Vinding, on the subject of *Work in Progress*, in 1936.

What are the functions of the term *character* as it operates in our literary criticism and conversations today? What does it enable us to think and to say, what does it prevent us from thinking or saying? What are the terms in our discursive system that it overlaps with and reinforces, what are the terms it comes into collision with? These are questions which I believe the writing of Joyce poses with particular force, perhaps with more force than any other set of texts assembled under a single authorial name. They are large questions, which, to be treated with the fullness they deserve, would require extensive answers. Let me simply assert that the term *character* crystallizes and enforces a number of assumptions about the human subject, whether one is discussing the characters in *Dubliners*, or writing a character reference for an employer, or exclaiming 'He's quite a character!' or admiring a politician as a 'person of character', or responding to Pope's notorious lines:

> Nothing so true as what you once let fall,
> 'Most women have no characters at all'.[1]

Of the related and mutually reinforcing assumptions that lie behind all these usages I want to isolate three (my reasons for doing so will emerge presently): the assumption that the subject, or the self, can be apprehended as 'self-bounded and self-contained', as 'one whole'; that it is 'made

---

[1] Alexander Pope, 'To a Lady: Of the Characters of Women', lines 1–2. Pope's epistle is concerned with the division and inconsistency forced upon women by their social existence; taught, as they are, 'but to please', and 'by man's oppression curst', they therefore lack the determining properties of character as it is commonly understood. Pope's treatment of gender roles can be read profitably alongside Joyce's.

up of its parts, the result of its parts and their sum, harmonious'; and that each subject is unique and self-identical, 'that thing which it is and no other thing'.

My quotations come, of course, from Stephen Dedalus's discussion of Aquinas and aesthetic theory in *A Portrait of the Artist as a Young Man*, in which the defining properties of beauty are said to be *integritas, consonantia*, and *claritas* (v.1345–1405). We should not be too surprised to find that the notion of beauty in the Western tradition of thought bears a structural resemblance to the notion of character, since the two concepts are historically and theoretically intertwined. They are both predicated upon a certain model of transcendence: the notion of character depends not only on consistency and therefore recognizability *within* a text, but also on consistency and recognizability *across* texts, and across history. The transcendence of the term *character* is closely related to the transcendence of *nature*, as that term has been used in Western writing: what constitutes a person (real or fictional) as a character is what he or she does 'naturally', when not under compulsion or acting a part, and the 'nature' of an entity (or its 'true nature') is the same as its character (or true character). The concept of human nature, moreover, involves a set of immutable character types and traits, independent of culture and history. Millions of schoolchildren have been taught to admire the plays of Sophocles and Shakespeare because they contain characters 'just like ourselves'. A favourite pedagogic exercise in literary classes is still the 'character sketch', whereby students are invited to give a consistent and rounded account of a character's uniqueness, bringing together widely separated parts of the text and explaining away all anomalies by means of strategies drawn from the same rhetorical armoury of character analysis they learn to apply, through the normal processes of socialization, to their neighbours. And among the immediate pleasures of *Ulysses* and *Finnegans Wake* are the quirks of character which the reader delights in for their immediate 'recognizability' – all the more in texts where so much is *not* immediately recognizable.

The pleasures of character recognition are not just directed outwards. Every time we apprehend a character in a literary text, we are reassured of our *own* self-boundedness, self-consistency, and uniqueness; our own knowability and undividedness; our own existence independent of history, social construction, and ideology. As Hélène Cixous puts it in her brilliant essay, 'The Character of "Character"', 'Through "character" is established the identification circuit with the reader: the more "character" fulfils the norms, the better the reader recognizes it and recognizes himself' (385). (Once again, this is not very different from what happens in the social sphere.) The strength of this satisfaction is suggested by the discomfort caused by those counter-examples where a character fails to come together as a unified entity. One well-known instance is Cressida, who, in the familiar story of her love for and betrayal of Troilus, turns from a figure of faithful love to a figure of treachery. Shakespeare's play, in particular, leaves the audience disturbed and puzzled – not that such transformations have never occurred in their experience, but that a literary character is expected to manifest the wholeness and consistency that life sometimes fails to deliver.[2]

But this process of 'recognition' crucial to the apprehension of character is not as simple as it may sound. As readers conversant with a given literary tradition at a given moment in history (in which the realist novel continues to play a dominant role), we deploy a battery of interpretative techniques to produce characters as we read, but in order for these to be effective, they must be occluded in an illusory experience of unmediated access to knowable human nature.[3] But Joyce's texts – especially the later chapters of *Ulysses* and all of *Finnegans Wake* – tend to interfere with this automatic process, and it requires unusual skill and commitment as a reader to preserve untroubled the illusion of character, as is evidenced by the many impressively subtle and thorough critical accounts of Joyce's writing with this aim.[4] (The same could be said of events within a plot, narrative voice, symbolic patterns, moral import, and so on.) But what if we wish to talk about character – and it is undoubtedly a phenomenon of great importance in Joyce's work – without buying into the whole ideological system which has hitherto given it its meaning and weight?

One possibility is to turn for assistance to the other meaning of the word *character*: a written sign.[5] Here we might say that the *conventional* nature of character is not obscured at all: the sign is not a transcendent

---

[2] For a valuable discussion of the effects, inside and outside the text, of Cressida's inconsistency, see J. Hillis Miller, 'Ariachne's Broken Woof'. In *The Poetics of Prose* (66), Tzvetan Todorov considers briefly a type of narration in which character is not a matter of psychological consistency but simply a reflex of particular actions, as in *The Arabian Nights*.

[3] This does not mean, of course, that we believe characters in a novel to be 'real', any more than we believe a film which uses illusionistic techniques to be a series of real rather than represented events. For an entertaining discussion of this point, see Stephen Heath, 'Le Père Noël'.

[4] Equally impressive is the way in which 'James Joyce' has been produced by the biographer's skill and patience as a complex but consistent and bounded character, most notably by Richard Ellmann.

[5] Jed Rasula has further elaborated upon this coincidence of meanings; see his perspicacious essay '*Finnegans Wake* and the Character of the Letter'.

and transparent value but a historically produced, unmotivated, dia-
critical one. Sophocles' dramatic characters may seem instantly recognizable to a modern reader, but the Greek characters of his text are
strange and mute, as Joyce's text will be, and would have been, in a
different time and place. So by allowing the two senses to overlap
(which, in spite of their sharing a single signifier, our discursive habits
usually prevent), by insisting that every time the term *character* is used to
mean an 'assemblage of consistent personal qualities' it should be
thickened and coloured by the sense of character as 'arbitrary sign in a
conventional, historically determined system', we may be able to talk
about characters in a novel without subscribing to the ideological
premises which habitually underpin such discussions. And this, of
course, is just what Joyce does: it is only in this *double* sense that we can
legitimately talk of HCE and ALP as 'characters' in *Finnegans Wake*: they
are persons only insofar as they are at the same time letters scattered
across the text. And Joyce goes further than this in foregrounding the
second sense of the term *characters* in the *Wake* (especially if we consider
the manuscripts as part of the Joycean text): he allows personal traits and
actions (or, more accurately, verbal statements about personal traits and
actions) to be grouped under *sigla*, written characters largely independent of any conventional sign system in daily social use – a triangle, an
inverted V, a T on its side, and so on.[6] These sigla, which make a limited
appearance in the final text[7] but proliferate in the notebooks, were more
than just handy ways to refer to figures who could have been called by
their full names; they enabled Joyce to remove the traces of personal
identity that linger even in the use of letters, which are always open to
being read as initials and therefore as no different from a proper name.
The employment of sigla also removes character from the realm of the
spoken, fixing it in a written text where it preserves an alien silence,
unassimilable to the aura of self-presence and self-knowledge granted by
the voice: we can convert the letters 'HCE' into the spoken syllables

---

[6] No reproducible sign could, of course, be entirely free from connections with existing sign
systems; ALP's triangle, for instance, is relatable to a long tradition of identifying the female by
means of a stylized representation of the pudendum. The major study of this aspect of Joyce's
work, Roland McHugh's *Sigla of 'Finnegans Wake'*, while extremely valuable in many ways, is
somewhat disappointing in its treatment of the sigla themselves. It is coloured by the conviction
that 'the correct interpretation of certain parts of *FW* is absolutely dependent upon Joyce's
manuscripts having survived' (134); it consequently fails to develop far enough the early observation that 'Joyce's technique of personality condensation is ultimately inseparable from his
linguistic condensation' (10), tending instead to use the sigla as a guide to the 'correct' interpretation of the book's structure.
[7] Notably, as 'The Doodles family, ⴍ, △, ⊣, ✕, □, ∧, ⊂' (*FW* 299.n4).

'aitch cee ee' (hence Jarl von Hoother's 'eacy hitch' (*FW* 23.04)), but we cannot do the same with a graphic symbol that has no alphabetic relation and no sonic equivalent.

It may be the case, however, that the assumptions about the subject upon which the notion of character as person is built are not so easily dislodged, at least within the world of discourse we inhabit, and have no choice but to inhabit. Let us scrutinize this second sense of the term *character* a little more closely: does it, after all, entirely dispense with the properties which the first sense depends upon? Would it not be true to say that the *word*, for instance, in order to function as a vehicle of communication, must also be self-bounded, self-consistent, and unique, and therefore recognizable? As traditionally understood, the word must have limits to set it off from other words (in both syntagmatic and paradigmatic systems); it must have internal structural coherence (the letters must occur in a fixed order according to rules known in advance by the reader), and it must be different from every other word in the language; without these properties, language could not be held to transfer clear and distinct meanings efficiently from one subject to another. Exactly the same is true for the letter or siglum. So the common conception of language – or, more generally, the common concept of the sign – is yet another instance of the power exerted by centuries-old assumptions that can be traced back to Plato and are still powerful today, in spite of the efforts of a number of philosophers and critics in the final third of the twentieth century to question them or at least place them in a historical perspective. Character in this sense, it seems, is not so different from character in the other sense, and both demand *integritas*, *consonantia*, and *claritas* in order to perform what is demanded of them.

If Joyce is truly to undermine character as personage, then, he must also undermine character as sign. This is most obvious in the case of the proper name: if the word under which character traits are assembled retains its transcendent discreteness, coherence, and uniqueness, the essential identity of character will survive all vicissitudes of behaviour. So Joyce dismantles that last refuge.[8] The name 'Bloom' in *Ulysses*, for instance, is capable of losing all the Thomist properties that Stephen enumerates: it can slide over its boundaries into other words (as in 'greaseabloom' (11.180) or 'Bloomusalem' (15.1548)); it can lose its internal coherence and consistency (as when it drops a letter to become

---

[8] See the suggestive discussion by Hélène Cixous under the title 'Le vrai nom de l'artiste', in 'Ensemble Joyce', *Prénoms de personne*, 256–63.

'Boom' (16.1260) or when it is distributed between 'Stoom' and 'Blephen' (17.549, 541)); and it can become indistinguishable from other words or names (as when it becomes part of a song title in 'Blue Bloom is on the rye' (11.230–1) or when it occurs with reference not to Leopold but to a Dublin dentist (10.1115)). However, *all* lexical items, not just proper names, are susceptible to this treatment, and what remains in *Ulysses* an occasional reminder of the frangibility of the word becomes in *Finnegans Wake* a generative principle: words are apprehended throughout as shifting, deceptive, illimitable, unpredictable, and uninterpretable (in any orthodox sense of 'interpretation'). Even the sigla are capable of merging and splitting: Joyce combined the marks for Shaun and Shem to create a composite sign representing their unification, or provided Issy's sideways T with a mirror image to indicate a narcissistic doubling. In the *Wake* letters, too, can be unstable, like the revolving Fs of *FW* 18.36, 121.03 and .07, and 266.22. The disappearance of the word as a self-bounded, consistent, and unique entity marks the disappearance of language as the communicator of clear and distinct meanings; or rather, it puts in question that model of language, just as the disappearance of character in the other sense puts in question the model of the subject as consistent, undivided, unique, and immediately knowable and self-knowable. And it is by breaking down the boundaries and structures of the word, by denying the absolute distinctions between words, by acknowledging and delighting in the multiplicity and uncertainty of meaning normally held at bay by those boundaries, structures, and distinctions, that the *Wake* is able to break down so effectively the notion of character as a way of conceptualizing the subject, and to reveal its multiplicity and uncertainty as a culturally produced, historically determined, signifying practice.[9]

At the same time, however, the *Wake* signals to us each time we (attempt to) read it the strength of our own ideologically generated but inescapable design for the stability, coherence, and recognizability of character in both senses, and brings to consciousness the powerful tools we have inherited for the retrieval of personages and words, however partially, temporarily, and tentatively, from even so decentred and shifting a text as this one. It shows us, too, that we can never simply move outside the system of discourse within which we are constituted as

---

[9] Though the *Wake* is often portrayed as denying historical change, it is difficult to read it without obtaining a strong sense of historical processes; this is in part because its language (including its proper names) is shown at every point to be historically (as well as geographically and culturally) determined, never standing as given or self-sufficient or transparent.

subjects and read as characters, that we can never wholly evade the
metaphysical assumptions that haunt our language. We may believe we
have done so, through our insistence upon the constructed, differential,
and historical character of character, for example, but to do this we have
had to treat words as stable and monosemous units in an act of assumed
communication. At which the *Wake*, always one step ahead of us, laughs
quietly back.

CHAPTER 5

'Suck was a queer word': language, sex, and the remainder in A Portrait of the Artist as a Young Man

One of the most remarkable events in the history of literary creativity occurred when James Joyce composed the opening pages of *A Portrait of the Artist as a Young Man*, pages that move from the earliest remembered experiences of Stephen Dedalus to a particularly memorable fever-ridden day during his first term at Clongowes Wood College. Much has been written about the extraordinary immediacy of these pages, which represent something stylistically unprecedented in Joyce's work, hitherto most notable for the 'scrupulous meanness' of *Dubliners* and the rather long-winded narrative of *Stephen Hero*. They mark a new departure for European literature, too, catapulting Joyce into the forefront of the modernist movement.

It would be satisfying to be able to date this extraordinary event exactly, and to contemplate the precise cultural and linguistic context within which it took place. Were the opening pages written out in a single burst of creative originality, or were they gradually and laboriously transformed from something very traditional to the radical departure they became? Firm evidence is lacking, however; it was only later that Joyce began scrupulously to keep his notebooks as a kind of huge extension of his published work. We know that he had five long chapters in mind from the start, and that he wrote the first version of chapter 1 in Trieste between September and November of 1907.[1] This version probably began somewhat later in Stephen's life than the one we now have: Stanislaus Joyce recorded in his diary that his brother planned 'to omit all the first chapters [of *Stephen Hero*] and begin with Stephen . . . going to school', and Joyce told his brother that the novel began at a railway station, 'like most college stories' (*JJ* 274). By 1909 he had three chapters

---

[1] On the dating of Joyce's composition and revision of the chapters of *A Portrait*, see Gabler's introduction to the Garland edition, 4–5.

to show Ettore Schmitz, who praised the second and third, but found the first much less successful. At some time in 1911 Joyce threw the entire manuscript into the fire, but it was rescued by his family, blackened though intact, and a final creative period involving extensive revision of what was already written ensued between 1912 and early 1914. From the surviving manuscript evidence, Hans Walter Gabler concludes that the revisions of the first chapter were made towards the end of this period, so it seems likely that the opening pages of the novel as we have them date from the year 1913. However, we can only guess how much of the writing belongs to this late stage, though there is some evidence that the exchange involving Simon Moonan as the boys go in from football – a passage to which I shall turn in a moment – was part of the original 1907 version.[2]

In this essay, I shall examine one feature of these pages which I think is of particular interest, and speculate on the conditions that made it possible for Joyce to achieve a singular breakthrough at this point in European cultural history.

SEX AND THE SCHOOLBOY

The passage I want to take for my particular text occurs a few pages into the novel, when the young Stephen Dedalus – not yet seven years old, if we can extrapolate from Joyce's own life – gives grave consideration to a word he has just heard from the mouth of one of his schoolfellows:

Suck was a queer word. The fellow called Simon Moonan that name because Simon Moonan used to tie the prefect's false sleeves behind his back and the prefect used to let on to be angry. But the sound was ugly. Once he had washed his hands in the lavatory of the Wicklow Hotel and his father pulled the stopper up by the chain after and the dirty water went down through the hole in the basin. And when it had all gone down slowly the hole in the basin had made a sound like that: suck. Only louder. (*P* 1.150)

From the point of view of modern linguistics, Stephen's theorizing is obviously false: ugliness does not inhere in the sounds of a language, and although a culture can imbue certain sounds with negative associations none of the three common phonemes in 'suck' is so affected. (Compare the same sounds in words like 'luck', 'sup', 'musk', and 'success'.) Nor would water going down a drain sound, in objective, measurable terms, like the word 'suck' uttered in any normal human voice or accent.[3]

---

[2] In the sole surviving manuscript the name 'Moonan' has been imperfectly altered from 'Mangan' in copying from a previous manuscript – presumably the 1907 version of the chapter. See Hans Walter Gabler, 'The Seven Lost Years', 34.

[3] A properly theoretical statement would, of course, place 'suck' between inverted commas or

Although Stephen's vigorous response cannot be explained in terms of inherent aesthetic and onomatopoeic qualities, we can find other reasons for it, reasons not consciously available to the six-year-old boy but still operative upon him. In particular, the word, as used in this schoolyard scene, evokes a realm of taboo sexuality, a realm of which Stephen would be slowly becoming aware in the schoolboy milieu of Clongowes Wood College, with the usual mixture of excitement, ignorance, guilt, and fantasy. Although its overt meaning in the sentence 'You are McGlade's suck', which Stephen has just overheard, is 'favourite, sycophant', and Stephen can make sense of it only in terms of the special relationship indicated by the prefect's tolerance of playful behaviour on the part of the schoolboy, it possesses for him an aura of the forbidden, the sinful, the unclean, for at least two reasons that derive from the culture to which he is becoming assimilated: it echoes the primary taboo word 'fuck', and it names a specific sexual activity that could have taken place between the two males in question. One can imagine – and later the reader is given an example of – the half-overheard conversations among the older boys that would have granted Stephen that partial degree of sexual knowledge whose lack of specific content can invest certain words with all the more erotic power.

That these subliminal associations are not just those of the grown-up reader is confirmed by Stephen's consequent train of thought, as he recalls the visit to the Wicklow Hotel. A hotel would have been a notably adult space, and thus already a source of some disquiet for Stephen; and a visit to the washroom with his father would have added to this the ambience of adult male sexuality. ('Lavatory' in this context probably means 'washbasin', and the term may well have had ecclesiastical associations for Stephen; at the same time, the word was already in use for a room containing a water closet as well as a basin, and the hotel no doubt provided both. It is not many pages before the school latrine, or 'square', is named as a locus for schoolboy homosexuality.) Young children regularly find in 'bathroom' activities and vocabulary a conduit for sexual impulses which at this age have no other outlet, and Stephen's adjective 'dirty' – 'his father pulled the stopper up by the chain after and all the dirty water went down through the hole in the basin' – traverses a well-established pathway between excretion and sex even while it consciously refers only to the condition of the escaping water. Stephen's unease is projected on to the sound of the draining effluent, or rather on

italicize it; that it appears undifferentiated from the rest of the sentences in which it appears suggests the untheoretical, undistanced way Stephen is treating it, causing it to hover between a use and a mention.

to the sound which emerges so disquietingly from the 'hole' (common schoolboy slang for the female genitals, of course), and its perceived ugliness acts as a focus or correlative for the entire experience – 'And when it had all gone down slowly the hole in the basin had made a sound like that: suck. Only louder.' The association of the word 'suck' heard on the playground with this earlier sound is an indication, therefore, not of objective aural similarity but of the mental impression made by a prior experience of taboo sexuality, now triggered in memory. That the sexual element is conscious in neither experience is an important connection between them: it means that for Stephen they have in common a troubling yet unfathomable quality that only hindsight (that of the implicit, but well-concealed, adult narrator) can account for.[4]

The paragraph that follows this one exhibits the same features: a surface from which sexuality as a subject is absent, coupled with a sexual suggestiveness that can hardly have presented itself as such to the young boy but which helps to explain the peculiar intensity of his remembered experience:

To remember that and the white look of the lavatory made him feel cold and then hot. There were two cocks that you turned and water came out: cold and hot. He felt cold and then a little hot: and he could see the names printed on the cocks. That was a very queer thing. (1.159–63)

Stephen makes no comment on the word 'cock', but it is hard not to suspect once more a subliminal awareness of its sexual meaning that is part of its fascination for him. Like 'suck' and most of the other words on which he does comment explicitly in this chapter – 'belt', 'rump', 'kiss', 'God', 'wine' – it is a monosyllabic noun with Anglo-Saxon roots.[5] 'Cock' echoes the word 'suck' in sound and is linked to it semantically through the sexual activity (or fantasized activity) that involves both. The two paragraphs are also linked, beginning to end, by the word 'queer' – 'Suck was a queer word' . . . 'that was a very queer thing' – and it may be hard for the present-day reader not to assume a homosexual reference here too. However, for Stephen this is not a new word,

---

[4] Kenner asserts that the connection between the two occurrences of 'suck' is the idea of 'the forgiveness of sins in the confessional' ('The *Portrait* in Perspective', 146); this link does not seem as 'obvious' to me as it does to him, and it ignores the sexual suggestiveness of the sound on both occasions. Kenner does, however, valuably stress the externality of language for the growing boy (see especially 143–9; a condensed version of these pages appears as pp. 116–19 of *Dublin's Joyce*).

[5] See Onions, *The Oxford Dictionary of English Etymology*. The exception in this list is *rump*, which appears to have entered the English language in the fifteenth century from the Scandinavian languages. In modern English, however, it has the characteristic qualities of the Anglo-Saxon portion of the vocabulary.

suffused with strange and disturbing qualities, but a common Anglo-Irish adjective which is part of his normal speech. If there is a sexual meaning to be read into it – some commentators argue that the word was already being used to mean 'male homosexual' by the end of the nineteenth century[6] – it can only be as a wink on the part of the adult author to the reader.

A number of studies of *A Portrait* have discussed the barely submerged allusions to homosexuality in these pages, as well as in some later portions of the novel.[7] The sexual associations forged in these paragraphs point backwards and forwards, links in a chain of related experiences and meditations. Thus the cold and hot streams of water in the lavatory recall the description of the effect of urine on the bed-sheets in the book's opening (1.13), and strengthen the *double entendre* of 'cocks'. They point forward to the hot and cold bodily sensations that accompany Stephen's interrogation on the subject of his mother's kiss (1.260, 271) – another word, incidentally, which prompts a linguistically false onomatopoeic explanation from Stephen ('a tiny little noise: kiss' (1.279)). Similarly, the 'white look of the lavatory', which has such an effect on the young boy (even in recollection), anticipates his dwelling on the whiteness of three characters' hands: those of Eileen Vance (1.1008, 1257), who is associated from the very beginning of the novel with both sexuality and sin; Tusker Boyle (1.1255–6), one of the boys caught 'smugging' – masturbating, presumably – in the latrine; and Mr Gleeson (1.1347–52), who is suspected of allowing his sexual attraction to another of the delinquents, Corrigan (himself the object of intense physical attention from Stephen (1.1669)),[8]

---

[6] Joseph Valente states that Elaine Showalter, in *Sexual Anarchy*, 'correctly contends' that this was the case ('Thrilled by His Touch', 72 n16). Showalter, for her part, refers to an essay by William Veeder as support for her contention that 'several scholars' have provided evidence for the early use of the word in the sexual sense (*Sexual Anarchy*, 223 n24). Veeder in turn refers to 'Spears' (but gives no further bibliographical details), and cites the eighth edition of Eric Partridge's *Dictionary of Slang and Unconventional English* to the effect that the word has had this meaning 'since ca. 1900' ('Children of the Night', 159 n19). In fact, the entry for 'queer' in the eighth edition of Partridge states, after the meaning 'a male homosexual', 'since ca. 1920'. In this it is in agreement with other dictionaries, including the *OED* (second edition), Ayto and Simpson, *The Oxford Dictionary of Modern Slang*, and Thorne's *Bloomsbury Dictionary of Contemporary Slang*. As Valente has pointed out to me, one way in which words in the adult world can possess a power similar to the unspecifiable suggestiveness they often have for children is by being in the midst of a semantic shift of the kind *queer* was probably undergoing around 1900.

[7] See, for instance, the essays collected in Valente, ed., *Quare Joyce*; Carens, '*A Portrait of the Artist as a Young Man*'; and Lamos, 'James Joyce and the English Vice'.

[8] It is possible that in Stephen's recollection – 'he remembered how big Corrigan looked in the bath' (1.1669) – 'big' refers not merely to the older youth's overall size. As a member of the higher line, Corrigan could have been as old as eighteen (*JJ* 31n). One can understand why Stephen

to abrogate his punitive responsibilities.

My purpose is not to develop any of these arguments further, but to investigate the relation between implicit sexuality and overt attention to language, especially to single words. For the sexual suggestiveness in *A Portrait* frequently occurs, as it does in the passage we have just examined, as part of Stephen's encounters with language. (It is notable that in the second paragraph, the 'queerness' of the lavatory cocks appears to reside in the actual words they bear.) How is it that language can produce physical sexual effects, as it seems to in Stephen, even though at this early age he has no sexual vocabulary by means of which to describe his reaction? And how is it that language, in the form of literary writing, can produce a similar effect upon the reader – if not an actual physical response, at least an intensity and immediacy of reaction which comes close to physical sensation? Readers of *A Portrait* have frequently found these paragraphs, like the rest of the opening pages of the novel, remarkably vivid, and it seems likely that this vividness stems from more than just the accurate evocation of a young boy's attempts to understand language and its relation to the world he is also trying to come to terms with. That is to say, something rings true, in the mind, in the body, about Stephen's false linguistic theorizing: Joyce makes it possible for the reader to share his protagonist's experience of a word's peculiar intensity and physicality when uttered in a certain context. The early reviews of *A Portrait* testify to the shock of an encounter with language that has an unwontedly direct effect, often combined with a sense of disgust that is itself perhaps testimony to the immediacy of the feelings and sensations conveyed. The following are a few snippets, which could be multiplied at great length, all from 1917 reviews: 'an astonishingly powerful and extraordinarily dirty study . . . absolutely true to life – but what a life!' (*Everyman*); 'Mr Joyce has a cloacal obsession . . . by far the most living and convincing picture that exists of an Irish Catholic upbringing' (H. G. Wells, *Nation*); 'like the unwilled intensity of dreams' (A. Clutton-Brock, *Times Literary Supplement*); 'brutal probing of the depths of uncleanness' (*Literary World and Reader*); 'What he sees he can reproduce in words with a precision as rare as it is subtle . . . Mr Joyce plunges and drags his readers after him into the slime of foul sewers' (*Freeman's Journal*).[9] We are less likely to be disgusted today, and perhaps the intensity of our reaction is to that degree dulled, but many readers continue to report that intensity and precision of physical and mental

---

regards the bath with a 'vague fear' (I.550).

[9] These reviews are all reprinted in *The Critical Heritage* I, 85–98.

evocation is what draws them repeatedly back to *A Portrait*, and particularly to its opening chapter.

THE REMAINDER OF LANGUAGE AND THE POWER OF
LITERATURE

I want to approach these issues with the help of a series of three important books by Jean-Jacques Lecercle which explore the repeated manifestation in nineteenth- and twentieth-century literature of what he calls the 'remainder' – those aspects of language to which most linguistic theories fail to do justice, but on which the working of language depends. These are: *Philosophy Through the Looking-Glass* (1985); *The Violence of Language* (1990); and *Philosophy of Nonsense* (1994).[10] Although Lecercle focuses on texts that take greater linguistic and generic liberties than *A Portrait*, such as the works of Lewis Carroll, Jean-Pierre Brisset, and Raymond Roussel (the only references to Joyce are to *Finnegans Wake*), his interest is primarily in the contribution these works make to our understanding of language. Any language, he argues, operates in accordance with four propositions, not all of which are compatible with one another (and here I summarize brutally):

(1) Language is a material product of the body.
(2) Language is an abstract system, independent of the body.
(3) The speaker speaks the language, saying freely what he or she means.
(4) The language speaks, and meaning belongs to the community before it belongs to the speaker. (See *The Violence of Language, passim*, but especially 105–6.)

What Lecercle calls the 'commonsensical' view of language (*Violence*, 107), which is at the heart of Saussurean and Chomskeian linguistics as well, combines propositions (2) and (3): a language is an abstract system of rules which the speaker utilizes in order to construct sentences – sentences which, as Chomsky influentially pointed out, can be different from all those that have ever been uttered in the prior history of humanity. The Saussurean dichotomy of *langue* and *parole*, and the Chomskeian dichotomy of *competence* and *performance*, map this dual character of language as at once, and interdependently, suprahuman system and human act. Both common sense and theoretical linguistics

---

[10] In the first of these studies, Lecercle uses the term *délire* for the excess which is overlooked by the dominant, instrumentalist conception of language; in the later two, he prefers the term *remainder*.

acknowledge that there is an element of truth in (1) and (4), but these propositions are kept firmly in their place: the bodily specificity of language is governed by its systematic organization, and the shared meanings of language are at the disposal of the individual speaker.

It is when (1) and (4) begin to transgress their allotted frontiers that we become aware of the *remainder*, that aspect of language's functioning which, in spite of its necessity, is normally suppressed from our conceptions of it. The remainder imparts to utterances powerful effects of various kinds, though they cannot be described in purely conceptual terms. This is not to say that the remainder is prelinguistic (or presymbolic); it may just as easily be manifested in an excess of meaning as in a lack of it. The fact that language necessarily employs physical signifiers which have their own complex interconnections (at a purely material level), as well as connections with the worlds of meaning, feeling, and action, together with the fact that the meanings conveyed by any item of language always depend on its context, and that contexts are variable and inexhaustible – these facts result in an ever-present possibility that an utterance, written or spoken, will convey more than could be understood in terms of a model of 'intention' or 'communication'. To take one relatively simple example: because of the nature of language, the pun is always waiting round the corner, and its effects can never be fully controlled; thus the reader can never *know* whether in the penultimate sentence of *A Portrait* – 'to forge in the smithy of my soul the uncreated conscience of my race' – the word 'forge' means not only 'make' but also 'fake'.

An obvious instance of the remainder at work is the speech or writing of many of those who are held – partly *because* they use language in this way – to be mentally ill: the language of delirium, schizophrenia, glossolalia. To let one's speech be dominated by the body which articulates it, rather than subordinating diaphragm, larynx, tongue, teeth, and lips to a system, is to be regarded as passing beyond the bounds of sanity; and the same judgement awaits anyone who surrenders the individual's power over the system, and instead allows the language (and hence the culture that has produced it) to determine what is spoken or written – which might be series of clichés, endless lists, or constantly repeated words and phrases (one thinks, in *Dubliners*, of Eveline's mother's eternal 'Derevaun Seraun! Derevaun Seraun!'). Both these proclivities may be present simultaneously, of course, and language may revert at once to its physiological and its cultural roots.

There are two other, more familiar, discourses which are rendered distinctive by their openness to the remainder: the language of children and the language of literature.[11] Here, of course, we find ourselves back with the young Stephen at the beginning of *A Portrait*. Stephen's bodily response to the word 'suck' (heightened by his feverish condition, and – as we have noted – expressed in part by the recall of an earlier, and more obviously physical, experience) does not belong to the linguist's domain of explanation and analysis. The young boy perceives the word as belonging to others, and as itself disturbingly other, and he finds himself strongly affected by the word's physical, acoustic properties, so much so that it can be associated with a purely non-linguistic sound, one which had also crystallized for him an intense experience of alienation.[12] Moreover, we have already seen that the word's physical potency is profoundly linked to the sexual and the erotic, even though this is not a way of thinking available to Stephen at the age of six – in fact, it is because the thought of sexuality itself is not possible that the sexual quality is felt so directly as a physical sensation. Joyce, one might go so far as to say, is proposing a view of the latency period that in some ways extends and particularizes Freud's rather exiguous account. The rapid development of linguistic ability in this period (from five or six to puberty), Joyce seems to suggest, coincides with a stage of sexual development in which intense physical sensations are not linked to specific sexual knowledge, images, or practices; words may therefore be experienced as *themselves* suffused with (unnamed and unnamable) sexual impulses, at once highly physical and beyond the control of the speaker. 'Rump', 'suck', 'kiss', and 'smugging' are all words which seem to be particularly charged for the young Stephen in this way.

If we turn back to the opening paragraphs of *A Portrait*, to what is presumably the beginning of Stephen's encounter with language, we find a response that contrasts with this somewhat later development. Language begins, certainly, as the language of the other – the language of the father, no less, telling him the story of the 'moocow' and 'baby tuckoo' – but it is immediately appropriated by the child: 'He was baby tuckoo' (1.7). Even if language is misappropriated, as when the phrase '*the wild rose blossoms*' becomes in the little boy's articulation '*the geen wothe*

---

[11] A third discourse which is strongly marked by the remainder is prayer and liturgy, and *A Portrait* has many examples. Here too, the speaker surrenders individual command over language to the community, and invests the precise words spoken with a peculiar power in excess of their ordinary linguistic functioning.

[12] For a good account of Stephen's entry into language, see Fritz Senn, 'Foreign Readings', 41–4. Maud Ellmann provides a vivid exposition of Stephen's language, and Stephen's sense of language, as bodily secretion in 'Disremembering Dedalus'.

botheth', there is no hint of anxiety. Rather, the sense of possession is complete: 'He sang that song. That was his song' (1.11). The bodily aspect of language is a source of pleasure, not unease, as the child discovers the physical gratification of rhythmic utterance. The result, of course, is nonsense, both at the level of the 'words' produced (especially if one accepts the recent editorial restoration of *geen* in place of the earlier printed texts' *green*),[13] and at the level of the sentence itself. As a more mature six-year-old, Stephen will correct himself by dismissing the possibility of a green rose, though his uncertainty at this later stage about the relation of language to the world emerges in an immediate retraction of this dismissal: 'But you could not have a green rose. But perhaps somewhere in the world you could' (1.197–8). In infancy, however, there are no such uncertainties. Nonsense, the product of Lecercle's propositions (1) and (4) impinging heavily on (2) and (3), so that creativity arises not from the imperious use of an abstract system but from a willingness to let both the body and the language community speak, is produced in confidence and celebration.[14]

Nonsense, together with repetition, also becomes the vehicle for rhythm and melody when, in the same initial sequence, Stephen dances to his mother's playing of the sailor's hornpipe: '*Tralala lala / Tralala tralaladdy / Tralala lala / Tralala lala*' (1.17–20). But very soon rhyme, rhythm, and repetition become invested with fear and guilt, and the sequence of paragraphs seems to suggest that these are associated with Stephen's incipient sexual attraction to Eileen Vance (whom, we later learn, was the object of Dante's disapproval on account of her family's Protestantism (1.999–1000)):

When they were grown up he was going to marry Eileen.
He hid under the table. His mother said:
– O, Stephen will apologise.
Dante said:
– O, if not, the eagles will come and pull out his eyes.
                    Pull out his eyes,
                    Apologise,

[13] Both Gabler, in the edition cited here, and Chester G. Anderson, in the text published in the 'Case Study in Contemporary Criticism' (edited by R. B. Kershner), restore the childish spelling. For a cautionary comment on this change, see Brockman, 'Composite Portraits', 371.

[14] Later, nonsense will be a sign of Stephen's disaffection, when words 'band and disband themselves in wayward rhythms: *The ivy whines upon the wall / And whines and twines upon the wall...*' (v.173–9), or when the jingle of the dean of studies' words seems to blend with the smell of his candle butts, 'bucket and lamp and lamp and bucket' (v.485). Some of Joyce's own highly repetitive passages of lyrical prose in *A Portrait* run the risk of the same kind of emptying out of meaning.

> *Apologise,*
> *Pull out his eyes.*
>
> *Apologise,*
> *Pull out his eyes,*
> *Pull out his eyes,*
> *Apologise.* (1.29–41)

Here the remainder of language overwhelms its rational communicative function: words are progressively emptied of their meaning through repetition, rhyming, and rhythmicization, and are transformed into the sounds of physical aggression and vindictiveness. Though the source of the utterance is not identified, it has all the markings of a children's chant – another manifestation, that is, of the speech of the linguistic community rather than of a single individual exploiting the creative possibilities of language.[15]

The other discourse which exploits the potential of the linguistic remainder – besides the languages of madness and childhood – is the one we are already dealing with: literature. Historically, it has been poetry which has found a variety of means to release the bodily dimension of speech from its domination by language's rational-communicative function, and it has been poets, above all, who have testified to a mode of composition in which the controlling consciousness of the language user is relaxed in order to allow the language's own proclivities – which is to say, those of the inherited culture, mediated by an individual and partly unconscious psyche and by the urgings of the body – to determine to some degree the words of the poem. The result, for the successful poet, is not, of course, the nonsensical or cliché-ridden speech of the schizophrenic, but it may be quite close to the intense engagement that characterizes some childhood involvements with words.

It is here that the historical dimension becomes particularly important. Although any culture within which language's primary function is direct and transparent communication will find itself having to come to terms with the linguistic remainder, the way in which this happens is strongly conditioned by the specificity of its place and time. In particular, current conceptions of language and current conventions of literature (whether articulated or not) will be of central significance in deter-

---

[15] In revising the early epiphany on which this passage is based, Joyce substituted Dante for Eileen Vance's father (who enters the house with a stick), and deleted the source of the chant: 'Joyce – (*under the table, to himself*)' (*Poems and Shorter Writings*, 161). These deletions render the episode less specific, and in particular introduce an ambiguity as to whether the chant is the product of internal defiance or external malice.

mining the options available to the writer, and in providing the resistant material against which creative originality has to work. Thus, to take an obvious example, one way of conceiving of the originality of Romantic poetry is as a revaluation of the remainder and of its literary potential. The new weight attached to the language of children, of drug-induced states, and of the mad; the exploitation of the sonic properties of language; the development of new rhythmic possibilities – these are just some of the ways in which the remainder was freshly exploited at the end of the eighteenth century and into the nineteenth. Among the conditions which made these new departures possible was the flowering of interest in language, which came to seem less a tool than a resource, with a complex history that could be mined for insights into human nature and national character.

During the course of the nineteenth century, language study in Britain – largely under German influence – became more scientific and more stringently historical. Individual words were invested with a new historical and material specificity as the science of etymology gained ground; each word (understood now as essentially spoken, not written) was seen to have a concrete history, not only in terms of shifts in meaning but in terms of changes in sound, occurring in accordance with strict historical laws beyond speakers' or language communities' control.[16] The great monument to English philology was, of course, the *New English Dictionary* (later the *Oxford English Dictionary*), the first volume of which was published in 1888 – the year in which the young James Joyce entered Clongowes Wood College (and perhaps overheard the word 'suck' in the school grounds). An important precursor was W. W. Skeat's *Etymological Dictionary of the English Language*, published in 1882, the year of Joyce's birth. In *Stephen Hero*, Stephen is said to have 'read Skeat's Etymological Dictionary by the hour' (*SH* 32), and there is every likelihood that this is an autobiographical statement on the part of James Joyce.[17] Another milestone was Henry Sweet's monumental study in

---

[16] Linda Dowling, in *Language and Decadence in the Victorian Fin de Siècle*, discusses the effect on late nineteenth-century Irish and English writers of the new German philology. It is interesting to note that Ferdinand de Saussure's influential *Course in General Linguistics*, which was an important founding text for a new synchronic linguistics, was published in the same year as *A Portrait* – and that although Saussure strove to keep language within the bounds of the rational and the systematic in the *Course*, he failed to exorcise the remainder: see, for example, Derrida's discussion of Saussure's attempt to discredit onomatopoeia in *Glas*, 90–7. (The entire right-hand column of *Glas* is an extended discussion of the remainder.)

[17] Stephen Whittaker discusses the importance of Skeat for Joyce in 'Joyce and Skeat', and Hugh Kenner has frequently made reference to Stephen's (and Joyce's) absorption in Skeat's *Etymological Dictionary* – see, for example, *A Colder Eye* (147, 191, 218). However, as Whittaker points out,

phonetics, *The Sounds of English*, published in 1908, between the first and the revised versions of the opening chapter of *A Portrait*. Also worth mentioning as late fruits of the historical method are George Saintsbury's massive *History of English Prosody from the Twelfth Century to the Present Day*, published in 1906–10, when Joyce was beginning *A Portrait*, and his *History of English Prose Rhythm*, dating from 1912.

The new etymology of the later nineteenth century represented a reaction against the speculative, 'metaphysical' etymology of the earlier part of the century, the most colourful representative of which was John Horne Tooke.[18] No longer is the point of etymological study the discovery of ultimate origins, which would illuminate the true meaning of the word; rather, it is to trace the history of change as something interesting for its own sake. The sounds and shapes of words, like those of zoological and botanical species, are physical entities subject to the vicissitudes of time and space; they are not indices of a nation's soul or reflexes of spiritual truths. Most important of all, perhaps, the new philology demanded a simultaneous fascination with and distance from words: stripped of their mystique, they nevertheless remained objects to be examined, charted, and cherished.

When Joyce was writing *A Portrait*, the only poet in English who had been able to capitalize fully on this new sense of the materiality and historicity of words was Gerard Manley Hopkins – who, interestingly, had been Professor of Greek at University College Dublin until his death some ten years before Joyce entered the college. However, Hopkins's work was not widely known until a collection of his poems was published by Robert Bridges in 1918 (four years after the serialization of *A Portrait* began). In France, Mallarmé – with whose writing Joyce certainly did have some familiarity[19] – had found ways to foreground individual words as both physical and semantic entities (and had written an entire study entitled *English Words* (1877), in which he set out his theories of the potential meaningfulness of the sounds of the English language). But the

Kenner uses the much-revised fourth edition, which would not have been available to Joyce at the time.
18 See Dennis Taylor, *Hardy's Literary Language and Victorian Philology*, ch. 4, 'The Historicism of Victorian Philology'. A transitional figure, influenced by German scientific philology but working in a popular style and with some of Hooke's imaginative flair, was Richard Chenevix Trench, who published a series of immensely popular books on the English language in the 1850s, and whose grandson, Richard Samuel Dermot Chenevix Trench, was the main model for the character of the Englishman Haines in *Ulysses*; see Downing, 'Richard Chenevix Trench' and Aarsleff, *The Study of Language*, 229–47.
19 For a detailed study of the influence of Mallarmé on Joyce – concentrating, however, on *Finnegans Wake* – see David Hayman, *Joyce et Mallarmé*.

most characteristic poetry, and poetic prose, of the turn of the century was closer to the verse that Stephen writes in *A Portrait* and in *Ulysses*, and to the style which Joyce employs later in *A Portrait* to convey the heightened moments of Stephen's career. One of the great achievements of this writing was the exploitation of the rhythmic potential of English verse, and in this respect it did capitalize on one aspect of the remainder, often allowing language to be determined by a strongly rhythmic impulse that derives both from bodily movement and from popular forms of poetry. Swinburne, Kipling, Dowson, Gilbert, and the early Yeats were all in their different ways masters of strongly musical rhythmic form, building on the metrical innovations of Tennyson and Browning. Joyce was certainly able to learn from them, but he also needed to find a way to break down the powerful rhythms of these predecessors. A carefully unpoetic prose, a style of 'scrupulous meanness', as in parts of *Dubliners* and *Stephen Hero*, was one possibility, but this did not open a door to a new literary practice.

A door did open, however, when (perhaps, as we have seen, as early as 1907, and certainly by 1914) Joyce wrote, or extensively revised, the opening pages of *A Portrait*, turning his account of early childhood into an engagement with language as an assemblage of words, each with its peculiar density and singular history, each functioning as a site where both physical articulations and semantic suggestiveness work together, where to heighten one is to heighten the other. The process is the opposite of the metaphorical: as Lecercle notes, 'The universe of *délire* [roughly equivalent to the remainder] may be wildly imaginative: it is also painfully literal. There are no longer any clear frontiers between words and things' (*Philosophy Through the Looking-Glass*, 162). Contrary to the assumption governing the realist tradition – that to draw attention to the language as such is to divert attention away from the reality it is attempting to represent – Joyce showed that an even stronger sense of the physically and emotionally real can be created in language that foregrounds its own materiality. In many passages in *Ulysses* and *Finnegans Wake* he demonstrates this with unequalled brilliance;[20] in *A Portrait* such moments are few, but they announce very clearly the break with the literary tradition and the new possibilities to be developed.[21]

---

[20] I have discussed some examples in *Peculiar Language*, chapters 5 and 7.

[21] The other major innovation that paved the way for his later works was the use of a paratactic narrative sequencing, allowing Stephen's life to be represented by very few scenes, each related in some detail but separated from those before and after by unexplained gaps. David Hayman has given a valuable account of this feature of the novel in 'The Fractured Portrait'.

To open his novel with a representation of childhood language, and to make Stephen's responses to and encounters with language such a cardinal part of his experience of early schooling, therefore, is not just to introduce a highly successful new technique for beginning a biography at the beginning, with particular relevance to the biography of a writer (or would-be writer); it is also to announce a fresh understanding of the literary potential of language, distinct both from what had gone before and from the other literary experiments of the time. (We might think of Imagism and Vorticism – Ezra Pound's collection *Des Imagistes* and the first issue of Wyndham Lewis's *Blast* both appeared in 1914 – or the writing of Gertrude Stein or T. S. Eliot – *Tender Buttons* came out in 1914 and 'Prufrock', written in 1910–11, first appeared in 1915.[22]) Literature, Joyce demonstrates, shares with childhood language the capacity to exploit the remainder, to allow the body and the language community to speak through and to some degree against the abstraction and instrumentalism of utilitarian employments, and most theories, of language.[23] 'Suck' *is* a queer word, not intrinsically but as Stephen encounters it in the schoolyard and as the reader encounters it in the pages of *A Portrait*. Joyce's failure to gloss it (beyond the indirect explanation that Stephen gives to himself), like his failure to gloss many of the other schoolboy terms in these pages, is not only the result of a strict adherence to the child's point of view; it is also a strategy designed to put the reader in the same situation as the boy and thus enhance the physical suggestiveness of the words. Of course, any word can be made strange; it is a matter of context and presentation. The child finds it happening in his or her daily life, while the artist has to develop and perfect the means to make it happen. However, it is not a skill that, finally, can be taught: the remainder is everything about language that is not reducible to rule, and the effectiveness of these moments in *A Portrait* can never be fully accounted for. The explanation of the intensity and erotic suggestiveness of 'suck' for Stephen does not *quite* explain its intensity for the reader; no literary effect can be wholly explained and remain literary.

We can only guess at the ingredients that went into this momentous

---

[22] The year 1913 also saw Joseph Conrad's *Chance*, D. H. Lawrence's *Sons and Lovers*, Igor Stravinsky's *Rite of Spring*, Robert Frost's *A Boy's Will*, William Carlos Williams's *The Tempers*, Jacob Epstein's *The Rockdrill*, and the first volume of Marcel Proust's *A la recherche du temps perdu*. In 1915, Dorothy Richardson's *Pointed Roofs* (the first volume of *Pilgrimage*) appeared, along with Virginia Woolf's *The Voyage Out*.

[23] One theory of language which does not occlude the remainder is Freud's, and Joyce may well have been influenced by the important part played by the material specificity of words in such works as *The Interpretation of Dreams* (1900), *Jokes and Their Relation to the Unconscious* (1901), and *The Psychopathology of Everyday Life* (1905).

act of creation. One would probably have been dissatisfaction with literary styles that either made language subservient to the massive body of 'reality' and thus diminished its power to delight and move with its own sounds and rhythms, or privileged language's sonorous patterns and thus cast a veil over the physical and emotional details of daily experience. Another ingredient would have been a growing consciousness of the complex interrelation in the spoken utterance among articulated sound, semantic associations, and the fears and desires of the mind and the body. The nineteenth-century philologists had tried – with a large measure of success – to corral these elements of language within the strong walls of a scientific discipline; Joyce (perhaps benefiting from the special vantage point granted by his linguistic marginality as a speaker of Anglo-Irish) found a way of capitalizing on the inevitability of breaches in the fortress.

THE ARTIST AS A YOUNGISH MAN

The irony that underlies this remarkable artistic breakthrough in *A Portrait* is, of course, that the artist whose portrait we are being asked to contemplate does not appear capable of it himself. Although the title of the novel repeats a common formula for a self-portrait, the work itself presents a disjunction between the author *of* and the author *in* the text. As we noted above, Stephen's earliest 'literary' productions are dominated by the remainder, and while he is a young schoolboy they remain formulaic and ritualized, such as the nine-line 'address' in his geography book (1.300–8), the prayer he murmurs before going to bed (1.411–16), and the poem on Parnell he attempts after the Christmas dinner quarrel, which turns into a listing of the names and addresses of some of his classmates (II.373–6). Two tendencies then develop in Stephen's use of language as a literary vehicle: a lyrical, repetitive, Paterian mode, and a hard-edged, unsparing, realist mode.[24] (Both of these are manifested in Joyce's own early 'epiphanies'; see *Poems and Shorter Writings*.) We become aware of the first style in Stephen's fantasies about the romantic heroine Mercedes (II.104, 166), and of the second in what are presented as transcribed epiphanies, introduced with the words, 'He chronicled with patience what he saw, detaching himself from it and tasting its mortifying flavour in secret' (II.252–3).

There is one other encounter with a single word in the novel that is worth noting, one that marks the changes in Stephen's relationship to

---

[24] For a discussion of these two tendencies in Joyce's earlier style, see John Paul Riquelme, '*Stephen Hero, Dubliners*, and *A Portrait of the Artist as a Young Man*: Styles of Realism and Fantasy'.

language and to sexuality when he reaches adolescence. While Simon Dedalus searches for his initials cut into a desk in the Queen's College anatomy theatre in Cork, Stephen finds a different inscription:

On the desk before him he read the word *Foetus* cut several times in the dark stained wood. The sudden legend startled his blood: he seemed to feel the absent students of the college about him and to shrink from their company. A vision of their life, which his father's words had been powerless to evoke, sprang up before him out of the word cut in the desk. (II.1049–55)

Stephen sees, as if present before him, a large student carving the word among his laughing peers. The image of the letters cut into the wood, and the vision it evokes, stays with him, at once exciting him by providing an external echo of his own fantasies and increasing the guilt and self-hatred that is an integral part of his adolescent sexual life. Although 'suck' and 'foetus' both affect Stephen powerfully, and both combine suggestions of forbidden sex with a male community from which he feels excluded, the differences are striking. The former is Anglo-Saxon, the latter Latin; the former is spoken, the latter is written; the former evokes a memory, the latter evokes a fantasy. Far from being barely conscious of sexuality, Stephen is now hyperconscious of it (though at this stage it seems centred on masturbation and masturbatory fantasies – it is only at the end of this chapter that he first has sex with a prostitute). The result is that he reads the word not as an item of the language with its own suggestive power and physical attributes but as a trace, the record of a past event, and as a provocation to fantasy and self-abuse (in both senses of the term). What is important for the purposes of my argument is that for the *reader*, the word 'foetus', as a word, has no particularly strong resonance (though the fact of its incision in the anatomy desk may). Stephen's reaction appears, in fact, to be excessive, an indication of the high pitch of his sexual angst. There is no remainder at work; just a train of associations. We witness the trials of adolescent sexuality, but we do not participate in the overflowing of the linguistic system and the genesis of the literary.[25]

Occasionally, the older Stephen has experiences which suggest the

[25] Another place in which a single word becomes the focus of Stephen's attention is the discussion with the dean of studies about the term 'tundish', a term with which the Englishman is not familiar and which Stephen therefore takes to be peculiarly Anglo-Irish (*P* v.507). (Later, of course, he discovers that it is 'good old blunt English' (v.1720).) Here it is the very familiarity of the word which produces a feeling of estrangement when Stephen is made to realize that this familiarity is not shared, and the significance of this moment of verbal foregrounding is political rather than sexual. However, the political and the sexual are often inseparable in Irish history, and historical memory itself can impinge on discourse in ways analogous to the eruption of the erotic (see Gibbons, "'Have You No Homes to Go To?'").

survival of his earlier sensitivity to the physical and erotic suggestiveness of individual words. Interestingly, two of these involve a foreign language. As Fritz Senn notes in 'Foreign Readings', 'What a foreign reader . . . tends to notice much more is that words are words, the only prime reality in literature' (*Joyce's Dislocutions*, 44); the same is true of foreign words in a native text. When the director uses the phrase '*les jupes*', it has a powerfully physical effect on Stephen, causing him to blush (IV.279–80); and something of the sensuous immediacy of the French word may relay itself to the reader (though perhaps not to the native speaker of French). In the meditation that follows on 'the names of articles of dress worn by women or of certain soft and delicate stuffs used in their making', we learn that the sensual quality of some words, as Stephen experiences them, is finer than reality: by contrast with the terms that name them, women's stockings are disappointingly coarse to the physical touch. A similar process occurs when Cranly responds to the sound of a woman singing with the words 'Mulier cantat' and the narrator continues: 'The soft beauty of the Latin word touched with an enchanting touch the dark of the evening, with a touch fainter and more persuading than the touch of music or of a woman's hand' (v.2479–83). (Here the strong punctual effect of the Latin phrase is described in Joyce's vague repetitive lyrical style.) In some of the diary entries at the close of the novel, too, there is an echo of the acute lexical attention that characterizes both Stephen and the novel at its opening. 'When he pronounces a soft *o* he protrudes his full carnal lips as if he kissed the vowel' (v.2653–4); 'Rather, lynxeyed Lynch saw her as we passed' (v.2695–6); 'I fear him. I fear his redrimmed horny eyes' (v.2754): these phrasings from the diary seem closer to Joyce's own most important stylistic achievement in this novel than the majority of Stephen's writings, thoughts, and utterances since chapter 1.[26] It is significant that when one diary entry falls into the style that has been typical of Stephen's 'literary' self ever since the romantic fantasies derived from *The Count of Monte Cristo* it is quickly mocked:

10 April: Faintly, under the heavy night, through the silence of the city which has turned from dreams to dreamless sleep as a weary lover whom no caresses move, the sound of hoofs upon the road . . . [etc.]
11 April: Read what I wrote last night. Vague words for a vague emotion. (v.2728–38)

[26] J. C. Squire, in a 1917 *New Statesman* review of *A Portrait*, makes the observation that Joyce's 'descriptive and narrative passages include at one pole sounding periods of classical prose and at the other disjointed and almost futuristic sentences' (*Critical Heritage* I, 101).

And later Stephen refers self-deprecatingly to his use of 'the spiritual-heroic refrigerating apparatus, invented and patented in all countries by Dante Alighieri' (v.2764–5).

When we meet Stephen again in *Ulysses*, Joyce's new technique of interior monologue – a development of the opening and closing sections of *A Portrait* – gives us access to a mental world that possesses a linguistic and cultural richness (and humour) well beyond anything in the earlier novel. Although his literary productions remain relatively unpromising, Stephen's internal ruminations and sometimes his speech suggest a pleasure in language, and a skill in its deployment, that represent a mature development of the schoolboy's reaction to 'suck' and 'kiss', and the college student's response to '*les jupes*' and '*Mulier cantat*'. Throughout the later text, Joyce exploits the remainder in a number of different ways, not only in the more linguistically and stylistically extravagant chapters like 'Sirens', 'Cyclops', 'Oxen of the Sun', and 'Circe', but continually as part of the texture of the writing, always alert to the possibility that a word can resonate physically and often erotically even as it points to a referent or expresses an idea.

And *Finnegans Wake*? The triumph of the remainder, without a doubt. Like 'suck'. Only louder.

CHAPTER 6

Joyce, Jameson, and the text of history

'History is what hurts': this is one of Fredric Jameson's many artfully phrased aphorisms in his influential study *The Political Unconscious*, a book that introduced a new, and seldom surpassed, sophistication into Marxist studies of literature in 1981 and that has to be taken into account by anyone working on the relation between 'literature' and 'history'. The passage continues, in characteristic Jamesonian vein, 'This is indeed the ultimate sense in which History as ground and untranscendable horizon needs no particular theoretical justification: we may be sure that its alienating necessities will not forget us, however much we might prefer to ignore them' (102).

History is 'a nightmare from which I am trying to awake': this is Stephen Dedalus's definition, produced for the benefit of Mr Deasy in 'Nestor', the Ulyssean episode for which, according to Joyce's schema for the book, history is the designated art. Stephen's comment is followed by the silent self-interrogation: 'What if that nightmare gave you a back kick?' (*U* 2.377–9).

Both Jameson and Stephen are vividly aware of the double manifestation of history in our lives: on the one hand as that which, operating from outside the human capacity to construct and construe signs, imposes limits upon – and, though this is less often emphasized, opens up possibilities for – thought and action; and on the other hand as that which communities make and remake under the shifting pressures of ideological and material needs. Taken in the former sense, history – which goes by many other names in literary, psychoanalytic, and political theory, including Jameson's 'Necessity', Lacan's 'Real', and Althusser's 'absent cause' – escapes, by definition, any conceptualization; to name it in language is already to textualize, to metaphorize, to narrativize it. (For Jameson it is figured in the sentences I have quoted as a watchful and malevolent being who 'hurts' and who 'will not forget us', for Stephen it becomes, through the revivification of the dead metaphor in 'nightmare', a vicious horse.) However, it is not difficult to agree with Jameson that our incapacity to name or to discuss history in this absolute sense in no way diminishes its force and effectiveness; it is indeed the ultimate untranscendable horizon within which all our actions, and all our words about those actions, occur.

The other sense of history provides more possibilities for discussion – indeed, the unbounded scope it offers for verbalization constitutes one of the major difficulties in dealing with it, difficulties quite as great as those involved in apprehending the ineffable non-textual history to which we are all subject. History in this sense is semiotically mediated: it is what the world and events in the world *mean*, or are taken to mean, or are made to mean. Its domain is that of ideology, of narrative in its most general sense, of the ceaseless creative activity of the human imagination working with – and upon – the materials of language and other sign systems to present to itself a version of experience with which it can live. The nightmare from which Stephen is trying to awake – in Catholic, British-ruled, Ireland during the first decade of the twentieth century – is a production of history in this sense, not merely a product of it: a narrative of exploitation, exclusion, and domination, of racial, national, gender, and class hegemony tricked out, by both oppressors and victims (categories which are not entirely separable), in the vivid colours of tragedy, epic, and romance. (The interspersed sequences of the 'Cyclops' episode of *Ulysses* present a few of the linguistic modes through which history is produced in a glamorous form, contrasting them with an apparently more neutral anecdotal style which is itself, of course, another potent mode of historical fabrication.) It is worth noting that Deasy's remarks on history occur just after he has given voice to his venomous anti-Semitism and just before he reveals his equally unpleasant sexism.

What is a nightmare to Stephen is, he implies, a comforting dream to many members of the community in which he lives, its function – to adapt Freudian theory along the lines of Jameson's project – being precisely to prevent the dreamer from awakening: if, Joyce seems to suggest, the Irish people as a whole at this time had been brought face to face with the contents of the political unconscious – realities that could be manifested only obliquely in cultural productions – the long sleep would be rudely ended. One is tempted to say that at times the slumber has become uneasy, forcing the dreamer to stir and turn over – dates one might cite are 1916 and 1919–23 – but that for the majority the sleep continues – as perhaps it must to some degree or other in any society, though Jameson may prefer to believe that a day will dawn, and must dawn, when dreams and nightmares are all dissolved in the brilliance of the postcapitalist era. One does not find that sense in Joyce; there is no likelihood that Stephen will wake from his nightmare (though it is to his credit that it does not subside into an assuaging dream), and dawn at the end of *Finnegans Wake* brings no daylight clarity or lucid and lasting truth.

That disagreement between Jameson (who stands here for the most culturally astute forms of late twentieth-century Marxism) and Joyce, I would argue, springs from a substantial difference in their understanding of the relation between the two senses of history. Some of Jameson's most strenuously rhetorical writing is devoted to the project of steering between two contrasting ideologies which treat these two histories very differently: what he calls the ideology of 'structuralism' – which would deny the existence of the first history or of the referent of any historical, or narrative, text – and the ideology of 'vulgar materialism' – which would reduce the second, textual, history to a mere mechanistically determined reflection of the first (*Political Unconscious*, 82). A successful middle course would, for Jameson, *not* be an instance of ideology, since it would be an acknowledgement both of the real contradictions that constitute History (or Necessity) and of the constitutive function of the texts in which those contradictions are represented (and disguised). Not surprisingly, these prove to be treacherous waters through which to navigate, and if we stay with Jameson on the voyage it is largely because the Scylla and Charybdis he has depicted for us are equally unappealing alternatives.

Joyce's texts, on the other hand, seem to imply that *all* versions of history are made in language and are, by virtue of that fact, ideological constructions, weavings and reweavings of old stories, fusions of stock character types, blendings of different national languages, dialects, and registers.[1] *Finnegans Wake* is the fullest statement in the world's textual archive of this view of history, exploiting the properties of the linguistic signifier to mix and conjoin narratives from a multiplicity of cultures, periods, disciplines, and discourses, at every level from the individual word to the several-hundred-page book. But the process can be seen at work in *Ulysses* and the earlier texts as well. Neither *Dubliners* nor *A*

---

[1] For a careful discussion of Joyce's awareness and exploitation of the competing varieties of historiography current during his writing career, see Spoo, *James Joyce and the Language of History*. Hofheinz, in *Joyce and the Invention of Irish History*, gives a useful account of some of the ways in which Joyce responds to Irish traditions of historical writing; see in particular chapters 3 and 4.

Portrait offers a position outside the histories they relate from which we can judge them as more or less ideologically determined, more or less true to reality; and the concrete evocation of a Dublin day in June 1904 in *Ulysses* is equally a textual achievement, in which the invented character Leopold Bloom is as alive as the historical individual George Russell, and the invented burying of Patrick Dignam in Glasnevin Cemetery as historical an event as Throwaway's documented winning of the Gold Cup. (Any reader of *Ulysses* who has visited the Martello Tower at Sandycove can testify to the way its historical reality appears to be enhanced, not diminished, through its recalling of Buck Mulligan and Stephen Dedalus; the knowledge that James Joyce once lived there for a short period has a much weaker effect on the touristic imagination.)

It might seem, then, that Joyce represents the first of Jameson's pair of unacceptable ideologies, that which denies altogether the existence of the referent or the Real. *Ulysses*, for instance, is sometimes seen as an extended dismantling of all the traditional assumptions of realistic fiction: it begins with the kind of fictional discourse, modelled on historical writing in the narrow sense, that treats the characters, events, and places it handles as if they pre-existed the narrative which in fact brings them into being, and moves on to modes of writing which insist that those existents and occurrences are constituted entirely by the language in which they are presented. Several chapters – 'Cyclops', 'Circe', and 'Ithaca', in particular – are characterized by a principle of endless generation: far from conveying the illusion that their language is tied to a set of events which predetermine their length and structure, it spawns actions, characters, speeches, memories, fantasies, speculations, and hallucinations in potentially limitless profusion – and at the same time problematizes the relationships among such categories. *Finnegans Wake* carries the process to an extreme, seeming to give language and its chance patterns and echoes absolute primacy over non-linguistic reality.

I would argue, however, that this does not constitute any kind of claim about the existence or non-existence, or the true nature of, the Real; what it does do is demonstrate a few facets of the immense power of language (and the systems of cultural signification with which it works) to create an impression of access to that inaccessible Real while at the same time drawing attention to the linguistic and literary processes through which this effect is achieved – the exploitation of narrative and descriptive conventions, the multiplication of allusions and references, the tapping of the obscure sources of sexuality and comedy. This power to fabricate a 'Real', to elicit and direct drives of eroticism, humour, or curiosity, is so strongly evident in *Ulysses* and *Finnegans Wake* that one cannot become aware of it without gaining some sense of the degree to which other kinds of narrative or description depend on the same power for the sense of the Real or the True which they convey – including works of history, criticism, and theory, and including what Jameson unashamedly calls 'the single great collective story' told by Marxism. Joyce could be said to dramatize and amplify Jameson's argument that although history is not a text, it is 'inaccessible to us except in textual form, and that our approach to it and to the Real itself necessarily passes through its prior textualization' (*Political Unconscious*, 35).

Instead of reading Joyce in the light of Jameson, then, it might be fruitful to read Jameson in the light of Joyce. Can we regard Jameson's text as a web of stories, archetypes, verbal strategies, rhetorical ploys, in which the skilful handling of history as a mode of discourse produces an impression of privileged access to truth or the Real? It might be possible to regard the narrative of the Odyssean intellectual journey between two unacceptable and opposed ideologies of history which I mentioned earlier, and which could be said to provide the rhetorical motor of *The Political Unconscious*, as itself an ideological construct, designed to preserve intact a comfortable but threatened position – a position which succeeds in retaining *both* the reassurance of an ultimately knowable ground outside all textual operations (guaranteed for Jameson by the insights of Marx) *and* the invigorating potential of a powerful creative and constitutive textuality. It might be, like ideology (in one of its many definitions), the imaginary resolution of a real contradiction. Jameson's balancing act could be related to another ancient rhetorical structure – one that has generated many a philosophical and political narrative – the Aristotelian 'Golden Mean'. (A somewhat surprising resource for Jameson to use, perhaps, since it is more often to be found in the armoury of the liberal pluralist than the committed radical.) Jameson does not, it is true, disguise the logical impossibility of his position in relation to the two alternatives: he calls it a 'paradox', and refers to its two dimensions as 'inseparable yet incommensurate' (82); but it would be naïve to think that ideology could be exorcised merely by the invocation of the term *paradox* – this was, after all, a favourite device of New Criticism, whose conservative ideological stance is now unmistakable.

Probably the most powerful narrative scheme in *The Political Unconscious* is the progression from point *a* to point *b*, where *b* preserves but subsumes, and thereby transforms, *a*. It is a familiar plot, where linear movement is accompanied by progressive widening, to produce an onward drive and to provide a conclusion of satisfying finality in which the entire narrative is recuperated yet transcended in a fresh perception of 'truth'. Jameson acknowledges one source of this structure: the medieval four-level allegorical system whereby the Old Testament was assimilated to the New; the more immediate source is of course the Hegelian and Marxian dialectic, in which the irreversibility of the progression is given particular emphasis. In the tradition of fiction, one obvious example is the *Bildungsroman*, in which errors are transformed into experience and thence into the achievement of adulthood and maturity.

Joyce, of course, uses the same narrative scheme, but, unlike Jameson, does so partly to draw attention to it *as* a storytelling device. *A Portrait of the Artist as a Young Man* offers itself as a classical *Bildungsroman*, and has often been read as such; it is possible, however, to read it – especially in the light cast backwards by *Ulysses* – as an undermining of readerly expectations of progress from innocence and naïvety to self-knowledge and success. If we take the two novels together, the later one can be said to perform an operation upon the former which is a kind of proleptic parody of Jameson's subsuming tactic: *Ulysses* certainly subsumes *A Portrait* into a much wider fictional whole, but the effect is to deny the anticipated narrative progression from fledgling poet to great artist, whose errors are volitional and are the portals of discovery. In 'Ithaca', Stephen and Bloom part without any fulfilment of the carefully generated expectations of mutual recognition or cross-fertilization, and by refusing this recuperative culmination the novel draws attention to the narrative structure, and the narrative hopes, which it evades. At another level, however, it could be said that *Ulysses* does obey the dictates of this narrative injunction: as Karen Lawrence has shown in detail in *The Odyssey of Style in 'Ulysses'*, the progression of its styles is itself a narrative journey, and the 'Ithaca' episode could be seen as the achievement of a final perspective from which all the earlier styles can be understood as relative – though the 'Penelope' episode comes where it does, perhaps, to challenge that claim of finality. It is only in *Finnegans Wake* that Joyce fully resists the linear, progressive, subsuming structure at the level of *discours* as well as at the level of *histoire*: no amount of ingenious analysis can make the language or the content of the later chapters encapsulate, transcend, or dominate that of the earlier ones. The sense of deepening insight, of closer and closer approximation to the Real, which is such a persuasive feature of a verbal structure like Jameson's, is jettisoned, and the bafflement and disappointment that *Finnegans Wake* so often produces in its readers is no doubt partly the result of this refusal.

What I have suggested, in effect, is that Jameson's text is subject to his own favourite manœuvre, and that it can be subsumed into the wider notions of textuality, ideology, and history that we find represented in Joyce. In particular, Joyce's writing (and those features of the literary which it exploits) enables us to challenge the separation of the two senses of 'history' implied in Jameson's argument and Stephen's Nestorian reflections. It does this by questioning the division of the world into signs and referents, language and existents; it reminds us that signs are referents and existents too, and history as text or ideology is as real as the unfathomable history that hurts us or gives us a back kick. Insofar as texts – Joyce's or Jameson's – have *effects* on their readers (and both writers seek and achieve effects that are extraordinarily powerful) – they are part of the Real. Novels and theoretical treatises can kick, too. Signs, texts, ideologies, interpretative methods – and the stories we tell about them – not only have histories, but make history. When we comment on the texts of Jameson or Joyce, we comment on the Real just as much as when we comment on the French Revolution or the price of books; equally, comments of either kind remain in the realm of textuality while they work their own effects in and on history.

Rather than an absolute division between the Real and the Text, along which we are obliged to tread a perilous path, rather than an irreversible progression from pure signification to an apprehension of Necessity, we learn from Joyce an appreciation of *difference*, which resists the narrative of progress and the claims of transcendence. And we learn that although the hurtful history to which we are constantly subject cannot be named, it can be changed – thanks to the historically gener-ated power of the texts we write and read. Jameson's version of the Scylla and Charybdis tale is, I submit, based on a false premise: that before we can act politically (and all action is to some degree political) we have to find a narrative which 'convinces' us as true and all-subsuming. I would contend, in the spirit, I believe, of Joyce's writing, that we can, and must, continue to find ways of rewriting ourselves, our history, our future, one another, in a constantly reworded engagement with the non-textual Real and with a constant alertness to the effects we are producing by our textual activity. One rich tradition which has an important part to play in that engagement is Marxism, and *The Political*

Unconscious is a superb example of the rewriting of that tradition for a particular time and place – a rewriting which, in its acknowledgement of the textuality of history, is testimony to the historical effectiveness of Joyce's own creative rewriting of history.

CHAPTER 7

Wakean history: not yet

- You, Cochrane, what city sent for him?
- Tarentum, sir.
- Very good. Well?
- There was a battle, sir.
- Very good. Where?
    The boy's blank face asked the blank window.
    Fabled by the daughters of memory. And yet it was in some way if not as memory fabled it. A phrase, then, of impatience, thud of Blake's wings of excess. I hear the ruin of all space, shattered glass and toppling masonry, and time one livid final flame. What's left us then?
- I forget the place, sir. 279 BC.
- Asculum, Stephen said, glancing at the name and date in the gorescarred book. (*U*2.1–13)

This passage opens the 'Nestor' episode of *Ulysses*, the episode in which the question of history – a topic explicitly raised at many points in the book – is posed most insistently. Is history a matter of dates and names in books ('279 BC', 'Asculum'), Blakean fables of memory, 'a tale like any other too often heard' (*U*2.46–7), a route of possibilities carved through infinite impossibilities (*U*2.49–51), an inescapable nightmare (*U*2.377 – and see chapter 6 above), humanity's movement 'to one great goal' (*U*2.380–1), a shout in the street (*U*2.386)? Although *Ulysses* keeps these and other options open, it does, as we saw in chapter 6, ultimately align itself with a particular conception of history: one which minimizes the gap between two radically different uses of the word 'history', on the one hand as the totality of events as they have occurred through time, and on the other as a story told about the past. Not that Joyce simply accepts that fusion of two disparate meanings; much of *Ulysses* puts it under considerable strain, threatening to pull the two senses of 'history' apart.

86

In 'Wandering Rocks', for example, history as narrative is exploded by the multiplicity of simultaneous unrelated events; in 'Sirens' it is undermined by the uncontrollable properties of the material signifier of language; in 'Cyclops' and 'Oxen of the Sun' it is unsettled by the transforming power of narrative and linguistic styles; in 'Circe' it is challenged by the uncertainty of the distinction between the real and the unreal; and in 'Ithaca' it succumbs to the proliferating energies of descriptive language itself.

Nevertheless, the decision to base the book upon the events of a dateable day in a specifiable location situates it firmly in the mainstream tradition of the novel, which has always been seen as the fictional counterpart of the historiographical tradition. *Ulysses* can thus be said to leave the conventional concept of history as the union of events and language intact, if somewhat shaken. It is *Finnegans Wake* that breaks decisively with that concept, refusing all the attempts made by its readers to bring it back to the recognizable configurations of history, insisting that the multiple and endless accumulation of events and beings in the world and the equally endless telling of stories belong to two quite different orders of reality, whose relationship is deeply problematic – as much so for the historian as for the novelist. The *Wake* achieves this by means of all the devices I listed for the chapters of *Ulysses*, but these devices now operate as consistent and constitutive textual processes rather than as sporadic adventures in this or that mode of writing. Shifts of viewpoint and location occur in mid-sentence or are combined in a single word; the material properties of the signifier continually play havoc with any attempt to ascertain a stable referent; narrative and linguistic presentation determines what can scarcely any longer be called the 'events' and 'characters'; and the endless capacity of language for self-generation is evident on every page of the text.

This difference between the two books' handling of historical material is crucial. As long as the text offers us, as does *Ulysses*, a clearly separable diversity of methods in linear sequence (helpfully labelled by Joyce in his schemas) we are left with the impression that the representation of the world in language is a matter of free agency, and this implies that behind all the variation is an unchallengeable, neutral base – call it the 'initial style' or 'traditional narration' or just 'history' – from which all these alternatives derive and against which they are measured. The *Wake*, however, offers no such metatextual or paratextual solace; there is not a single page of introductory scene-setting or of concluding explanation, no substantial oases of traditional prose in the text (though there are a few brief mirages), no chapter headings, no opening or closing sentence, not even a title that can be read outside the processes of shifting and ambiguous meanings that characterize the language of the entire book. This absence of any verbal bolthole, from which we might contemplate in security the crazy excesses all around, has not often been commented upon, yet it is a highly significant aspect of Joyce's creative decision-making; it would have been a very simple matter to provide the reader with such a refuge or vantage point, but Joyce refuses it – even though he expended much energy outside his book helping readers make sense of it.[1]

By this means, the model of the novel as simulacrum of history is shattered, and with it the model of historical writing as simulacrum of the novel. If the language which the historian has to use possesses all the properties revealed in *Finnegans Wake* – and revealed, I would argue, not as fortuitous side effects but as essential to the working of language in any context[2] – then the dream of capturing in words 'what really happened' must be abandoned. Words do not picture the world independently of their users, they do not hold reality in their grasp for our calm contemplation, they do not transmit to us the way things were or are. Even if they could and occasionally did, there is no way in which we could know they were doing so.

But *Finnegans Wake* undoes history in other ways, too. For all the efforts of the exegetes, the text does not contain within itself a clear determination of a time and place, of a sequence of events, or of a set of existents. It is not that history is absent; on the contrary, history is omnipresent, in all the forms in which it is named in 'Nestor', and more. It is there as names and dates, for instance:

1132 A.D. Men like to ants or emmets wondern upon a groot hwide Whallfisk which lay in a Runnel. (*FW* 13.33)

It is there as archive, as myth, as patriotic tale, as scabrous anecdote, as the pressure of a guilty past, as national destiny, as eternal cycle, as legal contract, as domestic detail. Above all, it is there as language, and language's own history is part of the account of history which the book gives – which must be the case in any historical writing, whether acknowledged or not. *Finnegans Wake* denies the historian's fiction that

---

[1] This argument is continued in chapter 11 below, where I examine the common appeal to the notion that *Finnegans Wake* is a dream in an attempt to control – or at least excuse – the multiplicity of interpretation.

[2] For an elaboration of this point, see my discussion of the status of *Finnegans Wake* in *Peculiar Language*, chapters 7 and 8.

the past can be seen as the past, that events possess meanings in themselves, and emphasizes continually the interpenetration of past and present, of diachrony and synchrony.

One early and recurrent motif of the *Wake* involves a historical placing in terms of what has *not yet* happened, which both parodies the tendency in historiography to present events in terms of what they lead to and at the same time demonstrates the centrality of this mode to any historical writing, which must always reconstruct after the event and can never bear witness to it in its own time and place. The motif begins as early as the second paragraph of the *Wake*, which is suffused with the 'not yet/*pas encore*' modality:

Sir Tristram, violer d'amores, fr'over the short sea, had passencore rearrived from North Armorica . . . : nor had topsawyer's rocks . . . exaggerated themselse . . . : nor avoice from afire bellowsed mishe mishe . . . : not yet . . . had a kidscad buttended a bland old isaac; not yet . . . were sosie sesthers wroth with twone nathandjoe. (*FW* 3.04)

It receives an extended treatment in a series of doggerel couplets in the Shem chapter (1.7):

In Nowhere has yet the Whole World taken part of himself for his Wife;
By Nowhere have Poorparents been sentenced to Worms, Blood and Thunder for Life
Not yet has the Emp from Corpsica forced the Arth out of Engleterre;
Not yet have the Sachsen and Judder on the Mound of a Word made Warre . . . (*FW* 175.07)

Other occurrences also refer to the passage of history or to the writing of history or biography:

Though not yet had the sailor sipped that sup nor the humphar foamed to the fill. (*FW* 124.32)

. . . offering the prize of a bittersweet crab, a little present from the past, for their copper age was yet unminted, to the winner. (*FW* 170.07)

His biografiend, in fact, kills him verysoon, if yet not, after. (*FW* 55.06)

The *Wake*, it seems, is situated before history, but that 'before', that recurrent 'not yet', implies within itself the whole of history.

In French, of course, *encore* passes very easily from 'yet' to 'again', and the cyclical view of history so prominent in the *Wake* is another device for unsettling our secure linear perspectives: if history comes to us only as narrative, it happens as often as it is told or retold, its repetitions stretching endlessly into the future. Part of the history narrated in the *Wake* is Shem's writing with and on his own body, but what he writes remains perpetually in the present thanks to the grammatical properties – the text specifies tense, voice, and mood – of the language he uses:

> ... by its corrosive sublimation one continuous present tense integument slowly unfolded all marryvoising moodmoulded cyclewheeling history. (*FW* 185.36)

Personal and social narratives are here conjoined: the wheeling cycles of history are equally Viconian eras and the individual sequence of birth ('unfolded'), marriage ('marryvoising' – with a nod to Marivaux), and death ('mould'). Shem's text is, as this description suggests, the *Wake* itself, though it is also any history and any story.

In thus drawing attention to its own production and reception (the story of Shem's writing is of course told by a disgusted yet fascinated Shaun figure), the *Wake* reminds us not only that in being made out of language it is made out of historical materials, but also that, for the same reason, it is made by history and through history. A text does not enter history as an object whose nature and future are determined at its moment of publication; as long as it is read, remembered, or referred to it is continually being made and remade, and this is its only mode of existence as a text, rather than as one physical object among many. Each International James Joyce Symposium prolongs the existence of Joyce's writings, but also changes them, even if what the participants claim to be doing is restoring them to their original or real selves. This is the paradox of the much-debated 1984 edition of *Ulysses*, which the editor Hans Walter Gabler describes, choosing his words carefully, as 'a non-corrupted counterpart to the first edition of 1922' ('Afterword' to *Ulysses: The Corrected Text*, 650) – that is, a text which has never existed before, but can be thought of as what *should* have appeared in 1922. Thus Gabler presents as the hitherto unrealized goal of the whole history of Joyce's labours a text which at the time of publication existed only as a 'not yet'. The new edition thus 'made history' in more than one sense; it rendered the 1922 text and all other texts derivations of itself, even though they predate it in the history of *Ulysses* publication. Nor has the text ossified as a result of the labours of Gabler and his team; the publication of the 'Corrected Text' in fact gave rise to the most productive era of *Ulysses* editing as Gabler's decisions were questioned, further corrected, or supplanted by yet more editorial ventures. As Gabler himself remarks (with a wisdom not typical of all his opponents), 'Grounded in historicity and shaped by critical judgement, such editions can neither claim nor attain definitiveness' ('Note on the Second Impression', *Ulysses: A Critical and Synoptic Edition*, vii).

Criticism works in the same way. It gives us a new reading and tells us that this is how the work should always have been read, and it tries to make all the other readings which it draws upon derivative of itself. The most history-making critical works may not be those of high scholarship, but the more mundane productions of anthologists, introductions, and prefaces. For example, when a reader opens Gabler's revised text of *Ulysses* in its most familiar British form, the Bodley Head and Penguin edition of 1986, he or she encounters first not Joyce's words but a preface by Richard Ellmann. For thousands of readers of *Ulysses*, no doubt, this preface became an integral and largely unquestioned part of the experience of reading Joyce's work, and the history of its appearance in this influential position – publishers' meetings, negotiations, financial transactions, and a whole anterior history of influence and reputation – remained an untold story. Because of the status of this preface and of its author, most of its readers would not think of asking what other possibilities it has ousted, what other kinds of preface Ellmann could have written, or what other authors might have chosen to write. We may, perhaps, feel inclined to ask what Stephen asks himself in 'Nestor', 'Was that only possible which came to pass?' (*U* 2.52) – was Richard Ellmann the only figure a leading publisher would turn to in the 1980s for this task, and was it inevitable that his preface would be an attempt, against the thrust of most recent studies of Joyce's writing, to identify the achievement of *Ulysses* as the expression of a simple theme – 'universal love' – and to present its extraordinary linguistic exploits as essentially mimetic devices of a traditional kind? Whatever its particular history, the preface stands as testimony to one kind of historical remaking of Joyce's text, its ideology part of our recent history and therefore of the history of *Ulysses*.

Texts make history; history makes texts. *Finnegans Wake*, in dramatizing this cycle-wheeling process, manages to make it an extremely funny business. The joke, finally, is on Stephen, whose meditations on the subject of history in Nestor, though they are tinged with grim humour, fail to engage with the productive potential of the past's inevitable textuality. The critical project of reducing the *Wake* to a reliable, and serious, historical record is subject to an eternal 'not yet'; but at the same time it is important to acknowledge that we miss a great deal of the *Wake*'s comedy if, in the name of some principle of polysemic free play, we overlook its multiple engagements with history as well as with the writing of history.[3] Recognizing the textuality of the history we know does not mean discrediting historical knowledge or denying the past; as Stephen says to himself, in the passage we began with, 'And yet it was in some way if not as memory fabled it.' *Finnegans Wake* is replete with fables of memory and memories of fables, and its own historical force is not lessened thereby, even if we can only tell more and more stories about it.

[3] To cite one example, Margot Norris demonstrates the way in which the 'Shem' chapter of *Finnegans Wake*, while criticizing the pretensions of historiography by parodying its interested rhetoricity in the hilariously exaggerated distortions of Shaun's biography of the artist, manages to weave into its texture a sense of the material as well as intellectual struggles that marked the rise of modernism ('The Critical History of *Finnegans Wake*').

CHAPTER 8

Molly's flow: the writing of 'Penelope' and the question of women's language

STOPPING THE FLOW

Descriptions of the style of Molly Bloom's interior monologue by critics, female or male, feminist or patriarchal, seem to be fixated on one particular metaphor, a metaphor usually signalled by the word 'flow'. Whenever the final chapter of *Ulysses* is being discussed, sooner or later, it appears, that term will crop up. Here are a few instances:

The rarity of capital letters and the run-on sentences in Molly's monologue are of course related to Joyce's theory of her mind (and of the female mind in general) as a flow, in contrast to the series of short jumps made by Bloom, and of somewhat longer ones by Stephen. (Richard Ellmann, *James Joyce*, 376)

If Bloom and Stephen, in their singularity and in their interchange, seem to represent language's two principles, Molly might represent the extreme of language at its loosest and most flowing. (Gottfried, *The Art of Joyce's Syntax*, 35)

To enter the mind of Molly Bloom after so much time spent in the minds of Stephen and Leopold is to plunge into a flowing river. If we have hitherto been exploring the waste land, here are the refreshing, life-giving waters that alone can renew it. The flow is the flow of Nature . . . (Blamires, *The Bloomsday Book*, 246)[1]

She has her own laws, which are not man's; the rhythms of her meditation despise man's dams and fences . . . Joyce has dared to think his way into a woman's mind: it would be dangerous to shape, use the artist's cunning: it is safer to leave the floodgates open and let the dark turgid flow have its will; otherwise the spell might be broken. And so we listen to an incredible torrent of reminiscence . . . (Burgess, *Here Comes Everybody*, 173–4)

We are told that the 'lack of punctuation symbolizes the lack in

---

[1] Blamires is even more graphic in *Studying James Joyce*: 'When we enter the mind of Molly Bloom we leave this world of masculine aridities and angularities for a world of fluidity. Molly's thought flows, gushes, spurts and tumbles headlong. It is a flood . . . If there is something sterile about Bloom's sexual life and Stephen's cerebration, then the antidote to both is here in the outflow of an unstoppable fertility' (131).

Molly's mind of the laws and rules of the "built" world, and the rhythms
flow like water' (French, *The Book as World*, 245); that the 'flow of
associations is assisted by an absence of punctuation and logical connection, allowing it to pursue its own unimpeded current' (Bolt, *A Preface to
James Joyce*, 145); that the 'most striking effect of Molly's utterance is the
flow' (Hayman, *Ulysses*, 118); that 'her thoughts move like the tide –
flowing forward, breaking, rolling back upon one another' (Henke,
Joyce's Moraculous Sindbook, 235); and that in this chapter the book's
strands 'seem to flow on, to be literally interminable' (Toynbee, 'A
Study of James Joyce's *Ulysses*', 282). Other critics refer to the 'formless,
flowing monologue that provides the "last word" of the book' (Lawrence, *Odyssey of Style*, 203), 'the long smooth flow of "Penelope"' (Peake,
James Joyce, 298), 'the words flowing through that mind' (Card, *An
Anatomy of 'Penelope'*, 54), 'the flow of its language, transgressing the
boundaries set by syntax and decorum' (Boheemen, *The Novel as Family
Romance*, 173), 'the flow of Molly's consciousness' (Humphrey, *Stream of
Consciousness*, 27), and 'a flow of "discours"' (Gabler, 'Narrative Reread-
ings', 67). For Tindall, 'her enormous flow is less stream than flood'
(*James Joyce*, 42), while for Shechner, 'The stream of her consciousness is
the displacement to language of her urinary and menstrual flow' (*Joyce in
Nighttown*, 217). Steinberg, discussing the style of the 'Penelope' episode,
manages to use the word 'flow' eight times in seven pages (*The Stream of
Consciousness*, 112–19).

Related metaphors of rivers, streams, and liquids – and of the barriers
they pour over – occur in almost every attempt to characterize the style
of the episode.[2] Interestingly, however, there appears to be no record of
a comment by Joyce – who didn't hesitate to give metaphoric handles to
his readers – that suggests this image. The famous description of the
'Penelope' episode which he gave Budgen refers to the earth, not to
water, and so does the Ithacan name for the embedded Molly, 'Gea-

---

[2] If the word 'flow' is not used, a water metaphor of some kind is usually present in attempts to
characterize the chapter's style. For example, 'Marion's monologue snakes its way through the
last forty pages of *Ulysses* like a river winding through a plain, finding its true course by the
compelling logic of its own fluidity and weight' (Budgen, *James Joyce and the Making of 'Ulysses'*, 269);
'The ruminations of Mrs Bloom [are represented by] a long unbroken rhythm of brogue, like the
swell of some profound sea' (Wilson, 'James Joyce', *Axel's Castle*, 164); 'The little cloud no bigger
than a woman's hand, observed by Stephen and Bloom, has filled the sky, come down in shower,
become a stream – not only the stream of Molly's consciousness but her more commodious
stream' (Tindall, *A Reader's Guide to James Joyce*, 233); 'In the whirlpool of the woman's expansive
thoughts *Ulysses* has its irresolute conclusion' (Bernard Benstock, *James Joyce*, 141); 'liquid,
unpunctuated prose' (Parrinder, *James Joyce*, 195); 'an abrogation of syntactic dykes', a 'fluent
amoral unsystematized self-cancelling outpouring' (Kenner, *Ulysses*, 148, 149).

Tellus'. Stuart Gilbert's chapter on 'Penelope' elaborates on Joyce's 'earth-mother' archetype; and although he does use the word 'flow' in this chapter, drawing a connection with a river 'whose waters at a certain period of each year flowed reddened as with blood into the sea' (*James Joyce's 'Ulysses'*, 400), he does so in order to describe not Molly but Stephen. The only fluid mentioned in the schemas for this chapter is milk, and it occurs as an adjective under 'colour' for both 'Ithaca' and 'Penelope' (see Richard Ellmann, *Ulysses on the Liffey*, appendix).

This is not to suggest that the urge to use the word 'flow' is necessarily erroneous or wilful;[3] on the contrary, the fact that it does not appear to have been initiated by Joyce and is not prominent in the early commentators he instructed might suggest that it is a widely shared and objective response to a specific feature of the text, or, more accurately, a conjunction between something in the text and the particular expectations readers have brought to it. But what *is* it that flows and overflows in the language of Molly's nocturnal reflections? Two possible answers suggest themselves immediately. One is that her sentences override the syntactic rules normally observed by language, and the other that they run on much longer than is usual. Neither of these answers survives any scrutiny of the text, however, if we take it that what the metaphor describes is the language we are invited to imagine passing, in the form of thoughts, through Molly's brain as she lies – and sits – awake during the early hours of 17 June 1904. It has been pointed out, for instance by Anthony Burgess in *Joysprick* (59), that once the missing punctuation and other typographical absences have been made good, the language of this episode is relatively conventional (especially when measured against the earlier linguistic experiments in *Ulysses*): the syntax, though it exhibits dialectal features and some of the ellipses, corrections, and changes of course that characterize spoken utterances, is not particularly transgressive.[4]

Here is a section that I think most readers would agree is typical of Molly's monologue, with graphic signs regularized:

[3] It is, nevertheless, refreshing to encounter a collection of essays on 'Penelope' in which other topics and tropes dominate the discussion: Richard Pearce, ed., *Molly Blooms*.

[4] An early acknowledgement of this fact came from Rebecca West, who commented: 'Most of the wildness of this chapter is typographical cheating, a surface effect which is created by the lack of punctuation, and would instantly disappear . . . if a few commas and full stops and dashes and exclamation points were inserted' (*The Strange Necessity*, 48). Karen Lawrence, in her study of the styles of *Ulysses*, observes that 'once we learn how to read the continuous rhythms of the prose, the style seems much less radical than it first appears', and argues, I think correctly, that this reversion to earlier and simpler stylistic techniques after the complexities of the preceding chapters is part of its function as a conclusion (*Odyssey of Style*, 204–5).

I'd love to have a long talk with an intelligent well-educated person. I'd have to get a nice pair of red slippers, like those Turks with the fez used to sell – or yellow; and a nice semi-transparent morning gown (that I badly want), or a peach-blossom dressing jacket like the one long ago in Walpole's (only eight-and-six, or eighteen-and-six). I'll just give him one more chance. I'll get up early in the morning – I'm sick of Cohen's old bed, in any case. I might go over to the markets to see all the vegetables and cabbages and tomatoes and carrots and all kinds of splendid fruits all coming in, lovely and fresh. Who knows who'd be the first man I'd meet? They're out looking for it in the morning; Mamy Dillon used to say they are, and the night too. That was her mass-going! I'd love a big juicy pear now, to melt in your mouth, like when I used to be in the longing way. Then I'll throw him up his eggs and tea in the moustachecup she gave him to make his mouth bigger. I suppose he'd like my nice cream, too. I know what I'll do: I'll go about rather gay, not too much, singing a bit now and then. 'Mi fa pietà Masetto'. Then I'll start dressing myself to go out. 'Presto, non son più forte'. I'll put on my best shift and drawers – let him have a good eyeful out of that to make his micky stand for him.[5] (*U* 18.1493–510)

To read the passage on the page in this form, or to hear it read aloud by someone who has marked it in advance for syntactic clarity, is certainly to be aware of free mental energy moving rapidly from topic to topic, but it isn't to experience a marked transgression of the fixed laws of grammar or a capacity to take language into new realms of freedom and formlessness. The syntactic deviations are characteristic of casual speech: thus the second sentence, instead of the written formulation 'red or yellow slippers' postpones the 'or yellow' until later, when the thought of the alternative actually strikes. This sentence also does without a verb before 'long ago' in the way that a spoken utterance might, and includes the kind of correction ('eight-and-six, or eighteen-and-six') that would not occur in writing.[6]

The interior monologues of Stephen and Bloom infringe grammatical conventions far more radically – you only have to rewrite a stretch of Bloom's monologue using the transcription conventions of 'Penelope' to get a piece of language that really does overflow the boundaries of orthodox English:

Howth Bailey light 2 4 6 8 9 see has to change or they might think it a house

[5] Normalizing the text is of course not simply a mechanical procedure, and I have chosen to emphasize the relative syntactic orthodoxy of Molly's monologue in this instance. A normalization truer to the rhythms of verbal thought would use more dashes and triple periods; such a rewriting would also conform quite closely to a tradition of representing thought or spontaneous speech in fiction.

[6] Fritz Senn has brilliantly demonstrated the importance of self-correction in *Ulysses*; see 'Righting *Ulysses*' and *Joyce's Dislocutions*, ch. 4, 'Dynamics of Corrective Unrest'.

wreckers Grace Darling people afraid of the dark also glowworms cyclists lightingup time jewels diamonds flash better women light is a kind of reassuring not going to hurt you better now of course than long ago country roads run you through the small guts for nothing still two types there are you bob against scowl or smile pardon not at all best time to spray plants too in the shade after the sun some light still red rays are longest roygbiv Vance taught us red orange yellow green blue indigo violet a star I see Venus cant tell yet 2 when 3 its night (*U* 13.1068–77)

It is evident that Joyce has adopted a very different set of conventions to represent Molly's thoughts from that utilized earlier for Stephen, Bloom, and occasionally – notably in 'Wandering Rocks' – for other characters. (This is to leave aside those techniques which involve refraction through another established style, as occurs in the first part of 'Nausicaa', periodically through 'Cyclops', and consistently through 'Oxen of the Sun'.) But the differences between these two styles of thought do not seem to warrant the obsessive use of the metaphor of 'flow' for the final chapter. Both styles involve associative leaps, and suggest a potential interminability. The rewritten passage from 'Nausicaa' suggests that, if anything, it is Molly's greater syntactic correctness and explicitness which conveys the sense of smooth transitions from subject to subject, whereas the jumps and ellipses of Bloom's thought processes disclose a more eccentric and unpredictable mind.

If the term 'flow' does not refer to an overspilling of syntactic categories, it might imply an extension of the sentence beyond its normal limits. Joyce himself encouraged such a perception by referring to the eight sections of 'Penelope' as 'sentences'. But sentences they are not, whether we think in terms of syntactic structure or graphic markings; the only unit they approximate to is the paragraph, and then only by virtue of some white space on the page. (No one given the text *without* these indications would be able to say where the seven breaks occur.[7]) If it is unusual sentence length that is implied by 'flow', the term would be more accurately used of earlier parts of *Ulysses*: some of the interpolated parodies in 'Cyclops', for instance, or the wordier pastiches of 'Oxen of the Sun'. (There is a 255–word sentence in the Gibbonesque section of 'Oxen' (*U* 14.955–77), and the account of the religious retinue in 'Cyclops'has a sentence of nearly 314 words (*U* 12.1689–712).) The most striking examples – where form and content seem carefully matched – are the 212– and 442–word Ithacan sentences (produced, it is interesting

---

[7] The single exception is the middle break, which in most editions is marked by a period. See the note that follows.

to note, after Bloom's action of 'turning the faucet to let it flow' and of the subsequent question 'Did it flow?' (*U* 17.162–228)). Molly's sentences, syntactically defined, are, on the whole, fairly short. Nor is her style more paratactic than earlier representations of thought in the book; the sudden burst of 'ands' in the passage quoted above is effective because it stands out from a syntactic texture that involves frequent postponed resolutions produced by interpolated thoughts or changes in direction (a stylistic feature increased during the process of composition by Joyce's insertions).[8]

We have to conclude, then, that the sense of an unstoppable onward movement ignoring all conventional limits is derived from the language, not as it supposedly takes shape in a human brain, but as it is presented *on the page*. Here is the passage I quoted earlier as it actually appears in compliance with Joyce's instructions to the printer:[9]

Id love to have a long talk with an intelligent welleducated person Id have to get a nice pair of red slippers like those Turks with the fez used to sell or yellow and a nice semitransparent morning gown that I badly want or a peachblossom dressing jacket like the one long ago in Walpoles only 8/6 or 18/6 Ill just give him one more chance Ill get up early in the morning Im sick of Cohens old bed in any case I might go over to the markets to see all the vegetables and cabbages and tomatoes and carrots and all kinds of splendid fruits all coming in lovely and fresh who knows whod be the 1st man Id meet theyre out looking for it in the morning Mamy Dillon used to say they are and the night too that was her

---

[8] In a linguistic and statistical comparison of Molly's interior monologue with that of Stephen and Bloom, Erwin Steinberg proposes that, in addition to the lack of punctuation, it is the 'comparatively long sentences' and 'the use of transitional words' (co-ordinating conjunctions, *yes*, and *then*) that give the impression of continuous flow in this episode (*The Stream of Consciousness*, 119). The second of these features is a part, though probably only a small part, of the effect of continuousness. However, the average sentence length in the samples he analyzes (omitting the exceptional opening and closing passages) is only 15.04 words (118): this is certainly longer than the more staccato style of Stephen's and Bloom's interior monologue, as he points out, but it is by no means unusually long for English prose. Taking an episode where Joyce *does* write unusually long sentences, 'Eumaeus', we find that the fourteen sentences of the first two paragraphs (which are not untypical of the chapter) have an average sentence length of 53 words.

[9] It is clear from the way editors have treated Joyce's manuscript inconsistencies with regard to these graphic features that there is general agreement about their nature: they are not stylistic choices indicative of specific characteristics of this or that thought, but a blanket convention for the whole chapter which Joyce could have achieved merely by giving the printers a list of rules. Editors have assumed, therefore, that inconsistencies must be ironed out – to the extent that the 1984 edition removed the period after the fourth section (18.747), although it is present in all the workshop and published versions to which this edition refers. It is back in the 1986 impression and the trade editions, however, presumably on the grounds that an exception can be made for punctuation at the chapter's mid-point (in terms of sections) as has always been done for its end (see *Ulysses: A Critical and Synoptic Edition*, 2nd impression, I, ix). Rabaté stresses the importance of this central period in 'Le nœud gordien' (134–5).

massgoing Id love a big juicy pear now to melt in your mouth like when I used to be in the longing way then Ill throw him up his eggs and tea in the moustachecup she gave him to make his mouth bigger I suppose hed like my nice cream too I know what Ill do Ill go about rather gay not too much singing a bit now and then mi fa pieta Masetto then Ill start dressing myself to go out presto non son piu forte Ill put on my best shift and drawers let him have a good eyeful out of that to make his micky stand for him (*U* 18.1493–510)

The actual experience of reading a text printed in this way is one of working to recover its lost signs – punctuation marks and upper-case letters – in order to make sense of it; a sequence of guesses, backtrackings, and corrections that renders onward progress much less smooth than we are accustomed to, even in this novel's linguistic carnival, and that no doubt gives rise to the feeling that its language is especially deviant. This process of interpretation is an attempt to recover what Joyce's instructions to the printer have obscured: the syntactic relations which are a necessary part of the thoughts we are to imagine passing through Molly's mind. *We* may be uncertain whether 'I suppose' in line 1507 refers to the reasons for Milly's gift of a moustachecup or to Leopold's desire for cream with his breakfast, but it makes no sense to assume that Molly shares our uncertainty.

If, then, the sentences seem to run on without a pause it is not because we have seized the qualities of Molly's thought that their unpunctuatedness represents, but because we have failed to seize – thanks to Joyce's mode of visual presentation – the syntactic articulations she may be assumed to be using. In other words, this effect relies on the strategies and techniques of an activity that has nothing to do with the continuities of unexpressed thought: the activity of reading.[10] The relation between the unpunctuated (and largely unparagraphed) text and the sense of a

[10] Similarly, the confusion which arises for the reader when the referent of the masculine pronouns changes without notice is not the product of any confusion we are to ascribe to Molly; it is, on the contrary, the product of her certainty, which needs no embodiment in the explicitness of a proper noun. (Bernard and Shari Benstock, in providing a key to these pronouns in *Who's He When He's at Home*, proceed on the assumption that 'she is clear in her own mind about their individual identities' (229).) Most of the time, *Ulysses* achieves readability by grossly falsifying this aspect of thought and language: Leopold's and Stephen's interior monologues are much more explicit than any transcription of thought would be – and at the same time they are extremely selective in their references, which involve either publicly shared knowledge or private concerns for which some explanation is provided within the covers of the book. Even Molly's monologue is much more explicit and transparent than real self-communing would ever be; by and large, that is to say, it has the linguistic characteristics of an address to another person (Glasheen calls it Molly's 'letter to the world' (*Third Census*, xxxviii)), and the 'ambiguous' pronouns – the Benstocks find very few that cannot be securely apportioned – are only hints of a type of language that would, if it could be exactly transcribed, remain totally obscure to other minds.

rapid and ungoverned passage of thought is therefore purely an analogical or emblematic one;[11] we read off from the visual signal an equivalent
aural one, we take the uninterruptedness of print as a conventionally
sanctioned sign for an uninterruptedness of thought. Replacing the
punctuation and capitals in fact makes our progression as readers more
'flowing', and does not affect the thoughts being represented (since the
ambiguities we struggle with are not ambiguities we attribute to Molly),
but it takes away that striking visual symbol of homogeneous continuity,
a feature which belongs to the printing not the thinking. We have no
difficulty in interpreting the symbolism, since the thought processes in
question are those of someone unable to sleep after an extraordinary
day that has stirred memories and provoked desires; we would expect
such thoughts to be insistent, helter-skelter, widely ranging, yet constantly circling around a few dominant preoccupations. That there is an
extremely strong tendency in criticism – evident in many of the brief
citations I have given – to associate this emblematically signalled continuity with 'the female mind' is a reflection not of any concrete characteristics of Molly Bloom's language but of the critics' gender assumptions. We shall return to this point in due course.

Some readers associate the absence of punctuation in 'Penelope' with
sleepiness, rather than with the freely moving continuities of wakeful but
unrestrained thought, an association which has the advantage of providing an explanation (of a kind) for the chapter's distinctive style that is not
related to gender stereotypes. And it is true that when Bloom is drop-
ping off in the 'Nausicaa' episode, Joyce has recourse to the removal of
punctuation as an emblematic device:

O sweety all your little girlwhite up I saw dirty bracegirdle made me do love
sticky we two naughty Grace darling she him half past the bed met him pike
hoses frillies for Raoul de perfume your wife black hair heave under embon
señorita young eyes Mulvey plump bubs me . . . (*U* 13.1279–82)

To interpret the absence of punctuation and capitals in 'Penelope' as an
emblem of sleepiness cannot be regarded as 'wrong', since the significance of these printing conventions is not a matter of established
agreement; however, Bloom's half-awake monologue is marked in addition by an even more deviant syntax than his normal style, implying a
much more complete breakdown of rational thought than is the case in
Molly's monologue. (The content of Molly's memories is hardly sugges-

[11] I have discussed emblematic, as opposed to mimetic, functions of literary language in *The
Rhythms of English Poetry* (287–95) and *Peculiar Language* (154–7).

tive of sleep either, and her efforts to 'doze off' by counting (18.1544–6) lead straight into more speculations, desires, plans, and memories.) In any case, by this stage in the book the reader is unlikely to assume a naturalistic connection between the technique of a chapter and the state of mind of its central character or characters: this traditional assumption has been under attack since the headlines of 'Aeolus'.[12]

The omission of the graphic signs that articulate sentences can be read, then, as an emblematic pointer to the kind of ungoverned thought that would be normal under these circumstances, though the visual realization of these thoughts cannot be the direct representation of mental processes. What the reader is encouraged to imagine or produce is a mode of spoken utterance that tries to suggest rapid thought by minimizing syntactically induced pauses. However, Joyce has adopted other conventions in the visual presentation of this chapter for which this explanation will not serve. Absent from the printed page are not only the punctuation marks and upper-case sentence beginnings that might make a difference to the way we speak the words, but the apostrophes in possessive and abbreviated forms that can make no difference to oral realization at all.[13] 'I'm sick of Cohen's old bed' will sound the same with or without its two apostrophes; the effect of removing them is a purely visual one, with no bearing on the mental utterance they represent. Even more clearly a matter of the eye alone is the use throughout the chapter of numerals and graphic signs where an orthodox written text might use words: 'only 8/6 or 18/6'; 'whod be the 1st man Id meet'. This technique is not limited to those cases where a figure and a word would be equally acceptable, or even cases where Molly might be visualizing rather than verbalizing a memory, like the price label on the dressing jacket in the passage quoted above, or Lieutenant Gardner's death notice – 'Gardner lieut Stanley G 8th Bn 2nd East Lancs Rgt of enteric fever' (*U* 18.389). (In the latter, we may note that the remover of stops is still at work, altering even the visual memory of the printed notice to conform to the Penelopean style.) They

[12] Another chapter in which the style (one that is very different from that of 'Penelope') is often said to represent tiredness is 'Eumaeus'; but here too there is a productiveness and proliferation of discourse that would be more accurately described as tireless (see my discussion in *Peculiar Language*, 172–84).

[13] As the Rosenbach MS shows, Joyce first of all included apostrophes (and periods at the ends of all sections), and only later made the decision to have them removed. The felicitous ambiguities which sometimes resulted may have led to the title of his last book. (To see what 'Penelope' looks like with all its apostrophes, it is now possible to consult Danis Rose's so-called 'Reader's Edition' of *Ulysses*; most readers familiar with Joyce's preferred text will probably find this editorial innovation a diminishment rather than an enhancement of the episode's special qualities.)

include instances that clearly contravene the norms of written English, like 'ı kiss then would send them all spinning' (*U* 18.190–1) and 'ı of the 7 wonders of the world' (*U* 18.551–2).[14] Moreover, the 1984 edition restores some idiosyncratic spellings that are also discernible only in their written form: 'neumonia' [*U* 18.727], 'an alnight sitting' [*U* 18.1196]; 'place' for 'plaice' [*U* 18.939], and 'carrot' for 'carat' [*U* 18.870]. There is also the matter of Molly's use of upper- and lower-case initial letters: sometimes an expected capitalization doesn't occur – 'the german Emperor' (*U* 18.95), 'the prince of Wales' (*U* 18.482), 'paris' (*U* 18.613) – and sometimes an unexpected one does – 'like a Stallion driving it up into you' (*U* 18.152), 'all for his Kidney' (*U* 18.568), 'I tried with the Banana' (*U* 18.803).[15]

What these visual effects suggest is a style not of thought but of *writing*: an unconventional orthographic practice which ignores the rules of punctuation, prefers the directness of figures to verbally presented numerals, and suffers from errors characteristic of the transcription of speech.[16] It is not, that is to say, the writing of someone who wields the pen with ease and confidence, but rather of someone without the training and practice necessary for perfect clarity and correctness on paper. If for Joyce writing of this kind was associated with women, as it clearly was,[17] we need not ascribe the association to a deeply rooted

---

[14] The substitution of figures for words is not absolutely consistent; we find, for instance, 'she kissed me six or seven times' (*U* 18.672–3), 'a villa and eight rooms' (*U* 18.721), and 'all upside down the two ways' (*U* 18.1475). No principle for these exceptions is discernible, however, and it seems likely that they were oversights on Joyce's part, though editors have, somewhat inconsistently with their practice elsewhere in the chapter, left them as they are. Kenner comments interestingly on the shock of seeing even the words of a song presented in accordance with this convention (*The Mechanic Muse*, 80–1).

[15] Perhaps the most important example of unorthodox capitalization is Molly's final 'Yes'; its significance is summed up (and related to another purely visual effect) by Derrida: 'The final "Yes", the last word, the eschatology of the book, yields itself only to *reading*, since it distinguishes itself from the others by an inaudible capital letter; what also remains inaudible, although visible, is the literal incorporation of . . . *yes* in *eyes*' ('Ulysses Gramophone', in *Acts of Literature*, 274).

[16] Rabaté, in 'Le nœud gordien', notes that Joyce's abbreviation for the chapter in the workshop material is 'Pen', and relates this both to the opposition between pen and sword and to Molly's writing (126). (He might well have cited a sentence from an Aeolian headline that foreshadows these interconnections: ɪᴛʜᴀᴄᴀɴꜱ ᴠᴏᴡ ᴘᴇɴ ɪꜱ ᴄʜᴀᴍᴘ' (*U* 7.1034).)

[17] 'Do you notice how women when they write disregard stops and capital letters?' Joyce asked Stanislaus after a brief unpunctuated interpolation by Nora in one of his letters (*Letters* ɪɪ, 173). Scott, in *Joyce and Feminism* (70–1), discusses the absence of punctuation in letters by Nora, by Joyce's aunt Josephine Murray, and by Joyce's mother, and several examples of such letters are given in Maddox's *Nora* (though Maddox also cites examples of a more careful, punctuated style from Nora's pen – see 203, 344, 465). These letters certainly resemble Molly's monologue in their tendency to omit punctuation and sentence initial capitals, and in their use of fairly short sentences whose boundaries are signalled not by graphic marks but by syntax. (It is incorrect, strictly speaking, to call the graphically indicated units 'run-on sentences' as Scott, following

sexism, as it was an accurate reflection of a social and economic inequality which still exists in other, related, forms today. The reader can choose whether to take from this an acceptance of the exclusion of women from the advantages of education or an impetus towards political action to change this situation; neither is obviously implied by Joyce's text.

Molly's main use for writing is doubtless correspondence, and letters are a significant feature of her monologue. Joyce takes advantage of his printed text to give us a more direct representation of them than a transcription of someone's thoughts could do. Near the start of the fourth section, a postcard from Hester Stanhope is recalled, complete with abbreviations – 'wogger wd give anything to be back in Gib' (*U* 18.616–17), 'yrs affly Hester x x x x x' (*U* 18.623) – and errors – 'still there [for theyre] lovely' (*U* 18.619). (We have no way of knowing whether the omission of punctuation is Mrs Stanhope's or the chapter's, of course.) Soon, Molly is remembering the letters she posted to herself to alleviate the boredom of life in Gibraltar after Hester's departure; significantly, the envelopes appear to have contained not writing but merely 'bits of paper' (*U* 18.699). And the recollection of the recent death of an acquaintance has her thinking of the letters she cannot escape writing:

its a bother having to answer he always tells me the wrong things and no stops to say like making a speech your sad bereavement symphathy I always make that mistake and newphew with 2 double yous in I hope hell write me a longer letter the next time . . . I could write the answer in bed to let him imagine me short just a few words not those long crossed letters Atty Dillon used to write to the fellow that was something in the four courts that jilted her after out of the ladies letterwriter when I told her to say a few simple words he could twist how he liked not acting with precipat precip itancy with equal candour . . . (*U* 18.728–44)

Molly's difficulties with letter-writing are clear enough: she finds composing notes of sympathy irksome, and relies on her husband to dictate

---

Richard Ellmann (*James Joyce*, 376), does – though we have already noted that Joyce referred to the sections of 'Penelope' as 'sentences'.) However, they do not display the habit of putting figures for numerals – Nora writes 'I was called five times but did not pretend to hear it is now half past eleven' – and there is evidence of an excess as well as a lack of punctuation in Nora's 'I ran off to one of the bedroom's to read' in the same letter (*Letters* II, 54). A female source is deducible for the occasional emphatic capital letter in 'Penelope' – Nora's mother wrote in a heavily capitalized style (see Maddox, *Nora*, 188, 197) – but if the use of figures where we might expect words comes from Joyce's family correspondence, the source is more likely to be a male one, as the following phrases from his father's letters suggest: 'the 3 little ones', 'the 3 young children', (*Letters* II, 222); '4 weeks in March', '2 months rent', 'your *3 youngest* sisters' (*Letters* II, 229).

them to her – a procedure she would find easier if he didn't forget to tell her when to punctuate ('and no stops'). She admits to making recurrent spelling mistakes (and once again Joyce employs a purely visual device, the cancelled letters in 'symphathy' and 'newphew' – which, in spite of his insistence in the margin, his printers failed to reproduce); and she decides to write 'just a few words' to Boylan.[18] The alternative would be a long letter written with the help of the 'Ladies' Letter-Writer', a useful aid to those whose education was limited – though one which required care in the transcription of unfamiliar words, as Molly's mimicry of a botched attempt to write 'precipitancy' suggests.[19] The strongly visual aspect of the chapter is once again brought out when Molly thinks about her misspelling of 'nephew', though in a manner that is the reverse of the figured numerals, since the letter *w* is transcribed in words: 'double yous'.

This is not to suggest, however, that the chapter can be understood straightforwardly as a representation of Molly's writing. For one thing, the orthographic errors are minimal; even Spanish, French, and Italian phrases (like the quotations from *Don Giovanni* in the passage quoted above) are, accents apart, correctly given. Numerous proper names are impeccably spelled. Moreover, there are some typical Joycean evocations of sound which do not belong to a written text (other than a modernist novel), such as 'I loved rousing that dog in the hotel rrrsssstt awokwokawok' (*U* 18.812–13) or the multilettered evocations of train whistle and fart (*U* 18.596, 874, 908). And the effect upon the reader of seeing epistolary errors and omissions in carefully set type is quite different from seeing them in handwriting.[20] 'Penelope' is a text which exploits readerly habits to fuse speech and writing, or more accurately to demonstrate the inseparability and interdependence of speech and writing in a literate culture. Through its visual techniques it is able to

---

[18] Milly's letter (*U* 4.397–414) shows that she is more assured on paper than her mother; although she asks to be excused for bad writing on account of her haste, there is only one example of the running together of two sentences (perhaps an indication of the fact that she is not telling all she might at this point): 'There is a young student comes here some evenings named Bannon his cousins or something are big swells'. Molly compares herself unfavourably with her daughter in educational terms when regretting that Leopold has sent the latter to work in Mullingar 'instead of sending her to Skerrys academy where shed have to learn not like me getting all 1s at school' (*U* 18.1006–7).

[19] Richard Ellmann reproduces a stilted and unconvincing (and uncharacteristic) letter of Nora Barnacle's dating from 1904 that is perhaps derived from such a manual (*James Joyce*, plates xiv–xv). One can see why Molly would prefer her own 'simple' (and deliberately ambiguous) words when writing to a lover.

[20] The critic who has been most alert to Joyce's awareness of the effects and possibilities of print is Kenner; for one such discussion, see *The Mechanic Muse*, 67–82.

suggest the unceasing passage of thoughts, impelled by strong opinions, desires, and memories, while at the same time revealing that thought, far from being a pure realm of subjectivity, is traversed by the material, differential, and cultural properties of language. The graphic marks that exist only in the written mode do not simply transcribe aural (or mental) features, but play a part in constituting it – which means that thought is subject to the accidents, deferrals, and absences that we prefer to pin on language. (This is an issue which the fifth chapter of *Finnegans Wake*, ALP's 'mamafesta', explores at length.) That most criticism of the chapter has ignored the significance of its status as writing bears witness to the power of the assumptions Joyce is both exploiting and testing: even more than speech, thought is the bedrock of our experience of identity and self-presence, and, in defiance of the text, Molly is quickly identified with nature, instinct, unselfconsciousness, and an idea of 'materiality' that has none of the resistant otherness of matter.

In showing how the chapter's graphic techniques give rise to the idea of undifferentiated continuity which is then transferred to Molly's mind, we haven't fully accounted for the privileging of the metaphor of 'flow' above all others, however. There are several contributory reasons for this marked preference. The phrase 'stream of consciousness' will already have implanted a watery metaphor in many readers' brains (though it is a term often applied to the equally associative thought processes of Bloom and Stephen), while the lack of evident structure or direction in the chapter encourages metaphors of indeterminacy. Critics are responding, too, to the sheer length of this continuous representation of thought (long by the standards of fiction, and even of *Ulysses* itself, though not those of psychological reality: an actual transcription of the thoughts of any of us during a sleepless hour would no doubt fill as many pages). Another reason is the prominence that has always been given to the closing passage of the episode, which is unusual in being an abnormally long paratactic sentence that could be described as syntactically 'flowing', from 'I was thinking of so many things he didnt know' to the final 'Yes' ('and' occurs 46 times in 27 lines).[21] The structure and rhetoric of this sentence is determined more by the demands of the entire book than by the conventions Joyce has set up for the representation of Molly's mind, which would lead one to expect not a climactic diapason but an endless proliferation. For those who are acquainted with *Finne-*

---

[21] This unbalanced view of the chapter is perhaps most vividly demonstrated by S. L. Goldberg, who, in discussing 'Penelope', complains about 'the pervasive factitiousness of the writing, apart from the last thirty or so lines on which so much of the chapter's effect relies' (*Joyce*, 100).

gans Wake, the riverine associations of ALP may well exert an additional influence: the emphasis on Penelope's 'fluidity' is much more noticeable in post-*Wake* criticism of *Ulysses* than in earlier comments. And one simple fact we should not overlook is that Molly is a woman, and a menstruating woman at that: would the word 'flow' crop up quite so often if the book had ended with a lengthy unpunctuated uncapitalized monologue from Blazes Boylan?

A FEMALE LANGUAGE?

Flow as against fixity, overflow as against observance of limits: this is one of the commonest figurations of gender opposition in our culture. Whatever its biological sources, which are evident enough, it plays a role in gender ideology which has left those sources far behind. It is one link in a chain of metaphors that associates the idea of 'woman' with such ideas as 'nature', 'physicality', 'irrationality', 'unreliability', and 'impulsiveness' – one of the many chains which bind women to specific, and subordinate, social and economic roles. Among the places where this stereotype has been most strongly reproduced is, of course, literature; and it is undeniable that some of its most notable appearances in modern literature are in the writings of James Joyce. (The question of the extent to which Joyce's texts *reinforce* the stereotype is, however, not one that can be answered without considering the various ways in which they are, and might be, read.)

One feminist response to this stereotype has been to embrace it, as offering a kind of language strategically appropriate at this stage of the struggle against the patriarchal order. Hélène Cixous, for instance, both employs and advocates for women a language of flow, relating it back to its distant origins in the female body. She imagines a woman exclaiming: 'I, too, overflow; my desires have invented new desires, my body knows unheard-of songs. Time and again I, too, have felt so full of luminous torrents that I could burst – burst with forms much more beautiful than those which are put up in frames and sold for a stinking fortune' ('The Laugh of the Medusa', 246). (Notice the carefully contrived oppositional imagery: overflowing torrents against the framed – and economically determined – artworks of the patriarchy.) From a perspective like Cixous's, the 'Penelope' episode of *Ulysses* is anything but reactionary in its gender politics: 'The feminine (as the poets suspected) affirms: ". . . And yes", says Molly, carrying *Ulysses* off beyond any book and toward the new writing; "I said yes, I will Yes"' (255).

But feminists have also frequently berated Joyce for his perpetuation of a male-created stereotype that demeans and disempowers women. We may take a well-known example from the first volume of Sandra Gilbert and Susan Gubar's *No Man's Land, The War of the Words*.[22] In documenting what they regard as male defences against the entry of middle-class women into the domain of literary writing, Gilbert and Gubar – who have elsewhere referred to the work of Kristeva, Cixous, and Irigaray as 'feminologist re-Joycings' ('Sexual Linguistics', 519) – offer this comment: 'Whether like Joyce's fluidly fluent Anna Livia Plurabelle, woman ceaselessly burbles and babbles on her way to her "cold mad feary father", or whether like his fluently fluid Molly Bloom, she dribbles and drivels as she dreams of male jinglings, her artless jingles are secondary and asyntactic' (232). The inaccuracy of this description of ALP's language (insofar as there *is* a characteristic style associated with ALP) will be evident to anyone who has read *Finnegans Wake*, as will the dubiousness of the implicit claim that Joyce's book upholds a stereotype of patriarchal dominance.[23] And we have already seen that Molly's monologue, far from being 'asyntactic', is more syntactically orthodox than those of the major male characters; while the implicit metaphor in 'fluently fluid' and 'dribbles and drivels' is a critical commonplace that reflects as much the critics' gender ideology as it does the language of the chapter. Linguistically speaking, there is no recipe in 'Penelope' for an *écriture féminine* that will undermine patriarchal structures; if we want to consider the possible implications of Joyce's experiments with language for feminism, we should not focus on his women characters alone.[24]

What Cixous is celebrating and Gilbert and Gubar are deprecating is a familiar stereotype of women's language, though there appears to be little evidence for it in attested speech characteristics. Studies of 'gender-

[22] Since this has been an influential work in feminist and modernist studies, and since it devotes a chapter to the question of gender and language in modernism, I am singling it out for comment; I should make it clear, however, that I am not treating it as 'representative' of any 'school' of feminist thought. The chapter I refer to, 'Sexual Linguistics: Women's Sentence, Men's Sentencing', is in part a revised version of the same authors' essay 'Sexual Linguistics'. It will be evident that my own discussion, including my reservations about Gilbert and Gubar's work, is heavily indebted to feminist criticism and theory; and my own participation in feminist debates is subject to all the hesitations and contradictions articulated by Stephen Heath in 'Male Feminism'.

[23] One way of interpreting 'cold mad feary father' might be as an anticipation of the Gilbert and Gubar argument that male modernism was driven by a terror of writing women: Lawrence, in 'Joyce and Feminism', has argued that Joyce's work is increasingly concerned to unmask the male anxieties about women's power that permeate his culture.

[24] As I noted in note 13 of the introduction above, the 1990s saw the publication of a number of feminist studies of Joyce that offered subtler accounts of the importance of gender in his work than these earlier celebrations and dismissals.

lect' are fraught with theoretical and methodological problems, but if there is any validity in the list of gender differences that has emerged from a range of empirical studies, they hardly support the notion of female speech as an untrammelled outpouring.[25] The features that tend to be identified in such studies include the use of more questions, especially 'tag-questions' (like 'isn't it?'), the use of more 'hedges' (like 'I mean' or 'sort of'), and the use of a more standard form of the language. (The last of these suggests that in making Molly's mental language less syntactically deviant than Stephen's or Bloom's Joyce might have been closer to social fact than many of his critics.) Females also characteristically talk less than males in mixed-gender groups (though are often *perceived* – for example, by class teachers – as having talked more than they in fact did). But the stereotype of the garrulous, effusive, and often ungrammatical female speaker lives on oblivious to this empirical reality, receiving plenty of reinforcement from literature across the centuries. It is the influence of this literary tradition, as well as its more widespread counterpart in the popular imagination,[26] that has made it easy for readers – whether they are decrying or extolling what they find – to categorize Molly's language as a 'female flow'. But if Molly's monologue simply reproduced these stereotypical characteristics, we probably could not endure – let alone enjoy – thirty-five pages of her ruminations.

In the chapter of *The War of the Words* that I have already mentioned, Gilbert and Gubar reinterpret Virginia Woolf's call for a 'woman's sentence' as the expression of a 'desire to revise not woman's language but woman's relation to language' (230). This is a promising shift of emphasis (though 'women's relations to language' or even 'languages' would be a preferable formulation), and it forms part of their admirably intentioned strategy of empowering women by countering the myth of their necessary exclusion from language. It might seem to open the way to a study both of the way gender as a culturally produced distinction operates in different kinds of language, including literary language, and of the way social and economic structures determine women's access to and use of language, including literary language. But they choose instead to trace the dual history of what they call male and female

---

[25] See, for example, Lakoff, *Language and Woman's Place*; several essays in McConnell-Ginet, *et al.*, eds., *Women and Language in Literature and Society*; Cameron, *Feminism and Linguistic Theory*; and Coates, *Women, Men, and Language*.

[26] Coates quotes some typical proverbs which enshrine this stereotype, like 'Foxes are all tail and women are all tongue' (Cheshire, England) and 'The North Sea will sooner be found wanting in water than a woman at a loss for a word' (Jutland) (*Women, Men, and Language*, 15).

'fantasies' about language, which, in their role as military historians, they see as weapons in the war of the sexes, ceaselessly wielded in two areas: in the language chosen for literary writing and in the comments made about language.

The distinctive female fantasy is about 'the possession of a mother tongue' (236) which will make its way against the dominant male language; instances include Gertrude Stein's 'fantastic experiments' which attempt to 'excrete a "nonsense" language' (246), Dorothy Richardson's project of creating a 'feminine prose' which would be (in Richardson's words) 'unpunctuated, moving from point to point without formal obstructions' (248), and Woolf's presentation of 'female figures whose ancient voices seem to endure from a time before the neat categories of culture restrained female energy' (250). These are all versions of the familiar stereotype of a 'woman's language': aligned with nature instead of culture, transgressive of the laws of linguistic form and rational sense, possessing an unrestrained energy. It sounds very like the conventional view of Molly Bloom's language. What is surprising is that it receives the strong approval of Gilbert and Gubar, who thereby align themselves with the French perpetrators of 'feminologist re-Joycings' and, it would appear, with their master, James Joyce.

Appearances are deceiving, however. The Gilbert and Gubar history of *male* fantasies about language reveals that though his female followers may be saved, Joyce himself is trapped on the other side of No Man's Land. His linguistic experimentation is not to be confused with that of Stein, Richardson, and Woolf (nor, presumably, with the games that Gilbert and Gubar themselves like to play with the signifier); it is described not as a flow of natural energy but by means of a phrase quoted – several times – from a speech by Merlin in Tennyson's *Idylls of the King*: 'densest condensation, hard' (257, 258, 259, 261). We are told, for instance, that Joyce's

'densest condensation, hard', with its proliferation of puns, parodies, paradoxes, and parables transforms what Hélène Cixous calls 'the old single-grooved mother tongue' into what we are calling a *patrius sermo* that can only be comprehended by those who, like Merlin and like Joyce himself, can translate what has been 'scribbled, crost, and cramm'd' on the margins of literature into a spell of power. (259)[27]

---

[27] The term *patrius sermo* is taken from Ong's *Fighting for Life*, a book which attempts to derive human adversativeness from a biological base, and which Gilbert and Gubar admire sufficiently to name one of their chapters after it. Ong has a footnote on contrasting terms for language in classical Latin (36–7), *patrius sermo* and *materna lingua*, in which he observes that the former 'does not mean "father tongue"' but 'the national speech bequeathed by ancestors who held it as a

And Joyce's puns 'suggest not a linguistic *jouissance* rebelliously disrupting the decorum of the text, but a linguistic *puissance* fortifying the writer's sentences with "densest condensation, hard"' (261).

Here, then, we have the opposite of the feminine language of flow: the masculine phallic language, condensed into a hard rod of power. One stereotype (which Gilbert and Gubar endorse) is opposed to another (which they attack). And what is it that determines whether a text that transgresses linguistic rules, exploits the materiality of language, and goes beyond rationality and sense, will be regarded as admirably fluid and overflowing or regrettably condensed and hard? The only consistent criterion which emerges from this chapter is the biological gender of the author.[28] The basis for this essentialism is a theory of the 'linguistic (as well as biological) primacy of the mother' (264), which explains how Gilbert and Gubar can claim that men 'usurp and transform the daily speech of women and children so as to make it into a suitable instrument for (cultivated) male art' (252).[29] Men, it seems, have no option but to acquire language by force, since it belongs naturally to women and children. We are left with a view of gender which, far from flowing over the rigid boundaries that have always facilitated women's oppression, reiterates and reinforces the oppositional stereotypes themselves.

I noted earlier that an appreciation of the written dimension of 'Penelope' can lead to a reading that – whatever Joyce's views on the matter – makes, in comic vein, a practical and historical point about women's education. It seems to me that a similar point could have emerged from the discussion of gender differences in language by

kind of property', while the latter signifies 'the tongue you interiorized as it came to you from your mother'. (The distinction between language as legal entity and physical activity is, of course, an early version of the gender stereotype that is the subject of this essay.) Gilbert and Gubar (ignoring Ong's careful distinction between *patrius* and *paternus*) adroitly redefine *patrius sermo* as a 'father speech', and apply it to the classical languages themselves as they function in modern Europe, drawing on Ong's work elsewhere on the teaching of classical languages as an initiation ritual (*The War of the Words*, 243–4, 252–3). This enables them to align the *materna lingua* with the vernacular (252). Gilbert and Gubar's skill in co-opting Cixous in their campaign against Joyce is also remarkable; the passage in 'The Laugh of the Medusa' from which they are quoting is actually a call to women to 'make the old single-grooved mother tongue reverberate with more than one language' (256), to do, that is, what Cixous believes Joyce has done.

[28] Male authors giving voice to female characters pose a problem for Gilbert and Gubar: thus Molly's monologue is at one moment an exemplification of a male stereotype of woman's language (232) and at another a parody of it (260); it also bears a strong resemblance, as we have seen, to a female fantasy of woman's language which meets with their approval. For an alternative view of Joyce's representation of women's language, see Lawrence, 'Joyce and Feminism'.

[29] This biological theory itself has all the trappings of the 'female fantasies' about language that have just been discussed, but it is not clear whether Gilbert and Gubar would be prepared to accept it as no more than a fantasy.

Gilbert and Gubar if it had not been occluded by their own unexamined gender stereotypes. A glimpse of how this happens can be gained from their use of the lines from Tennyson's *Idylls*. Tennyson describes a book

Writ in a language that has long gone by
. . .
And every margin scribbled, crost, and crammed
With comment, densest condensation, hard
To mind and eye; but the long sleepless nights
Of my long life have made it easy to me.
And none can read the text, not even I;
And none can read the comment but myself;
And in the comment did I find the charm.[30]

This is not exactly how Gilbert and Gubar quote the passage: I have included two lines – the fourth and fifth – which they omit. Although their repeated use of the truncated phrase 'densest condensation, hard' to attack male writing would not lead the reader to suppose it, the primary meaning of the word 'hard' in Tennyson's poem is 'difficult', as the full phrase 'hard to mind and eye' indicates. The issue that is really at stake here is not some phallic language which all men, and only men, speak, but the long history of exclusion from education that women have suffered; the accusation against Joyce and the other male modernists which ought to follow is that their work assumes a level of education which their potential women readers would have been less likely to possess than their male counterparts. To develop this charge – which clearly has some force – in an interesting and valuable way would require an analysis of the kinds of 'difficulty' that different texts, by male and female writers, pose, and the ways in which these would have had different consequences for male and female readers (which itself might form part of a study of other distinctions, such as class, race, and region). But to assume the alignment of difficulty with masculinity as an unquestioned given is not to undermine but to collaborate with the patriarchal domination of educational and intellectual institutions.

OVERFLOW

Critics may associate the word 'flow' with femininity, but *Ulysses* makes no such association. 'Penelope' is one of only five chapters in which the word makes no appearance in any of its forms (nor, for that matter, does it occur in Gerty MacDowell's section of 'Nausicaa'). However, Leopold

---

[30] *Idylls of the King*, Book VI, 'Merlin and Vivien', 672–80.

Bloom is, as we have seen, registered in 'Ithaca' as an admirer of the fluency of water; and it is in a chapter in which his mental world figures extensively – 'Sirens' – that the word achieves its greatest salience in the book, especially in Bloom's orgasmic involvement with Simon Dedalus's song (*U* 11.705–9). It also figures prominently in connection with Stephen's urination towards the end of 'Proteus' (*U* 3.453–69). This is not to say that we should identify Leopold or Stephen with the stereotype that more commonly gets attached to Molly, but that Joyce's treatment of the notion of the flow that transcends differences is not gendered in any simple way. It is possible, that is, to read *Ulysses* as a text in which, on the one hand, the cultural stereotype of the female flow is foregrounded, literalized, demystified, and parodied; while on the other a more potent ungendered flow – or set of flows – operates throughout the text to erode the cultural and ideological barriers between the sexes. In two suggestive essays, Maud Ellmann has discussed what she calls 'the economy of flows' as it operates, in relation to other economies, in *A Portrait*. She describes it in the following terms:

Semen, blood, urine, breath, money, saliva, speech and excrement provide the currencies for this economy. Menstruation also figures among these flows, for the text at this level (though not at others) is as indifferent to gender as to the formal separation of excrement and sexuality. ('Disremembering Dedalus', 193)

[T]he economy of flows lays siege to all distinctions which anatomy or prudery uphold. No function can maintain its semiotic chastity. The boundaries between the genders, or sex and excrement, or word and flesh, succumb to impudent and restless violations. ('Polytropic Man', 88)

In *Ulysses* the seepage across boundaries – especially the gender boundary – is even more marked.

Language is both a flow and an articulation: a material substance – neural discharges, muscular pulses, vibrating cords and membranes, sound and light waves, ink, paint, stone, liquid crystal – which threatens always to eliminate difference and identity, and a system of differences and identities that in order to function has to mark a resistant substance. (This is a materiality quite other than the idea of materiality that underwrites logocentric notions of 'nature', 'flow', 'presence', etc., though there is no way of representing it without contamination by that idea. I have already discussed its importance as one aspect of the linguistic remainder in chapter 5 above.) Some kinds of writing give the materiality of language a stronger role than others – verse, for instance, as Leopold Bloom dimly perceives:

But then Shakespeare has no rhymes: blank verse. The flow of the language it is. The thoughts. Solemn.

> *Hamlet, I am thy father's spirit*
> *Doomed for a certain time to walk the earth.* (*U* 8.64–6)

Although he ascribes the power of Shakespeare's lines to their 'thoughts', he has misremembered the actual words while retaining their metrical form.[31] Joyce's writing is another example: the sounds, the rhythms, the arrangement of the words on the page, play an important role in the reader's experience. Yet these features are fully engaged with the abstract system of meaningful articulations (as is not the case in nonsense verse or 'transrational' language); with the result that 'meaning' ceases to be a prelinguistic category given embodiment in a material envelope, and is dispersed across different aspects of the text (across both speech and writing, as 'Penelope', for instance, demonstrates), inexhaustible, unfixable. It is this materiality of language that produces slippages between words (in puns and portmanteaux), or between proper and common nouns, or between pronouns with different referents. To take pleasure in this aspect of Joyce's writing is not to espouse or promote feminism, but it is to identify and celebrate a property of language denied by the hegemonic linguistic ideologies of our time – ideologies which are fully complicit with sexism. One has only to look at the educational philosophy promoted by Republican and Conservative (and more recently, many Labour) politicians in the USA and Britain to see the interlocking web of assumptions about the primacy of the individual human subject, the transparency and instrumentality of language, the supremacy of the market economy, and the biological determination of gender roles.

Leopold Bloom's phrase 'language of flow' (*U* 11.298) is one example among hundreds in the 'Sirens' episode of the apparently contingent properties of English being harnessed to render diffuse the centred meaning of 'purely instrumental' language. (*Finnegans Wake*, of course, has tens of thousands of such examples.) Here the second syllable of 'flowers' has been cut off – by whom we cannot say, since the material of language does not tell the story of its own marking – so that the word flows into the word 'flow', to recall Bloom's earlier comment on the flow of the language. This in turn alerts us to the fact – otherwise obscured by

---

[31] Similarly, in 'Sirens' Bloom is unsuccessful in his attempt to reduce the materiality of music to the abstraction of mathematics; his thoughts proceed from 'Numbers it is. All music when you come to think' to the conclusion 'But suppose you said it like: Martha, seven times nine minus x is thirtyfive thousand. Fall quite flat. It's on account of the sounds it is' (*U* 11.830–7).

our rush from signifier to signified – that the word spelled 'flower' can
mean 'one who flows'. As we have seen, Henry Flower is also a flow-er;
and Molly Bloom in 'Penelope', though she is usually discussed by critics
as a flow-er, is also a flower, a 'flower of the mountain'.[32] The words
'flower' and 'flowers' occur more often in the 'Penelope' episode than in
any other, and if we were seeking a metaphor to guide us to an
understanding of the female in _Ulysses_, this one might take us further
than 'flow'. Flowers traverse the division between nature and culture,
not by flowing across it but by demonstrating that permeability is a
constitutive feature of it. Most of the flowers that Molly thinks about are
cultural artefacts: they are sold out of baskets, worn on the bosom,
depicted on wallpaper, or put around the house. They also feature in
songs and compliments, and at one point they figure in a paean to
nature that moves between clichés of wilderness worship to an admiration for efficient agriculture (it is another of those bursts of parataxis
that seem to parody the stereotype of 'natural' 'feminine' utterance):

I love flowers Id love to have the whole place swimming in roses God of heaven
theres nothing like nature the wild mountains then the sea and the waves
rushing then the beautiful country with the fields of oats and wheat and all kinds
of things and all the fine cattle going about that would do your heart good to see
rivers and lakes and flowers and all sorts of shapes and smells and colours
springing up even out of the ditches primroses and violets nature it is (_U_
18.1557–63)

Like gender, like language, the 'natural' origin of flowers is already
culturally inscribed; the nature they belong to is an idea we inherit from
a long cultural history. Molly Bloom is not one to strive after a nature
from which culture has been evacuated, as some Romantic poets tried
to do (with consequences that we still feel today). Her attitude to her own
'female flow', for instance, is scarcely Romantic; although for some
readers it seems to reinforce the mythic quality of the chapter, and
doubtless has something to do with critics' predilections for the metaphor we have been discussing, Joyce allows us to read the event of
menstruation as a literalizing and demystifying of the myth:

have we too much blood up in us or what O patience above its pouring out of

[32] She is well aware of the flow between proper and common nouns, and therefore of the potential
of her own married name: 'what did I tell him I was engaged for for fun to the son of a Spanish
nobleman named Don Miguel de la Flora . . . theres many a true word spoken in jest there is a
flower that bloometh' (_U_ 18.772–5); 'bloomers . . . I suppose theyre called after him I never
thought that would be my name Bloom when I used to write it in print to see how it looked on a
visiting card or practising for the butcher and oblige M Bloom youre looking blooming Josie
used to say after I married him' (_U_ 18.839–43). (See also Rabaté's discussion of the way the name
'Bloom' is disseminated through the chapter (_James Joyce, Authorized Reader_, 108–9), and my
consideration of proper names in chapter 4, above, pp. 56–7.)

me like the sea anyhow he didnt make me pregnant as big as he is I dont want to
ruin the clean sheets I just put on I suppose the clean linen I wore brought it on
too damn it damn it . . . O Jamesy let me up out of this pooh sweets of sin . . . (*U*
18.1122–9)

O but I was forgetting this bloody pest of a thing pfooh you wouldnt know
which to laugh or cry were such a mixture of plum and apple . . . (*U* 18.1533–5)

Through Molly's thoughts Joyce both alerts us to the myth ('like the sea')
and reduces it to a messy and inconvenient reality, for the introduction
of which the author himself seems to accept some blame ('O Jamesy let
me up out of this'). Molly's only consolation is that her flow demonstrates that she's not pregnant: not what any self-respecting fertility
symbol would be expected to feel.[33]

Flow and fixity, nature and culture, female and male, speech and
writing, material and system: *Ulysses* asserts neither an absolute difference between these opposed terms nor a transcendence of all difference.
Rather it shows – or can do if we are able to read it this way – that each
pair is linked and separated by a hymen that both unites and divides
(rather as the Masque of Hymen in *The Tempest* celebrates the union of
the lovers while prolonging their chaste separation).[34] The marriage of
Molly and Leopold is also cemented by that which divides them: most
readers feel that Boylan's punctual phallic insemination of Molly's body
is less valorized by the novel than Leopold's disseminative play on its
surfaces.[35] Although the narrative is located firmly within the context of

---

[33] Richard Ellmann, in a section of *Ulysses on the Liffey* entitled 'Why Molly Bloom Menstruates',
proposes an alternative interpretation of the relationship between the mythic and the literal: 'In
allowing Molly to menstruate at the end Joyce consecrates the blood in the chamberpot rather
than the blood in the chalice' (171). But it is difficult to read Molly's comments as any kind of
celebration of human substance. Neither the early response to *Ulysses* as a degrading portrayal of
men and women at their most bestial nor the corrective movement of emphasis upon the
celebratory aspects of the book represented by Ellmann do justice to Joyce's interest in the way
human character is culturally produced, and the consequent possibilities for comic deflation and
juxtaposition. Boheemen's discussion of Molly's linguistic and menstrual flow and of the
punning relation to 'flower' (*The Novel as Family Romance*, 183–4) also misses this dimension (see
my consideration of Boheemen's argument in 'Joyce's Other'); and even Rabaté's rich account
of the book – which stresses the problematized relation of eye and ear – takes 'Penelope' to be an
'affirmation of the fluxes and of the "oceanic"', providing the book with a maternal supplement
in which speech displaces writing (*James Joyce, Authorized Reader*, 109). Rabaté's later discussion of
the chapter ('Le nœud gordien') gives more weight to writing.

[34] Jacques Derrida has followed through some of the endless unfoldings of the hymen with the aid
of Mallarmé in 'The Double Session' (*Dissemination*, 209–85).

[35] See MacCabe's comments on 'Bloom's desire to write on the membrane rather than burst
through it' (*James Joyce and the Revolution of the Word*, 123), and Maud Ellmann's account of the way
he 'supplants the phallus with the omphalos' ('To Sing or to Sign', 67). The latter's observation
that Bloom's 'Greek ees' cross the opposition of speech and writing may be related to the
printing conventions of 'Penelope' examined earlier.

early twentieth-century linguistic and mental habits, and is largely a parodic recycling of contemporary clichés, it manages to point beyond the strongly patriarchal structures of that world – which is to say beyond the patriarchal structures of our world – to the possibility that gender might be less rigid, less oppositional, less determined by a political and economic system.[36] Paradoxically perhaps, this might mean giving biology more of a say rather than less, since it is the crude abstractions of a dual and oppositional gender system (linked to the economies of fashion, glamour, pornography, and so on) that prevent the multiplicity of human physical traits from providing a basis – one of many possible bases – for an equivalent multiplicity of interpersonal relations. Derrida has sketched the thought of a revaluation of gender which would 'neutralize the sexual opposition, and not sexual difference, liberating the field of sexuality for a very *different* sexuality, a more multiple one. At that point there would be no more sexes . . . there would be one sex for each time' ('Women in the Beehive', 199).[37] To read Joyce's works as a questioning of the boundaries which structure the dominant Western conception of language, including the boundary between speech and writing, is to glimpse that other possibility: not because grammar is patriarchal, and must be overflowed by female torrents, but because the linguistic ideology which those rigid boundaries serve is continuous with the gender ideology that gives us, over and over again, two sexes in fixed and unproductive opposition.

[36] In *James Joyce and Sexuality*, Richard Brown gives evidence of Joyce's conscious criticism of simplistic notions of a separate female identity, and discusses his attempts at a redefinition of gender opposition (98–102). Of course, Joyce's writing may achieve more (or less) than he would have wished.

[37] Derrida also refers to this 'dream' in an interview with Christie V. McDonald: 'The relationship would not be a-sexual, far from it, but would be sexual otherwise: beyond the binary difference that governs the decorum of all codes, beyond the opposition feminine/masculine, beyond bisexuality as well, beyond homosexuality and heterosexuality which come to the same thing' ('Choreographies', 76).

CHAPTER 9

The postmodernity of Joyce: chance, coincidence, and the reader

In the 'Ithaca' episode of *Ulysses*, Stephen Dedalus narrates two short fictions to Leopold Bloom (*U* 17.611–41), one a scene in a solitary hotel, the other his *Parable of the Plums* (with which the reader is already familiar from Stephen's telling of it in 'Aeolus' (*U* 7.923–1058)). Bloom, occupying for a moment the place of the reader of *Ulysses*, has two responses to these stories. The second, an entirely typical one for Bloom, is to speculate on the commercial possibilities of a collection of Stephen's works; it is the first, however, that interests me here. What strikes Bloom most forcibly about the initial story is Stephen's choice (as far as we know, quite unmotivated) of the name 'Queen's Hotel' for his fictional setting, a name which evokes in the older man a detailed memory of his father's suicide – recounted in the clinical detail typical of the chapter – in the Queen's Hotel, Ennis. This recollection is followed by an enquiry from the catechistic voice: 'Did he attribute this homonymity to information or coincidence or intuition?' The answer is concise and unambiguous: 'Coincidence'.

To the two distinct modes of knowledge that might explain the unexpected chiming between the worlds of narrator and audience, 'information' and 'intuition', Bloom prefers that unaccountable falling together of events that we call coincidence. This notion is evoked not only by the chance matching of the hotel scene with the circumstances of his father's death but by some aspect of *The Parable of the Plums*, though we learn about it only indirectly from the question, 'Did he see only a second coincidence in the second scene narrated to him . . . ?', and thus do not learn what it is. (One possibility is that it is the similarity between the interest shown by the Dublin dames in the statue of the 'onehandled adulterer' Horatio Nelson and his own earlier investigation of the mesial

grooves of classical sculpture.[1]) Without wishing to claim that the passage offers us anything as precise as an allegory of the reading of *Ulysses*,
I would suggest that it draws attention to an aspect of Joyce's art that is
becoming more evident as we look at it in retrospect, from a cultural
viewing platform for which 'postmodernism' seems the best name,
however contentious and ill-defined the term remains. I wish to argue
also that, although no works of modernism remain unchanged in this
perspective, *Ulysses* and *Finnegans Wake* come out looking more different
than do their illustrious companions of that period, and hence more
different *from* them as well.

I do not intend to offer any totalizing description of postmodernism;
all I wish to observe is that one feature of some of the most interesting
and pleasurable art of recent times has been an openness to the operations of chance, including an openness to the contingencies of the
particular context in which the work is enjoyed by a particular reader.
That is to say, the fact that the work of art is experienced every time as a
singular *event*, by an individual with specific (and changing) needs,
expectations, memories, and associations, at a particular time and place,
is not factored out as far as it is possible to do so – which I see as the goal
of most modernist and pre-modernist art – but is factored *in* as an
essential part of the work's mode of operation. I am not thinking of the
kind of neo-Dadaist aleatory art that flourished briefly in the sixties (play
your own notes or assemble your own book), but on the contrary of an
art in which it is the very complexity and heterogeneity of the forms and
representations crafted by the artist that produce possibilities of connection and correspondence when they engage with an individual consciousness at a given moment. Postmodernism's commerce between
elite and popular culture, its amalgamation of the exceptional and the
quotidian, its employment of pastiche and quotation, its games with
self-referentiality, its preference for mixed and open forms, its courting
of the arbitrary and the random, its resistance to the 'serious' or the
'natural': all these features of recent art in a variety of media could be
thought of as producing not the sense of *necessary* cohesion that characterizes most modernist and pre-modernist art, but a sense of the constantly renewed *possibility* of connection, in which the history and situ-

---

[1] Bernard Benstock states that this 'second coincidence' lies in the alternative title of Stephen's
parable, *A Pisgah Sight of Palestine*, since Bloom 'has just burned the image of Palestine in the
advertisement for the fruits of Agendath Netaim' (*Narrative Con / Texts in 'Ulysses'*, 117). But Bloom's
burning of the Agendath Netaim prospectus – in order to light a cone of incense – does not occur
until later, well after Stephen's departure (*U* 17.1321–9).

ation of each interpreter provides one set of elements in the network of potentialities. Rather than art which exploits its culture in an attempt to transcend it, it is an art which celebrates its embeddedness in that culture, and remains open to changes within it. Among the many writers in English one might think of in connection with such an art are John Ashbery, Donald Barthelme, Angela Carter, Alasdair Gray, Thomas Pynchon, and Salman Rushdie.

While the complex texturing of works like these is clearly dependent upon the new possibilities first introduced by modernism and then left relatively undeveloped for about forty years, they seem to be reacting *against* the modernist deployment of these new resources in the service of a transcendentalizing or monumentalizing urge. Modernist works like *The Cantos* or *The Waste Land* or *The Waves* stake a claim against time and chance: they are stamped with the will to specify, to capture, to purify, to preserve. Proust and Lawrence, though their novels are minutely responsive to their cultural moments, struggle to determine psychological constants. Yeats searches for moments of transcendence in the ephemeral round; Kafka (and Freud) attempt to exemplify and enunciate laws of familial and social relations encompassing every human community. In spite of their obvious differences, all these modernist attempts to secure permanence, purity, and absoluteness, as well as many others, entail, ultimately, a resistance to ungrounded effects of meaning, even though we may now be able to read them against the grain of their grand projects, finding in their failure a success of another and more relativist kind. In particular, their aims entail a driving of the specificities of the reading situation to the margins, rather than an embracing of those specificities as part of the experience of art (which, of course, they always are, whether acknowledged or not). This is not to say that the major works of modernism have fixed meanings, but rather that even their *avoidance* of fixed meanings is something that does not, in principle, change from reader to reader, period to period, does not willingly interact with the concrete situation in which text and interpreter find themselves. Though meaning may be suspended, everything in the text is presented as self-justified, immune from grafting or dividing. The artwork wrests necessity from arbitrariness, permanence from the historical flux, universality from culturally specific detail. Think of the superb certainty of a Mondrian painting, the self-authenticating power of a Mies building, the assured self-validation of every note of a Schoenberg twelve-tone composition.

Now it would be palpably wrong to deny that *Ulysses* and *Finnegans*

Wake have similar 'modernist' pretensions. They assert their own massive monumentality, their own pre-programming of every interpretative
move. The unparalleled scholarly attention that *Ulysses* and *Finnegans
Wake* have attracted bears witness to their aura of achieved certainty:
every detail is assumed to be worthy of the most scrupulous editorial
consideration, the most minute genetic tracing, the most careful historical placing, the most ingenious hermeneutic activity – all in the name of
greater fixity, permanence, and truth. Yet the particular manner in
which Joyce accumulates details, multiplies structures, and overdeter-
mines interpretation achieves something else as well, and something
that I believe sets his texts apart from most other modernist works while
it relates them to our own cultural moment: it makes possible, and
relishes, the random, the contingent, and – emerging out of these as a
necessary effect – the coincidental. Rather than attempting to control
the mass of fragmentary detail to *produce* meaning, Joyce's major texts
allow meaning to arise out of that mass by the operations of chance.[2]

This is not to say that *Ulysses* and *Finnegans Wake* are torn apart by two
drives, one towards Joyce's grand encyclopedic schemes and the other
towards the haphazard and the coincidental working to undermine
them (which would be a version of the tension in modernist writing I
mentioned earlier). Rather, it is the rich systematizations of *Ulysses* and
Finnegans Wake, their ordered heterogeneity and multiplicitous coherence, that render their meanings forever unsystematizable – because of
the inevitable outbreaks of coincidence that defy all predictability and
programming.[3] Joyce's own ambiguous attitude towards the structural
frameworks of these texts – his removal of Homeric chapter titles from
the published *Ulysses* while circulating them in the schemata, for instance, or his avoidance in *Finnegans Wake* of any metatextual indications

---

[2] For two very different considerations of Joyce's work in relation to chance and coincidence, see
Monk, *Standard Deviations*, and Rice, *Joyce, Chaos and Complexity*. The former approaches the history
of the novel as a series of attempts to represent chance, understood as the other of narrative, and
rightly regards *Ulysses* as a breakthrough in its elaboration of a 'throwaway aesthetic' (see
especially chapter 4 and the 'Conclusion'). The act of successful representation, however, is
posited on the possibility of escaping chance effects; my argument is that in Joyce's later work
representation *itself* is rendered subject to chance. Rice, in his chapters on *Ulysses* and *Finnegans
Wake*, traces connections between Joyce's complex literary systems and the kinds of system that
are the focus for attention in the sciences of complexity and chaos theory. His overriding aim,
however, is to show that apparent chance effects in Joyce are in fact elements in a controlled and
orderly system, and he leaves out of account the contingency that necessarily marks the events of
writing and reading.

[3] In this respect, Joyce's two later works imitate the complex processes of culture, which depend on
the operation of what Derrida calls the iterable mark, always open to recontextualization and
therefore always open to chance. See, in particular, Derrida's essay 'My Chances'.

other than the title and book numbers while feeding his supporters with interpretative suggestions – merely confirms the texts' own ironic play with their ordering principles, whether Homeric comparisons or Viconian cycles. Monuments they may be, but they are also, and in the same gesture, comic dismantlings of the urge, so prominent around Joyce when he was writing them, to monumentalize.

It is from this open network of possibilities that the text's engagement with the reader's own situation arises. No single reader can comprehend every possibility of felicitous conjunction in *Ulysses* or *Finnegans Wake*. The specific situation you are in as you read, fed into by your personal history, the configurations of your knowledge, your cultural context, highlights certain connections both within the text and between the text and the constituents of that situation (though the distinction between what is inside and what is outside the text is precisely what collapses at these moments). It is this that accounts for that frequent experience of *recognition* that characterizes the reading of these two works, which is not an experience of finding one's own beliefs (or ideology) confirmed in the text, but of being surprised at the sudden public manifestation of what one took to be a private memory or quirk. This process is most obvious in *Finnegans Wake*, whose portmanteau style is entirely fabricated out of the multiple coincidences of language, both within single languages and across diverse languages. Rereading the 'Anna Livia Plurabelle' chapter recently I came upon the phrase 'bakereen's dusind' (*FW* 212.20), and there before me was the name of the South African river near whose banks I grew up (the Umsindusi, or in its familiar abbreviated form, the Dusi), and, like the small boy Joyce imagined in just such a situation, I felt a momentary pleasure in this unlooked-for bond between the work and me – a pleasure in no way diminished by my awareness that, if asked whether I was responding to an intended allusion or to a coincidence thrown up by the chapter's dense web of names, I would probably have to answer, like Bloom in his response to Stephen's story set in the Queen's Hotel, 'coincidence'. But the opposition between the 'intended' and the 'accidental' begins to break down at this point: if Joyce intentionally builds a machine of such complexity that unforeseen connections are bound to arise when it comes into contact with a reader possessing equally complex systems of memory and information, we cannot call them 'unintentional' in any straightforward sense of the word. And this means we cannot say that the openness to chance and to the reader that I am arguing is Joyce's link with postmodernism is only an 'accidental' effect of his overloaded monumentalization; that would be to re-erect precisely the opposition that his writing, and the notion of coincidence, undermine.

Of course coincidence is, as my discussion of the 'Ithaca' passage will have suggested, first of all an internal and fully thematized principle in these works. The chimings and echoes that criss-cross *Ulysses*, gradually revealing themselves to the assiduous reader and rereader, and the extraordinary multiplication of such effects in the *Wake*, invite a relishing of coincidence while constituting the network of detail that makes possible an infinite series of new coincidences. In *Ulysses*, it is Bloom who functions as Vergil to the reader's Dante while they explore the world of the coincidence. (Bloom's pleasure in coincidences is in no way opposed, as I hope will now be clear, to his enthusiastic appreciation of grand systems.) The word *coincidence* itself is something of a Bloomian leitmotif: its fourteen occurrences in the book are all associated with Bloom's consciousness, prompted by a dozen different events during the course of the day.

None of these is a major coincidence, on the scale of the parallel between quotidian Dublin peregrinations and heroic Greek journeyings: they are the little comings-together that characterize any excursion on the busy streets of a metropolis. Thus, for instance, in 'Lestrygonians', Bloom is walking the Dublin streets thinking of a thousand things including – very briefly – the political charisma of Charles Stewart Parnell, when he notices John Howard Parnell: 'There he is: the brother. Image of him. Haunting face. Now that's a coincidence. Course hundreds of times you think of a person and don't meet him' (*U* 8.502). Having thus rationalized away the coincidence, Bloom is startled a few moments later when another recent occupant of his mental world, George Russell, materializes in the flesh: 'And there he is too. Now that's really a coincidence: second time. Coming events cast their shadows before' (*U* 8.525). The coinciding of coincidences is something that cannot be explained away, and prods Bloom towards the realm of the occult (though even this involves not a rejection but an expansion of the realm of scientific explanation). Bloom goes on to indulge in a fantasy in which this new coincidence is multiplied, imagining that the young woman to whom AE is holding forth is one of the unsuccessful respondents to his solicitation for feminine aid in the columns of the *Irish Times*.

The other coincidences that Bloom remarks on are of a similar kind. In the Ormond Hotel he is about to begin writing to the successful respondent to his ad, whom he knows as 'Martha', when Simon Dedalus launches into a song from the opera of that name (*U* 11.713). In the same chapter he remarks to himself on the coincidence of seeing Blazes Boylan three times that day (*U* 11.303), and in 'Circe' uses coincidence as a defence against the charge of peeing into a bucket of workmen's porter (*U* 15.593). In 'Eumaeus', he remarks on no less than four 'coincidences' in the course of his unsuccessful attempts to engage Stephen in conversation (*U* 16.414, 890, 1222, 1776) – though, caught up as they are in the web of misinformation and bathos that characterizes the chapter, they do not qualify very obviously for the label. In 'Ithaca', in addition to the response to Stephen's narratives that I have already mentioned, he recalls the coincidences that might have led him to predict the result of the Gold Cup that afternoon (*U* 17.322).

These occurrences of the term *coincidence* are, of course, only explicit namings of a constant preoccupation; Bloom is always on the look-out for connections across time and place, verbal echoes, patterns in the heap of fragments that characterize his consciousness and his surroundings. Stephen, by contrast, seems driven by the traditional (and I include here the modernist) artist's need to *make* connections, to fuse and shape them, rather than to find and celebrate them in passing; his performance in the library, postmodernly self-parodying though it is, offers his audience pleasure and satisfaction in its achievement of just such a willed and wrought integrity. The enigmatic fictions he relates to Bloom in 'Ithaca' are more modernist than postmodern, and to this extent Bloom's response is wildly inappropriate, its insistence on the specific connections between the story and his own situation deflating Stephen's earnest, if ironic, narrative art.

What, then, is the importance of coincidence to Joyce? As Bloom's experiences indicate, a coincidence is an instance of contingency bearing the marks of necessity, or, as the *OED* has it, 'a notable concurrence of events or circumstances having no apparent causal connection'. Notice the hedging implicit in that 'apparent': part of the fascination of coincidence is that it always *may not be* a coincidence – it thrills or chills us with a sense of hidden connections, loops in time, secret correspondences. 'Coming events cast their shadows before', muses Bloom after seeing AE, momentarily denying that what he has experienced is in fact a coincidence – not, as when seeing Parnell's brother a moment before, because the connection is not marked enough, but because it may be a real (if supernatural) connection between apparently distinct phenomena. Though the Ithacan catechist definitively excludes 'information' and 'intuition' in the curious doubling of the name 'Queen's Hotel', there must remain a suspicion that Stephen, perhaps even subliminally, has absorbed the gossip about Bloom's father's suicide, which only that morning had passed from Martin Cunningham to Jack Power just out of Bloom's hearing (*U* 6.529–30); or that the insistence on coincidence is actually a reflex of Bloom's uncanny sense of something like telepathy at work.[4] Who can say of any apparent coincidence that it is not in fact the punctual culmination of a vast and perhaps ancient system of connections? (At least one writer usually classed as postmodern, Thomas Pynchon, has made of this question a rich narrative resource.) *Finnegans Wake*'s portmanteau style is a continuous exploitation of this potential in language and culture, languages and cultures.

Joyce values coincidence precisely because of this undecidability between chance and necessity; he is offering us not a Romantic theory of inherent correspondences, but a staging of their ever-present, though always uncertain, possibility. Meaning is never grounded or guaranteed; but, as the product of the complexity of our cultural systems, it is always available, always utilizable. One has only to compare Yeats's use of the gyre with Joyce's use of the Viconian cycle to gauge the difference between an attempt to wrest coherence from the chaos of history and a rejoicing in the ceaseless patterns of repetition thrown up by the chaos of history. Joyce may find the motif of the fall occurring at every level of cultural narrative, from the Crucifixion to Humpty Dumpty, from *Paradise Lost* to his father's jokes, but he is not offering a psychological or historical paradigm that will control and encompass that abundance of storytelling. On the contrary, the motif of the fall is precisely an encoding of the inevitable collapse of such attempts, narrated over and over in human history. *Finnegans Wake* can be understood as one great coincidence, if we allow the word its etymological sense of *coincidere*, 'falling together'. And the inevitable failure of the grand designs of Modernism is only one more example of Tim Finnegan's ignominious plunge from the ladder.

Coincidence has a venerable history in comedy, of course, but its traditional use in the genre is precisely to suggest the providential hand – clasped firmly in the authorial hand – that guides the paths of men and women, thus draining it of its contingency and arbitrariness. Joyce's comedy is very different: it celebrates precisely that contingency and arbitrariness, offering us an alternative to set beside the modernist bid for transcendence (which so frequently involved a reactionary politics of

---

[4] On the relation between chance and telepathy, see Derrida, 'Telepathy', and Royle, *Telepathy and Literature*.

transcendence as well): a future-oriented opening of new spaces in which difference, otherness, the unexpected, the unknown, the comic, the coincidental, may flourish.

CHAPTER 10

Countlessness of livestories: narrativity in Finnegans Wake

Most readers of *Finnegans Wake* would probably hesitate to call it a novel, and one of the reasons for this reluctance is that it lacks anything that could unproblematically be called a *narrative*, something which even such exceptional texts as *Tristram Shandy* and *Ulysses*, for all their oddity, can be said to possess. Yet narrative is hardly absent from the *Wake*; indeed, in the words of the text itself, at one of its many auto-descriptive moments, 'Countlessness of livestories have netherfallen by this plage, flick as flowflakes, litters from aloft, like a waast wizzard all of whirlworlds' (*FW* 17.26). *Finnegans Wake* is a great mound of stories, a gigantic accumulation of the world's narratives, but it seems that it is not one of them.

To explore this paradox, it will help to establish a working definition of narrative: let us say that it is a linear (though often multilevelled) account of recognizable characters and events, engaging with the reader's pre-existing mental schemata to arouse expectations, and to modify, complicate, defeat, or partially satisfy those expectations, arriving at full satisfaction – or something like it – only at the end (thereby constituting it as the end). Individual narratives work in different ways to produce pleasure and perhaps some form of understanding or insight, but what they all have in common is the condition of being narratives, of engaging with the world and the mind in the specific manner of narrative. I propose to call this quality *narrativity*, and my suggestion is that narrativity, so defined, is a crucial element in our enjoyment of any narrative *as* a narrative. The word *narrativity* is not recognized by the second edition of the *Oxford English Dictionary*, but it does appear in the titles of a few books and in the work of some narratologists. Gerald Prince, for instance, defines it as 'The set of properties characterizing narrative and distinguishing it from nonnarrative; the formal and contextual features making a narrative more or less narrative, as it were' (*A Dictionary of Narratology*, 64). Though the final phrase reveals Prince's uncertainty about his own definition, this remains a more technical (and perhaps emptier) employment of the term than the one I am suggesting; my interest is not so much in a 'set of properties' as in a quality or timbre, inseparable from the operation of readerly desires and satisfactions, that is precisely not reducible to any objectively ennumerable features or rules.[1]

⌐Narrativity, that is to say, has everything to do with the reader's performance of the text as he or she reads it – a strange kind of performance, since it involves being performed by the text as well.⌐Our consciousness that we are experiencing not a series of events as they might unfold 'in the real world' but a dynamic structure built out of inherited cultural materials according to (but also in deviance from) known codes, a series of events possessing a certain phantasmal quality, is not a hindrance to our full enjoyment of the narrative but on the contrary a precondition of it;⌐and our appreciation of a skilfully deployed narrative sequence in a literary text is in part a savouring of this quality of narrativity as it is foregrounded and exploited.⌐

Among the many other things they do with narrative, Joyce's first three books of fictional prose all practise a certain stretching of it, to produce an experience of controlled exiguousness. To take one example from *Dubliners*, 'The Sisters' arouses a host of expectations as it encourages its readers to recall familiar plots involving youthful induction into the mysteries of the adult world (of knowledge, of sin, of death), yet it ends with those expectations unfulfilled, with an awkward silence whose awkwardness is not just that of social intercourse brought up against a deeply embarrassing event but also that of a structural closure which fails to satisfy narrative norms. *A Portrait of the Artist as a Young Man* offers more in the way of accepted narrative satisfactions than *Dubliners*, but has many sequences that stretch – and thereby raise for a kind of questioning – narrativity itself; the extended recitation of Father Arnall's sermons would be one obvious example. Moreover, the central narrative of *A Portrait* – the familiar story of the growth of the artist through obstacles and false starts to maturity – is one that is constantly ironized by other forces in the book, questioning Stephen Dedalus's own exploi-

---

[1] Bill Readings gives a good account of the elusiveness of narrativity in his discussion of the importance of narrative for Jean-François Lyotard: 'Narrativity is . . . both constitutive and disruptive of representational discourse (the representation of an object to a subject by means of a concept). A deconstructive figure rather than a concept, narrative necessarily intervenes to disfigure the legitimation of representation' (*Introducing Lyotard*, 80). In the second sentence, I would use 'narrativity' again rather than 'narrative'.

128 *Narrativity in* Finnegans Wake

tation of that narrative as a guide to life even as they question Joyce's exploitation of it as a novelistic schema. *Ulysses* plays at extraordinary length with the familiar narrative patterns of sundering and union, departure and home-coming, trust and betrayal, and in that extraordinary length it too foregrounds narrativity itself: we do, it is true, experience a certain traditional kind of tension as Bloom continues to find more and more ways of postponing his return home, and we are aware of rising expectations of conventional resolution as his and Stephen's paths converge more and more closely, but to read *Ulysses* for its narrative tensions and resolutions (or non-resolutions) would be like reading *Middlemarch* for its eroticism. The sequence of tensions and resolutions do constitute, however, an essential cord on which everything else is strung, a cord stretched almost to breaking point without actually snapping. And the final word of the novel does somehow manage to release the multiple tensions built up throughout the book's extraordinary length.

In *Finnegans Wake* the connecting cord is gone. The broad scheme of day (perhaps), evening, night, and morning which structures the text is not a *narrative* scheme at all; it arouses no tension (we are not asking 'Will night fall?' 'Will morning come?'), it hooks onto no pre-existing narrative formulae, it offers no enigma to be solved or human crisis to be resolved. Heroic and ingenious efforts have been made to derive from the multifarious and ambiguous episodes an overarching narrative – for instance, the story of a publican who dreams epic dreams after a hard day's work, waking only in the penultimate book to make somewhat unfelicitous love to his wife – but apart from its thinness as it is spread over several hundred dense pages, any such derived sequence of events fails to engage with the traditional resources of narrative, and hence lacks momentum or drive.[2] What is more, this kind of simple linearity

[2] Michael H. Begnal, who has worked assiduously to find within the overdeterminations of the *Wake* a relatively straightforward account of the actions and speeches of a determinate set of characters, offers the following as the 'basic plot of *Finnegans Wake*' (after the preliminary material of Book I):

ii.1, the children are outside in the yard, playing a game after school until their parents call them in at dusk for supper; ii.2, after dinner, Shem and Shaun do their homework, while Issy sits on a couch, knitting and kibitzing; ii.3, Earwicker presides in his pub until closing time, finishes off the drinks left around by the patrons, falls down drunk, and staggers up to bed later; iii.4, the Earwickers are awakened by the cries of Shem in the throes of a nightmare, and they soothe him, return to bed, make love, and once again fall asleep as dawn is breaking; iv.1, Anna Livia awakens, and her thoughts form the monologue which concludes the book. (*Dreamscheme*, 51–2)

Not much narrative drive or proairetic complication there. And, as we shall see in the next chapter, some of the connecting links that produce a linear account of domestic life derive more from a tradition of commentary initiated by Edmund Wilson and by Campbell and Robinson's *Skeleton Key* than from clearly articulated statements in the text – for example, the 'supper' or hardly corresponds to the experience of reading the text of *Finnegans Wake*, page by page, sentence by sentence. This is not to deny the sense of a beginning at the beginning and the sense of an end at the end (which are not overridden by the syntax that links – fairly weakly, I would argue – unfinished end and uninitiated beginning); but my argument is that these are *structural*, not narrative, features of the book.

[On the other hand, *narrativity* abounds in *Finnegans Wake*; the book's very texture is a tightly woven web of stories. Through his extraordinary development of the portmanteau technique, Joyce found a way of interweaving narrative possibilities at several levels simultaneously: a paragraph, a sentence, a phrase, or even a word can offer a mini-narrative to the reader. Linearity – a crucial feature of narrative – goes out the window.]There are two requirements for this technique to work successfully: (1) most of the narratives must be familiar ones, so they can be triggered by the smallest fragment or allusion (and we might note in connection with this that among the books Joyce owned in Trieste was Georges Polti's *Thirty-Six Dramatic Situations*, which claimed to derive all the world's narratives from thirty-six basic situations);[3] (2) the book must be a long one, so that it can produce its own multiply reiterated versions of familiar plots (the sin in the park, the captain and the tailor's daughter, Buckley and the Russian General, and so on), and set up its own complex network of allusions and easily triggered associations.[The result is a certain emptiness of narrative – the stories are not new ones, and they keep coming back again and again – and a fullness of narrativity, a rich layering of stories allowing narrative echoes to fly back and forth among holy scripture, ribald joke, national history, pantomime, literary masterpiece, nursery rhyme.]I am reminded of the opening of Barthes's 'Introduction to the Structural Analysis of Narratives':

Numberless are the world's narratives. First of all in a prodigious variety of genres, themselves distributed among different substances, as if any material were appropriate for man to entrust his stories to it: narrative can be supported by articulated speech, oral or written, by image, fixed or moving, by gesture, and by the organized mixture of all these substances; it is present in myth, legend, fable, tragedy, comedy, epic, history, pantomime, painting . . . stained-glass window, cinema, comic book, news item, conversation. (95)

Of course, the *Wake* for the most part uses one substance, the verbal

'dinner' which joins II.1 and II.2, the continuity of the name 'Earwicker', and the event of the publican's staggering up to bed (presumably so that he can be found there in III.4).

[3] Joyce owned the French original, *Les Trente-six situations dramatiques*, published in 1912; see *JJ* 48, 124. (Thanks to Jorn Barger for bringing this book to my attention.)

(though there are visual and musical narrative effects too); but it can certainly be said to be 'an organized mixture' of all these sources of narrative – there is not one in Barthes's list that's not mined by Joyce.

The effect of this excess of narrativity over narrative could be described as a *staging* or *performing* of narrative, a putting it into play, a testing of its limits.[4] (In a similar fashion, one might say that the *Wake* has an excess of, for instance, referentiality over reference, metaphoricity over metaphor, descriptivity over description, ethicity over ethics, that results in a kind of staging of reference, metaphor, description, and ethics.) A single sentence, chosen more or less at random, will help clarify my argument:

Fudder and lighting for ally looty, any filly in a fog, for O'Cronione lags acrumbling in his sands but his sunsunsuns still tumble on. (415.20)

Different narratives of death and succession intermingle here: Cronos succeeded by his son Zeus; John Brown's body mouldering while his soul lives on to inspire his followers; the topos of monumental statuary (Ozymandias, perhaps?) crumbling into the sand while humanity persists regardless of individual claims to greatness. Two of these stories – Cronos and Ozymandias – entail disrespect for patriarchal authority, and the carnivalesque scene after the death of the father is depicted also in 'Fudder and lighting for ally looty' – food (or fodder) and illumination made available for everyone (*für alle leute*), with a suggestion of 'loot' as well – and in the (male) sexual promiscuity of 'any filly in a fog'. But there's a story of authoritarian rage here as well, in the initial thunder and lightning; and perhaps one of circumnavigation (reinforced by the immediate context of this sentence) in the tumbling suns and in the allusion to Phileas Fogg, whose voyage around the world in eighty days is another one of our culture's recycling and recycled narratives, going back, of course, to the *Odyssey* itself.

Within the context of the whole book the narrative texture of this sentence is even richer, since other stories of fathers and sons, parental anger and filial disrespect, sexual adventures and circuitous travels are evoked. We note the Irishness of the fallen hero ('O'Cronione'), and the tripleness of his male offspring ('sunsunsuns') who, in two contrasting

---

[4] A parallel in another medium might be the heightened apprehension of the possibilities and the limits of the dodecaphonic system in an inventive piece of tonal music (even if the hearer possesses no technical musical knowledge at all), where we might say that we enjoy not only the unfolding of harmonic sequences and melodic patterns but also the staging of harmonicity and melodicity. On the question of inventiveness, see Derrida's 'Psyche' (*Acts of Literature*, 310–43), an essay to which I am much indebted in my thinking about Joyce.

stories that depend on the ambiguity of 'tumble', either dance on his grave, or, in their turn, fall as well. (The twins Shaun and Shem often become a trio, as when they are manifested as the three soldiers observing the father-figure's indiscretion in the park.) Yet in none of these stories do we make any narrative *progress*; we know their beginnings and ends already (and where there is more than one end in the tradition, Joyce usually gives us both, simultaneously and undecidably). [What provides the special pleasure of reading *Finnegans Wake* is the way these stories in so many different registers map onto one another, and the way the power and fascination of narrativity is by this means instanced, exploited, and ironized.]When we consider sections of the text larger than the short sentence, of course, this complex texturing of narrative, and resultant heightening of narrativity, operates even more intensely and (if you're in the right frame of mind) enjoyably.

One cannot read *for* narrativity, however; it is like that dim star in the corner of the sky that disappears as soon as you look directly at it. *Narrative* is what one reads for: the particular narrative or simultaneously unrolling narratives that are engaging the attention at the moment of textual contact, with the exercise of recognition, memory, and prediction that they entail. Even in the *Wake*, narrativity is never present as such, but its effects are more strongly felt than anywhere else in literature, as the narratives keep short-circuiting, overlapping, exploding into multiple destinies, and blocking any attempt to turn them into transparent accounts of how it is with people and events in the world.

[Does this pushing of narrativity as far as it will go make the *Wake* unlike any other fictional text? I don't think so – as I have argued before in relation to other features of the book, the *Wake* represents an extreme of the literary that reveals with particular clarity the characteristic modes of literature's functioning.[5]]Foregrounded narrativity is that which marks literary narrative as distinct from other kinds of narrative. (However, this is not to make any 'high art'/'popular art' distinction – foregrounded narrativity can be found in the productions of the mass media as much as in those of the exclusive salon, as Kimberly Devlin has demonstrated – in a response to an earlier version of this argument – in using the concept to discuss the endless and multilayered narratives of television soaps.[6]) Thus it is not merely a question of fictional as opposed to non-fictional narrative: we might find no staging of narrativity at all in a wholly uninventive story or anecdote. At the same time, there are

[5] See chapters 7 and 8 of *Peculiar Language*.
[6] This response was made in a talk at the 1982 International James Joyce Symposium in Dublin.

non-fictional narratives of which we might wish to say that narrativity is being performed and tested, though only, I would argue, if they had a certain 'literary' quality and thereby encouraged a 'literary' reading. The accurate recounting of a sequence of real events – even a story-shaped sequence – would not be likely to produce the experience of foregrounded narrativity I have been describing; but Rousseau's *Confessions* or Gibbon's *Rise and Fall* might. We might risk the assertion that a *literary* narrative – fictional or not – is a narrative in which narrativity is played out at some distance from itself, a process which does not in any way inhibit its power to excite, to move, to delight.

Finnegans Wake is thus the limit case of literary narrative, as it is the limit case of literature in so many other ways. We put it down and turn with pleasure to other fictional constructions where narrative is strong and narrativity weak. But our pleasure in these other stories is not entirely that of relief, since reading the *Wake*, learning how to enjoy its excess of narrativity, is also a schooling which can enhance all the other narratives we encounter – not because it gives us lessons on what narrativity *is*, but because it diminishes our dependence upon what Joyce called 'goahead plot' and attunes our faculties to the dance of narrativity wherever it is to be found.

CHAPTER 11

Finnegans awake, or the dream of interpretation

Nor does it seem to me quite legitimate to get *arse* out of *heart*. Have you read any of those books about Baconian ciphers in Shakespeare? Those theories can sometimes be made to seem quite plausible.

Edmund Wilson to Thornton Wilder on the latter's
interpretation of *Finnegans Wake*, 1940

By the mid-1980s it seemed that the notion that *Finnegans Wake* is the representation of a dream, or a night's sleep, was beginning to lose the secure hold it once had over the book's interpreters. Two general introductions, both entitled *James Joyce*, may serve as evidence. In 1984 we find Patrick Parrinder observing that the idea of the *Wake* as 'night-language' – which, he says dismissively, 'is still heard from time to time' – 'reflects the same rather crude notion of imitative form that Joyce invoked to defend some of the later chapters of *Ulysses*' (*James Joyce*, 207). In 1985, Bernard Benstock, writing about 'what commentators insist on referring to as dream language', comments disparagingly on 'the easy conclusion that "*Finnegans Wake* is a dream"' (*James Joyce*, 148, 152).[1] The three essays on *Finnegans Wake* in the 1984 Bowen and Carens *Companion to Joyce Studies* also suggest that by the mid-1980s the idea of the dream commanded less support than it once did: one pointedly ignores the idea, one discusses it briefly to reject it, and the third makes use of it, but with a note of scepticism.[2] But 1986 saw the appearance of two books on

---

[1] One of the commentators who came to that conclusion was Bernard Benstock himself in 1965 (*Joyce-Again's Wake*, 8 *et passim*), another sign of how much times, and interpretative methods, had changed between the sixties and eighties.

[2] Barbara diBernard, 'Technique in *Finnegans Wake*' (diBernard quotes critics who refer to the notion of the dream, but makes no comment on this fact; see 654, 663); Michael H. Begnal, 'The Language of *Finnegans Wake*' (see especially 637–8 for his dismissal of the view that the *Wake*'s language is 'dream language'); and Patrick McCarthy, 'Structure and Meanings of *Finnegans Wake*' ('the concept of the dream form alone is insufficient to unlock many mysteries' (563)).

the *Wake* which attempt to resuscitate the idea of the dream – or at least of the night – as the major interpretative key to the work, John Gordon's *'Finnegans Wake': A Plot Summary* and John Bishop's *Joyce's Book of the Dark*. The former is an indication of the need which many readers, especially those who are not Joyce scholars or literary theorists, still feel for a machine which will reduce the book's dizzying multiplicity to a single, traditional plot line, while the latter is a bold attempt to breathe life (and, indeed, death) into the old idea of the *Wake* as a night book. It is too soon to announce the wake of the Wakean dream, then, but it is time that the idea itself was examined with the historical and theoretical scrupulousness it requires. This essay attempts to do so by way of three propositions discussed in three sections.

FIRST PROPOSITION

My first proposition is this: a reader approaching *Finnegans Wake* without any prior assumptions as to its content and method would be unlikely to regard the text as the representation of a dream.

I would guess that, since the publication of *Finnegans Wake*, the majority of those who have made the attempt to read it have had the idea of a dream somewhere in mind, whether as part of general cultural lore or as specific information received from a critical study or a helpful teacher. To test my proposition fully, this interpretative context would have to be wholly erased, and Joyce's words read without any extratextual presuppositions. But this is an impossible exercise, since we cannot simply clear the mind of its contents like a magnetic disk, and for most of us the idea of the dream has already become an inseparable part of the text we encounter. There isn't a two-stage process whereby we read in some neutral fashion and then add interpretative colouring; words come to us already clothed in the interpretative garb that endues them with sense.[3] The best we can do is try to get a degree of leverage on the problem by imagining a reader of *Finnegans Wake* who has managed, through some freakish circumstance, to avoid exposure to the tradition of *Wake* commentary before tackling the book. (In doing so we should bear in mind just how easy it would have been for Joyce to signal unambiguously, *within* the text, that what we are reading represents a dream or a night's sleep: a few words would have sufficed.)

Our hypothetical decontextualized reader will start, of course, with

---

[3] This point is forcefully argued by Stanley Fish in the title essay of *Is There a Text in This Class?*

the title. Read as a sentence in indicative mood without punctuation, it seems to refer to a group of people called Finnegan ending a period of sleep, with the apparent implication that this is a book about consciousness, day, the start of activity, the cleansing of perception. Although a reader unfamiliar with Joyce might stop there, let us imagine him or her acting with some boldness and inserting additional punctuation. A comma between the two words turns it into an imperative: the Finnegans are being ordered to rouse themselves. An apostrophe in *Finnegan's* (or the supposition that the first word is German) makes the structure a genitive one, and the subject a ceremony around a corpse – with the Irishness of 'Finnegan' pointing to an event neither solemn nor somnolent; alternatively, the phrase might refer to the effect of a remarkable individual upon the world, figured as the track left by a ship in water. Any knowledge of the ballad 'Finnegan's Wake', alluded to further in the first chapter, would strengthen the implications of arousal and energy: since the climax of the ballad is Tim Finnegan's revival on being splashed by whiskey, it is clear that we are not about to read a tragedy focused on death, but a comedy focused on the irrepressible force of life. (More sophisticated multilingual interpretations of the title would not disconfirm such a reading.[4])

Next in importance in establishing an interpretative context when we are faced with an unfamiliar book is the opening, which establishes rapidly what kind of work it is – largely by immediately establishing all the kinds of work it is not. Among the many genres to which this book does *not* claim allegiance as it opens is the dream relation, a rich tradition in Western literature. *Finnegans Wake* provides no waking, daylight frame – no 'Ac on a May mornyng on Malverne hulles / Me biful for to slepe, for werynesse of walkyng', or 'Alice was beginning to get very tired of sitting by her sister on the bank'. It introduces us to no identifiable dreamer – no Scipio or Chaucer who is about to relate how he fell asleep and the experiences that followed. It offers none of the vivid visual imagery that characterizes the convention of the dream relation (capitalized upon in this century by the film industry). It initiates no sequential narrative, in which the dreamer passes through strange

---

[4] *Fin-negans* suggests, through French and Latin, a negation of the end, rather as 'wake' suggests consciousness after sleep and revelry after death; while the darkness of night is contradicted by the whiteness suggested by the Irish *fionn*. There is also the returning hero of *Finn-again*, or the portmanteau hero in *Finn-Egan* (Finn MacCool and Kevin Egan). The advanced reader of the *Wake* would of course recognize how characteristic are the double suggestions here of night and day, death and life, sleep and waking, individual and group, native language and foreign language, mournfulness and cheerfulness, ending and beginning.

and shifting adventures. Nor could it be argued that the opening attempts some kind of 'realistic' evocation of the dream experience as a challenge to a highly literary convention: there is little similarity between the opening page of the *Wake* and anything recorded in the history of actual dream recollection. While it is true that one can find in the *Wake* equivalents of the processes of symbolization, condensation, and displacement identified by Freud in the dreamwork that turns latent into manifest content, and that Freud on occasion used puns and portmanteaux in his practice of dream interpretation, no one has attested a real dream that uses these processes so richly and relentlessly. Freud's own concept of 'secondary revision' posits a narrativizing and character-constructing agency that produces something much closer to the traditional story than anything in *Finnegans Wake*.

One might, in fact, imagine a reader deriving from the opening word of the text an alternative explanatory metaphor for the flow of language, the fluid melting of times and places and people, the jumble of flotsam strewn over every page: and a quick look at the end of the book – one strategy available to the puzzled reader – might, since the closing passage is clearly concerned with the movement of water, strengthen such an assumption. *Finnegans Wake*, our reader might decide, is modelled on a river, which carries with it the disordered detritus of human civilization to sea; the river which represents the watery grave of all society's attempts to erect firm structures and fixed principles. And both traditional figurative conventions and the opening pages of the book would further suggest that the river is also the river of time, the river of history, beginning with Eve and the Fall, and ending only with the final dissipation of individual death or the demise of humanity; except that in such an ending would lie a new beginning, just as the sea's waters eventually fall as rain to return to the river's source. If this interpretative hypothesis were appealing enough, it could serve as a framework for the whole text, to produce a reading quite different from that provided by the notion of the dream.[5] This is only one example of an alternative reading hypothesis: the opening paragraph alone could provide many more.

Sleep is certainly mentioned in the opening pages, but it appears as the condition of the fallen figure called Finn or Finnegan, advised to

[5] Richard Ellmann speculates on the possibility that a discarded plan for *Ulysses* 'had envisaged a theme of riverlike flow' and that *Finnegans Wake* 'was perhaps the legatee of this unused idea' (*JJ* 545) (though it is hard to fathom how he derives this from Joyce's comment to Budgen about a short *matutine*, *entr'acte*, and *nocturne* at the beginning, middle, and end of the book (*Letters* I, 149)).

remain prone because of the advent of a lively, if guilt-ridden, individual whose name – as a topic for gossip – takes us into the second chapter. There are numerous sleeping figures throughout the book, but there are far more waking figures; there are as many references to battles and bar-rooms as there are to beds and bedrooms – and even in the beds, much more takes place than sleep and dreams. Moreover, the existence of sleepers in the book would hardly induce our innocent reader to assume that the book itself represents a dream; dreams are not typically about sleep. When a dream *is* narrated, it is clearly announced as such, even in the dense and confusing texture of the *Wake*. At the beginning of 3.i we find the following:

And as I was jogging along in a dream as dozing I was dawdling, arrah, methought broadtone was heard and the creepers and the gliders and flivvers of the earth breath and the dancetongues of the woodfires and the hummers in their ground all vociferated echoating: Shaun! Shaun! Post the post! (*FW* 404.3)[6]

This dreamer, who uses conventional terms for recounting his dream – methought, meseemed, when lo! – turns out to be the donkey (*FW* 405.6); not an identification that would lead our reader to place great weight on dreaming as an explanation for the *Wake*'s oddness. (What follows this introduction, in fact, is no more like a dream than any chapter in the book: Shaun's lengthy answers to fourteen brief choral questions.)

Now it is certainly true that our innocent reader is likely to notice that after the coming of darkness at the end of Book I – a third of the way through the text – there is a frequent emphasis on *night*. The first three chapters of Book II have many suggestions of evening (albeit a wide-awake evening of games, homework, and bar-room debate), and after sporadic nocturnal suggestions in the first three chapters of Book III comes a chapter that seems to focus very specifically on a household at night-time. Book IV, of course, is shot through with suggestions of dawn, waking, breakfast. Given the repeatedly changing settings and characters, there would be little inclination to suppose that the whole book reflects the experiences of a single brief span of time – a night, or a day and a night – but if we imagine our hypothetical reader coming to the *Wake* with expectations derived from *Ulysses*, some sense of equivalence

---

[6] Bernard Benstock points out that in spite of the presentation of this sequence as a dream, it contains 'hardly a gram of psychological dream content'. He observes that 'it is characteristic of the *Wake* that . . . the invocation of a dream should result in language of least similitude to traditional assumptions about dreams' (*James Joyce*, 153).

might be set up between the latter parts of the two books (we are, after all, still in the first half of *Ulysses* when we learn, via the lush rhetoric associated with Gerty MacDowell, that 'The summer evening had begun to fold the world in its mysterious embrace' (*U* 13.1–2)). In both books, however, most of what is related in those later chapters has nothing to do with the notional nocturnal setting. And in neither case – whatever extravagances of language occur – is there any reason why the reader should wish to explain the oddity of the writing by reference to a dream. The fact that the first eight chapters of *Finnegans Wake*, before dark, or the last chapter, at daybreak, are no more lucid that the rest makes such an explanation a particularly unpromising one.

A final source of clues for the bemused reader looking for an explanatory schema would be apparent self-references in the text, as the word *paralysis* has helped readers of *Dubliners* and the phenomenon of parallax has helped readers of *Ulysses*. For instance, question 9 in the sixth chapter – the quiz show – might propose itself as a description of the whole work (an interpretative move which would itself be based on a prior assumption about the book's methods, of course):

> 9.   Now, to be on anew and basking again in the panaroma of all flores of speech, if a human being duly fatigued by his dayety in the sooty, having plenxty off time on his gouty hands and vacants of space at his sleepish feet and as hapless behind the dreams of accuracy as any camelot prince of dinmurk, were at this auctual futule preteriting unstant, in the states of suspensive exanimation, accorded, throughout the eye of a noodle, with an earsighted view of old hopeinhaven with all the ingredient and egregiunt whights and ways to which in the curse of his persistence the course of his tory will had been having recourses, the reverberration of knotcracking awes, the reconjungation of nodebinding ayes, the redissolusingness of mindmouldered ease and the thereby hang of the Hoel of it, could such a none, whiles even led comesilencers to comeliewithhers and till intempestuous Nox should catch the gallicry and spot lucan's dawn, byhold at ones what is main and why tis twain, how one once meet melts in tother wants poignings, the sap rising, the foles falling, the nimb now nihilant round the girlyhead so becoming, the wrestless in the womb, all the rivals out to allsea, shakeagain, O disaster! shakealose, Ah how starring! but Heng's got a bit of Horsa's nose and Jeff's got the signs of Ham round his mouth and the beau that spun beautiful pales as it palls, what roserude and oragious grows gelb and greem, blue out the ind of it! Violet's dyed! then *what* would that fargazer seem to seemself to seem seeming of, dimm it all?

Answer: A collideorscape! (*FW* 143.3)

The trouble about appealing to such a description to explain what the book is about is that it poses exactly the same problems as those which, on a wider canvas, it is being used to solve. A choice among the many possible readings of this passage could be made only on the basis of a prior, and externally derived, interpretative decision. If one has already decided – or been told – that the book is about dreams, one can trace a thread of appropriate references: the passage seems to concern a human being fatigued by his day in the city, who has sleepy feet, is helpless behind dreams, is in a state of suspended animation, and sees sights through the Roman watches of the night (Vespera, Conticinium, Concubium, Intempesta Nox, and Gallicinium).[7] And there is a theorist of dreams smuggled into the portmanteau 'reconjungation'. But if one feels that the key to the book is the panoramic history with which it opens, one will stress, among other references to 'his tory', the allusions to Poyning's Law, Hengest and Horsa, and the Viconian cycles or 'recourses' (birth, marriage, death, and *ricorso* occur in 'the reverberration of knotcracking awes, the reconjungation of nodebinding ayes, the redissolusingness of mindmouldered ease and the thereby hang of the Hoel of it'). If language seems most important, one will seize on 'flores of speech', 'futule preteriting', the verb in 'reverberration' and the conjugation in 'reconjungation'. If family relationships are central to one's approach, a daughter and competing twin sons can be found in 'the girlyhead so becoming, the wrestless in the womb, all the rivals out to allsea'. (In that last phrase we also have the river flowing out to sea once more.) Should Bruno's general principles of union and opposition seem to be the key, there's 'byhold at ones what is main and why tis twain, how one once meet melts in tother wants poignings'. An eye on the lookout for religious traditions will find the question of judgement after death a central concern – hearing 'dayety' as 'deity' and 'hopeinhaven' as 'hope in heaven', finding goats and sheep in 'gouty hands and sleepish feet', and putting 'the dreams of accuracy', 'camelot', and 'the eye of a noodle' together to produce dreams of avarice disturbed by the parable about the camel and the needle. Other preconceptions might lead the reader to the literary tradition – *Hamlet, Prince of Denmark*; or to Denmark itself, since 'hopeinhaven' is also Copenhagen; or to Joyce's own eye problems – 'earsighted view'; or to politics – 'whig' and 'tory'; or to courtly romance – Camelot, Galahad (in 'girlyhead'), and Hoel, the father of Isolde of the White Hands; or to the rhetoric of abuse – 'noodle', 'sap', 'foles', and perhaps '*oie*', goose, spelled out by 'awes', 'ayes', and 'ease'; or to objects in the sky – night and dawn, nimbus

---

[7] I acknowledge the standard reference works on *Finnegans Wake*, which I have used in commenting on this passage.

clouds and the cloud in *Hamlet* iii.ii, 'in shape of a camel', star in English and Greek (the *aster* of 'disaster'), the storm in 'oragious' and the colours of the rainbow.

If one is not seeking, consciously or unconsciously, to marshal one's responses to the passage's polysemy in such a way as to substantiate a particular interpretation, all these lexical explosions remain relevant (and part of the pleasure of reading), and what becomes most striking about the *Wake*'s language is the inseparability, even at the lexical level, of these different emphases: in this context 'camelot' points *simultaneously* to Arthurian legend, to Shakespeare (by two routes), and to the New Testament; 'poignings' participates *at once* in proverbial lore (poison), Irish history (Poyning's), Shakespearean allusiveness (poignard), and emotional description (poignant and pinings).[8] The *Wake* can turn the most ordinary word into a pun, so that after 'nihilant' the term 'becoming' refers both to the attractiveness of the girlyhead/curlyhead/ Galahad and to a philosophical theory. The answer to the question – 'A collideorscape!' – is equally ambiguous (and highly relevant): is our 'human being' looking at something real out there – a landscape of collisions (history, myth, family life, politics, religion, a changing rainbow) – or at something that he has created himself by shaking the kaleidoscope, a projection of his own interpretative activity, a colourful dream? (Notice, though, that the only dreams mentioned as such in the passage are the ones that the *Wake* both invites and resists, 'the dreams of accuracy'.)

The *Wake*'s moments of self-reference, then, replicate rather than resolve the multiplicity of perspectives the book offers in such abundance. Our innocent reader will doubtless note that one of its self-images is the dream, but will have no reason to privilege this over all the others that are available: the letter, the manifesto, the midden, the illuminated page, the photograph, the ballad, the children's game, the television programme, the riddle, the radio broadcast, the bedtime story, the geometrical theorem, the anecdote, the quiz show, the lecture, the homily, the mailbag . . . the list could go on as long as the longest list in *Finnegans Wake*.

It would seem unnecessary to spend time emphasizing something so obvious as the undecidable polysemic richness of the *Wake* were it not that so much commentary pays little more than lip-service to this property, before going on to press the claims of this or that particular

---

[8] I have discussed the operation of the Wakean portmanteau more fully in *Peculiar Language*, chapter 7.

and exclusive reading. We seldom think through the consequences of Joyce's having written, with great effort, a text whose meanings occur in the form of alternatives between which it is impossible to decide. I shall return to some of these consequences later, but it is time to move on to my second section and my second proposition.

SECOND PROPOSITION

The second proposition, which follows directly from the first, is this: the importance of the idea of the dream to our understanding of *Finnegans Wake* at the end of the twentieth century is a direct historical consequence of extratextual commentary, by Joyce and by others. It ought to be possible to trace this history, and to ascertain whether it proceeds from actual engagements with the text or, driven by needs other than accurate representation, in parallel with the text but at some distance from it.

For nearly four years, from early 1923, when Joyce began work on his last book, to late 1926, by which time he had perfected his stylistic technique, completed versions of twelve of the seventeen chapters, and worked out an overall structure, there is very little evidence to suggest that he associated his laborious project with the night, sleep, or dreams. He frequently explained what he was attempting, especially in correspondence with Harriet Shaw Weaver, and although the structure which was emerging involved nightfall at the end of the ALP chapter and a series of evening scenes (in June 1926 Joyce mentions plans for 'children's games, night studies, a scene in the "public", and a "lights out in the village"' (*Letters* I, 241)), no references to sleep or dreaming as a key to the technique or content of *Work in Progress* occur in his letters, or are reported, during these years. It might even have been his brother's hostile reaction to the project which put the idea into Joyce's head; in 1924 Stanislaus had called it a 'nightmare production' (*Letters* III, 102), and Joyce wrote to Weaver in April 1926, 'My brother says that having done the longest day in literature I am now conjuring up the darkest night' (*Letters* III, 140). In any event, when in November of 1926 Pound expressed his dismay with the growing work in characteristically forthright terms, and Weaver, too, indicated doubts, a deeply hurt Joyce had recourse to the idea of sleep as an explanation for the writing that was baffling even his friends and supporters: he defended what he was doing to Weaver in the well-known statement, 'One great part of every human existence is passed in a state which cannot be rendered sensible by the

use of wideawake language, cutanddry grammar, and goahead plot'
(*Letters* III, 146).

Sleep and dreams still do not seem to become a prominent motif in
discussion of *Work in Progress*, however. The most extensive publication
of extracts began in *transition* in April 1927, and towards the end of that
year the magazine began publishing a series of articles on the new work.
It is significant that these take very little advantage of the notion of the
sleeping mind in their undisguised attempts to gain acceptance for what
Joyce was doing: of the twelve pieces that had appeared by February
1929, only Budgen's (in the summer issue of 1928) makes a brief reference to the experience of dreams and sleep.[9] These essays formed the
basis of *Our Exagmination Round His Factification for Incamination of Work in
Progress*, published in May of 1929 with Joyce's encouragement, and it
may have been the author's participation that produced the slight
increase in the number of references to sleep and dreams; not only does
Budgen now have two-thirds of a page on the subject, but Jolas has
about a page. However, the notion is still largely absent from the book;
eight of the other essays make no mention of it, and the other two – by
Llona and Sage – contain a passing reference each.[10] To these sparse
references between 1926 and 1929 one can add a few others,[11] but the
strong impression one gets is that by 1929 the idea of the dream had
become an explanatory strategy which Joyce occasionally took advantage of, and allowed others to use, but that it was of considerably less
importance to him than, say, Viconian views of history. (As early as 1923
Joyce had suggested to Harriet Weaver that the answer to the puzzle of
his new project lay in the historical theories of Hegel and Vico, as well as
the idea of metempsychosis (*Letters* I, 205).)

After the publication of *Our Exagmination*, however, the attractiveness
– both to Joyce himself and to others – of the idea of nocturnal
experience as a way of explaining the peculiarities of *Work in Progress*

[9] See the essays by William Carlos Williams in no. 8 (November 1927), Elliot Paul in no. 9
(December 1927), Eugene Jolas in no. 11 (February 1928), Marcel Brion in no. 12 (March 1928),
Frank Budgen and Stuart Gilbert in no. 13 (summer 1928), Robert Sage, Thomas McGreevy, and
John Rodker in no. 14 (fall 1928), and Robert McAlmon, William Carlos Williams, and Eugene
Jolas in no. 15 (February 1929).

[10] See Beckett, *et al.*, *Our Exagmination*, 45–6, 91, 101, and 155–6.

[11] In 1927 Gorman refers to 'the differing degrees of the mind at sleep in the night' (*Critical Heritage*
II, 367); in 1928 AE writes of the 'strange slithery slipping, dreamy nightmarish prose' (*Critical
Heritage* II, 396); and Padraic Colum, in his preface to the 1928 publication of *Anna Livia Plurabelle*,
notes that 'the work in its entirety deals with what is nocturnal – with the night-side of our lives,
and with no other side' (xix). It is interesting that this comment by Colum, which ends his
preface, seems not to follow from the preceding discussion, as though it were the product of
external suggestion rather than his own reading.

appears to have grown.[12] Doubtless, the few hints about sleep and dreams in *Our Exagmination* were more useful to readers than discussions of medieval poets or Enlightenment philosophers, while Beckett's famous formulae ('His writing is not *about* something; *it is that something itself*' (14) or the 'absolute absence of the Absolute' (22)), however appealing they became in the post-structuralist era, must have seemed to many as baffling as the writing of *Work in Progress* itself. The idea of the dream offered a simple and effective strategy of recuperation: here was a categorization by means of which the suspension of the normal rules of language and literature could be excused, and Joyce's book placed in quarantine so that it could mount no challenge to the reading of other books, whose task was the quite different one of dealing with the daylit, wide-awake world. There are several reports of Joyce appealing to this idea in his last years.[13]

There is a significant extension of the idea of the dream still to be accounted for, however. The essayists in *Our Exagmination* concentrate largely on the language and technique of *Work in Progress*, and neither in their discussions nor in any of Joyce's recorded or reported comments (at this time or later) do we find the suggestion that the new work concerns *a* dream or *a* dreamer, *a* night or *a* day-and-night period. There is nothing about a series of dreams or a box of dreams-within-dreams either, let alone any references to a drunken publican asleep above his bar in Chapelizod one spring night. The nearest we come to a suggestion from Joyce that the book represents a single dream, perhaps, is a remark by Dr Dan O'Brien which Adaline Glasheen reports at second hand (*Third Census*, 92) to the effect that *Finnegans Wake* is 'about' – these are Glasheen's sceptical quotation marks – Finn lying dying next to the Liffey while history cycles through his head; a remark which

---

[12] Thus C. K. Ogden refers to 'the timeless condensation of the dream' (x–xi) and the 'night mind of man' in his 1929 preface to the Black Sun edition of *Tales Told*. Others who refer to the night or the dream in 1929 are Padraic Colum (*Critical Heritage* II, 488), C. Giedion-Welcker (*Critical Heritage* II, 498), and Michael Stuart (*Critical Heritage* II, 500, 505). And 1930 sees references by Leon Edel (*Critical Heritage* II, 406), Rebecca West (*Critical Heritage* II, 536), Stuart Gilbert (*Critical Heritage* II, 539), and Padraic Colum (*Critical Heritage* II, 543).

[13] See, for instance, the comments recorded by Ole Vinding in 1936 and by Jacques Mercanton during the late 1930s (Potts, *Portraits*, 149, 207–9, 213). Not all of Joyce's 'explanations' give prominence to the idea of sleep, night, or dream, however. A different emphasis emerges from the comment reported by Eugene Jolas, for instance: 'I . . . am trying to tell the story of this Chapelizod family in a new way. Time and the river and the mountain are the real heroes of my book. Yet the elements are exactly what every novelist might use: man and woman, birth, childhood, night, sleep, marriage, prayer, death' (*JJ* 554). Here night and sleep are only two elements in a longer list. Of course, reports of conversations with Joyce are likely to be distorted in the direction of the reporters' own favoured interpretative stances.

points rather more clearly to the metaphor of the river and to Viconian cyclic history than to the idea of a dream. (Ellmann appears to have embellished this report in incorporating it into his biography, and to have assimilated it to the idea of the dream; he tells us, without identifying his source, that Joyce informed a friend that 'he conceived of his book as the dream of old Finn, lying in death beside the river Liffey and watching the history of Ireland and the world – past and future – flow through his mind like flotsam on the river of life' (*JJ* 544).) Many of the reports of the role of the dream in the *Wake* in fact seem opposed to the idea of the single dream: Harriet Weaver commented to James Atherton, for instance, 'My view is that Mr Joyce did not intend the book to be looked upon as the dream of any one character, but that he regarded the dream form with its shiftings and changes and chances as a convenient device, allowing the freest scope to introduce any material he wished – and suited to a night-piece' (Atherton, *The Books at the Wake*, 17). Ole Vinding reports Joyce as saying in 1936, 'There are, so to say, no individual people in the book – it is as in a dream, the style gliding and unreal as is the way in dreams. If one were to speak of a person in the book, it would have to be of an old man, but even his relationship to reality is doubtful' (Potts, *Portraits*, 149). 'It is as in a dream' is not the same as 'It is a dream', and to name – reluctantly – 'an old man' as a character is to put him within the text and not outside it as a dreamer. Louis Gillet's report accords with these: Joyce, he states, gave him 'the clue to his work. He explained the mystery of his immense H.C.E., this unrivalled hero, thick-textured, of boundless embodiments, whose master-key character lends itself to all kinds of metamorphoses and is up to every role, like a kind of universal Fregoli. He spoke of the language he had used in order to give to vocabulary the elasticity of sleep, multiplying the meaning of words, playing with glisterings and iridescences, making of the sentence a rainbow where each drop is a prism assuming a thousand colours' (Potts, *Portraits*, 178).

Where, then, did this idea of a single individual's single dream arise? Was it the product of careful readings of the book when it finally appeared as a whole in 1939?

It seems not. Seven months after the publication of *Our Exagmination* – with nine years of work still ahead for Joyce – there appeared a brief description of the new book. In December 1929, *The New Republic* printed an essay on Joyce by Edmund Wilson, which ended with a discussion of *Work in Progress*. Wilson's summary of what the book would contain when it appeared provided a simple explanation for Joyce's complicated proceedings: 'It is a sort of complement to *Ulysses*; Joyce has said of it that, as *Ulysses* deals with the day and with the conscious mind, so his new work is to deal with the night and with the subconscious. The whole of this new production is apparently to occupy itself with the single night's sleep of a single character' ('James Joyce', 91).

Wilson thus presents the new book as a symmetrically opposed companion to *Ulysses* (in the process misrepresenting the latter as a book about the day), and follows through the logic of this symmetry by claiming that the new book will also be limited to a single short span of time. In one respect, it is to be even simpler than the earlier work: instead of reflecting the minds of a number of characters, it is to remain with one consciousness (or unconsciousness) throughout. Wilson is even able to name and place the dreamer: 'The hero of the night's sleep in question is, it would appear, a certain H. C. Earwicker, a Norwegian living in Dublin' (92). That 'apparently' and 'it would appear' are intriguing: they half-suggest that these ideas come from Joyce himself, but leave open the possibility that they are Wilson's own deductions.[14] Wilson clearly followed the gradual appearance in print of *Work in Progress* very carefully: in 1925 he had written an article on 'James Joyce as a Poet' for *The New Republic* which included a long quotation from the recently published 'Anna Livia Plurabelle' section – and even this early he was making guesses about the structure of the book, here that it was to begin with 'a description of the River Liffey chattering over its stones' (*Critical Heritage* II, 322–4).

There is, however, no evidence that Joyce communicated any clues to Wilson about *Work in Progress*. Joyce had written gratefully to Wilson after the latter had reviewed *Ulysses* in 1922, but when Wilson wrote to Joyce in 1928, while preparing to write the essay that was to appear the following year, to ask for a copy of his 'outline of *Ulysses*' and for information about publication of the new book, he received only a somewhat curt and uninformative dictated reply.[15] In the absence of evidence for any other source, then, one has to assume that the idea of the single dreamer's single dream, and the location of the whole book in one sleeping head in Chapelizod, is an invention of Wilson's dating from

[14] John Bishop cites a letter of Joyce's to Harriet Weaver in 1927 as evidence that Joyce conceived of the book as a publican's dream: '"The vintner's dream" is a phrase that Joyce used himself to characterize this passage (and, presumably, the *Wake* as a whole)' ('Reading *Finnegans Wake*', 257 n4). But Joyce's phrase does not refer to the passage on which he is commenting, let alone the whole book; it is part of a gloss on a single word: 'bottles (battles) = the vintner's dream of Satan & Michael' (*Selected Letters*, 322).

[15] See Edmund Wilson, *Letters on Literature and Politics*, 179–81, and Joyce, *Letters* I, 264–5.

1929.[16] A trigger for Wilson's theory can be conjectured, however: a month before his essay appeared, *transition* had published the last chapter of Book III, the chapter which figures most prominently in all attempts to pin the text down to a specific time and place and dreamer. The same issue contained an extract from Stuart Gilbert's forthcoming book on *Ulysses*, with a footnote which states that '*Work in Progress*, which deals exclusively with the night-hours, is thus the complement of *Ulysses*, an epic of the day' (130 n1).[17]

In any event, Joyce did not explicitly repudiate the newly provided narrative framework, though he was later to complain about some of the details of Wilson's post-publication review of *Finnegans Wake*, and the notion that the entire book was going to represent a night's dreaming began to make frequent appearances – especially after 1931, when Wilson's essay was republished with some revisions in his widely read *Axel's Castle*. Michael Stuart, for instance, also in 1931, reveals to his readers a few more specific details: the work is to be a 'miniature *universal* history as recalled by a sleeping Dubliner in a series of dreams lasting from about eight o'clock in the evening till four in the morning'.[18] (One wonders if this specificity is an effect of the Linati schema for *Ulysses*, published not long before by Gilbert.)

When in 1939 the whole text eventually appeared, the critics were well prepared to envelop it in the protective embrace of the dream theory – though the massive, wildly diverse, and inconclusive book can hardly have been what the promulgators of the 'single night's dream' idea were expecting. (Wilson had supposed in 1929 that 'the book is to end with [the hero's] waking up' (93).[19]) Wilson himself was quick to provide what must have been for many the definitive account of the book, first in two parts in the *New Republic* in the year of publication, and

---

[16] Arthur Vandevelde, in 'De dromers en de Wake', argues that the idea of *Finnegans Wake* as a dream 'does not stem from a close reading of the text', and although he disclaims any knowledge of its origin, he does implicate Edmund Wilson (though he cites nothing earlier than 1939) (112). One can only speculate, of course, on what suggestions Wilson might have received from friends he and Joyce had in common, notably Eugene and Maria Jolas, and Padraic and Mary Colum.

[17] In 1931 Max Eastman reported a conversation with Joyce, in which the latter contrasts *Ulysses* as 'a day in the life of a man' with *Finnegans Wake* as 'the night'. The difference in articles may be significant (*Critical Heritage* II, 417). Vinding's record of a similar comment has 'the' for both day and night (*JJ* 695).

[18] 'Mr Joyce's Word Creatures', *Colophon*, Part 7 (1931); reprinted in *Critical Heritage* II, 567–9. It is interesting to note that Budgen, in his discussion of *Work in Progress* in *James Joyce and the Making of 'Ulysses'* (1934) (282–313), makes no reference to the 'single night's dream' idea, though he does again refer the book's unusual effects to the experience of dreams.

[19] When he revised the essay for *Axel's Castle* he decided to be more cautious: 'Are we to leave him on the verge of waking or are we finally to see the fantasies of the dream closed down into the commonplace fate which we have already been able to divine?' (233).

later in another highly successful collection of his literary essays, *The Wound and the Bow*, published in 1947, as well as in Seon Givens's collection, *James Joyce: Two Decades of Criticism*, in 1948. The title of the essay has possibly been as influential as its content: 'The Dream of H. C. Earwicker'.[20]

The idea of the dream and the dreamer can be traced, then, by a somewhat circuitous route, back to Joyce; it seems likely that he planted it in some form in the heads of three or four of the *Exagmination* contributors, and when he saw it burgeon so promisingly he may well have given it further encouragement in conversations. But he refrained from public explanatory pronouncements; as with *Ulysses*, he seems to have preferred any advice on reading the *Wake* to come from some source other than the author. It is always easier for readers to discard interpretative guidance, should they find it inadequate to their needs, if they do not see the author standing behind it. (The intentional fallacy may be susceptible of demolition by theoretical argument, but as Joyce knew, direct authorial comments have a habit of dominating the text in a way that no theory can dislodge. As we have already noted, one of the striking features of Joyce's two big books is their lack of metatextual signposts; in the *Wake*, apart from the two words of the title and the Paris dateline at the end, all words are equal – none offers itself as a more secure term by which to explain the others.) The particular framework of a single night's sleep by a single individual seems, however, not to be a Joycean suggestion, but the result of American critical ingenuity, in-creasing the book's accessibility by means of a framework which at once renders it *more* like conventional novels – it is about an ordinary man and his family – and *less* like them – it belongs to the strange world of the dream. In both these ways, its apparent oddness is constrained and controlled.

What is also evident is that the interpretative approach which takes the *Wake* to be a dream is not, historically, the product of a close analysis of the text, since the text did not exist when this approach started on its highly successful career. Had Joyce picked on another aspect of his work to explain its bizarre form – and there were many to choose from – the critical history of the *Wake* (and the way it is commonly read today) might be different. Let us imagine, for instance, that Joyce had never

---

[20] Another early reviewer who referred to the 'publican's dream' framework was Harry Levin, who was probably following Wilson (*Critical Heritage* II, 693–703). Levin's 1939 review, which gives much less prominence to the idea than Wilson's, was praised by Joyce (*Letters* III, 464, 466, 468, 470).

mentioned dreams or sleep, but on several occasions indicated that he was interested in the language of jokes and slips of the tongue. Instead of turning first to Freud's *Interpretation of Dreams*, commentators would turn to *Jokes and their Relation to the Unconscious* and to *The Psychopathology of Everyday Life*.[21] They would no doubt be impressed to find that at the beginning of the former, serving as Freud's starting point in analyzing the structure of the joke, is nothing other than a portmanteau word. And as the argument turns from 'innocent' to 'tendentious' jokes, the materials of the *Wake* flow forth in profusion – guilt, hostility, family relationships, political quarrels . . . and all, of course, manifesting in one way or other the unconscious sexual impulses that it is possible to see as primally active in the *Wake*. Freud's study of slips of the tongue would be equally fertile; the *lapsus linguae* is a perfect analogue for the fall that recurs throughout the *Wake*, producing deformations that at once conceal and reveal unconscious drives and desires. In this scenario, our keys to the *Wake* would show that the book is concerned throughout with the uttering (and writing) of language that is both nonsense and sense, like the Freudian joke and the slip of the tongue, where the pleasure is both a childlike pleasure in the nonsense that has been wrought out of adult forms, and an adult pleasure in the sense that can be retrieved from childish nonsense. At the heart of the verbal deformations, it would be demonstrated, are the impulses and desires we are obliged to hide from ourselves as adults, and as builders of civilization: the sexual and aggressive urges that are initially directed towards those closest to us, and are then displaced onto others beyond the family or the national group. We laugh because those potentially destructive forces have been rendered nonsensically harmless – for a moment – through language, that same language which can itself be a potent means of domination and destruction. An account of the *Wake* along these lines would undoubtedly mention dreams as a third form in which the unconscious manifests itself, but a form less relevant to Joyce's text than jokes and parapraxes for two obvious, if not always acknowledged, reasons: unlike the other two, and unlike Joyce's book, the dream is a largely non-verbal and non-comic text.

THIRD PROPOSITION

It might seem that my third proposition should be something like this:

---

[21] Among those who have used these works in discussing the *Wake* are Paris, 'L'agonie du signe'; Rabaté, 'Lapsus ex machina'; and Norris, *The Decentered Universe*, ch. 5. An exemplary discussion of Joyce's use of Freud's case histories is Ferrer, 'The Freudful Couchmare of ∧ d'.

there is no internal evidence to support the use of the dream as the overriding interpretative context for *Finnegans Wake*, and no historical evidence to suggest that it was of major importance in the writing of the book, or that it arose from a close reading of the whole work; it should therefore be abandoned henceforth. But that is not the conclusion I wish to draw; in fact, such a conclusion would rely on precisely the kind of logic – the absolute separation of internal and external – that the *Wake* itself undermines. I would prefer to emphasize how productive the idea of the dream has been, in spite of its inadequacies as an interpretative frame, in creating an audience for one of the most complex of all literary texts, and in allowing commentary to flourish in the face of a work that might have been greeted with silence. To show, as I did earlier, that standard interpretative procedures applied to the text in isolation from any specific preconceptions do not foreground the notion of the dream is not to dismiss that notion as useless or invalid. It may be that standard interpretative strategies have no purchase on *Finnegans Wake*, and that we *have* to read in terms of some prior framework, derived from critics or from Joyce himself. It may be that what we think of as conventional interpretative strategies working on the text in isolation *always* make more use than we realize of already acquired schemata, and that what the *Wake* does is merely to render us conscious of this fact. If this is so, the concept of 'correct' interpretation is complicated for every work of literature: different assumptions produce different readings, each of which may be perfectly correct in terms of its prior set of assumptions. If I read the *Wake* as Earwicker's dream, I will make a certain sense out of it that will be different from the sense which would emerge if I read it as the passage of the river or an exploration of jokes or the wheeling of the Viconian cycles; and in none of these cases would it be true to say that the framework emerges unaided from the text itself. Nor can we simply dispense with interpretative contexts and read line by line for local pleasures – even local pleasures depend on an interpretation in terms of something less local (the rules of English, the conventions of narrative, assumptions about the proper names in the text, and so on), and if the text works cumulatively, as most of those who enjoy the *Wake* would insist, it must do so by building up larger schemata into which to fit specific details.

We can find a familiar parallel in the history of *Ulysses* criticism. Had Joyce never made public the Homeric titles of his chapters, there can be no doubt that a large proportion of those who are at this moment reading the book around the world would be undergoing a different experience. One reason for this is that the Homeric titles provide an interpretative context for the often difficult writing of the chapters, and for the structure of the book as a whole, that seems to work. If readers who tried to make use of the titles in this way had found that the text remained as strange and structureless as before, it is reasonable to assume that the Homeric schema would have withered away. (As it is, some elements of the published schemata are perceived as relatively arbitrary, and tend to be ignored – even though the text is dense enough to allow an ingenious commentator to justify all of them, and probably in any order).[22] But it would also be true to say that if these titles had appeared with less impressive authorial credentials – merely as one critic's suggestions, say – we might also be reading the text differently, since we would then find it easier to set aside the specific Homeric parallels, and this would open up more freely other possible interpretative contexts. In other words, our reading of a text is historically conditioned by the tradition of commentary within which it comes to us, and the emphasis we give to the different possibilities which that tradition allows is governed not just by the degree to which each seems to work for us, but also by the degree of authority we assign (perhaps unconsciously) to their various sources. It is therefore always a useful exercise to challenge accepted interpretative contexts, as I have done with regard to the idea of the dream; such challenges help to free interpretation for fresh scrutiny of the text and new thinking about its implications. The same cause is aided by playing down the significance of authorial comment – either by a theoretical argument against intentionalism or by a sceptical examination of reported comments in their historical context. It is likely that the new interpretations thus made possible will be less geared to a project of assimilating and regularizing what is difficult and unorthodox. But what we cannot claim is that we are replacing *error* with *truth*.

With the *Wake* we have both a more overdetermined text than *Ulysses*, allowing numerous alternative interpretations all to seem convincing, and a wider range of only semi-authorized frameworks – Viconian cycles, the family in Chapelizod, the language of the night, and so on. It is in the nature of the text to allow none of these dominance over the others, as I have already argued with respect to a specific passage; Joyce did not spend some sixteen years weaving multiple threads into his work only to have a single one emerge as supreme over all the others.

---

[22] In this spirit, Daniel Ferrer demonstrates that a number of the techniques assigned in Joyce's schema to other chapters are just as valid for the 'Sirens' episode as the '*fuga per canonem*' which is its official technique; see 'Echo or Narcissus?'

However, we can still conduct meaningful and valuable discussions about rival frameworks – not in order to settle, once and for all, upon the right one, but to ascertain which are useful in which particular ways. How well particular approaches work is also a matter of time and place, since our interpretative practice is imbricated with all our other intellectual and social practices, which change as we change, and as our own historical and geographical contexts change. The dream framework served a useful purpose in acclimatizing readers to Joyce's eccentric text, but I would argue that intensive critical and textual work on the *Wake* – and much else that has happened since it was published – has rendered it a less satisfactory interpretative scheme now than it once was. It either offers too little to the interpreter (the whole book is a dream seen entirely from the inside, in which case all the interpretative work remains to be done), or too much (the book is the dream of a particular individual at a particular time and place, in which case all its details have to be traced back to a single character's waking life). As an explanation of language and technique it is little more than a metaphor (less useful, perhaps, than the metaphor of the unconscious to which it is related); as a narrative backbone it leaves large parts of the text unaccounted for.[23] At this point in the history of our culture we do not need to be shielded quite so much from the assault which the *Wake* makes on our general habits of reading, and we are more able to understand it as an exemplification rather than a denial of the special qualities of literature.

My third proposition, then, is that the notion of the dream as an interpretative context for *Finnegans Wake* is one among a number of such contexts which, though incompatible with one another, all have some potential value. Or to put it another way, *Finnegans Wake* is, indeed, a 'collideorscape'. The question of the relative usefulness of these approaches cannot be separated from the cultural history from which they arise and in which they are, and always will be, embedded.[24]

Attempts to revive the flagging fortunes of the dream as an explanatory context for *Finnegans Wake*, therefore, have a significance which they would not have had twenty or thirty years ago. John Gordon's *Plot Summary* shows that it is still possible to proffer an interpretation – presented as *the* interpretation – by using the notion of the dream in a

---

[23] For further discussion of the dream and narrative structure, see chapter 8 of my *Peculiar Language*, especially 210–17.

[24] This is why the reading imagined in my first proposition – a reading 'without any prior assumptions as to the content and method of the book' – is, strictly speaking, impossible; as readers we are constituted by a particular cultural history, and our reading of any book is governed (both limited and made possible) by the interpretative context that history provides.

literal-minded way, tracing elements in the text back to a mundane setting (a pub in Chapelizod, a day in late March 1938, and so on). Gordon follows another familiar convention by tracing elements back to Joyce's life as well; thus we learn, in a bizarre mingling of the literary and the biographical, that 'the Original Sin of *Finnegans Wake* is the act of intercourse which produced Lucia Joyce' (81). As so often, the idea of the dream licenses some complex specular manœuvres: here the dream is dreamed both by James Joyce and by his father, the former dreaming that he is the latter dreaming of being the former (92). The book seems too long to be a deliberate parody of *Wake* criticism, but it is perhaps as parody that it performs its most useful function, for it demonstrates how easily interpretations of this kind may be generated out of the mound of meanings that constitute the *Wake*. The arbitrariness with which Gordon carves a route through Joyce's text carries with it the shadow of a hundred other interpretations, all as committed and all as capable of massing evidence in their favour.

John Bishop's study, *Joyce's Book of the Dark*, is another matter altogether, although it too could be called 'literal-minded'. Its project is to treat as seriously as possible, and to push as far as possible, Joyce's reported remarks about the importance of the night and sleep in *Finnegans Wake*, and to avoid some of the obvious weaknesses of the dream framework by insisting that a night's sleep, understood literally, is not the same thing as a dream or even a series of dreams. Though Bishop lays much emphasis on Joyce's comments, he advances no case, historical or theoretical, for using them as a basis for interpretation.[25] More important than the question of Joyce's authorization of this or that interpretation, however, is whether Bishop's way of dealing with the text itself is convincing and useful (it can only be the latter, of course, if it is the former). What is particularly impressive about Bishop's study is that it is not an attempt to simplify or bracket off the *Wake*; the pleasurable difficulty of Joyce's text (and of the author's deep involvement with it) is evident on every page of this long and intricately argued book. Much of his discussion uses strategies of interpretation which represent something new in *Wake* criticism, while at the same time throwing light on earlier attempts to make sense of the book, and it is these that I wish to focus on. The main innovation in Bishop's critical method is a practice

---

[25] Bishop is also prone to exaggeration; he claims, for instance, that 'Joyce himself, whenever he was asked to clarify the book, problematically said that it was "about the night"' (*Joyce's Book of the Dark*, 19), and asserts that the notion that 'the dreamer is a single sleeping man' (as opposed to other kinds of dreamer) 'is most consistent both with Joyce's remarks on the subject and with the remarks of Joyce's co-workers and publicists (Budgen, Gillet, and all the writers represented in *Our Exagmination*)' (417 n3). As we have seen, the evidence supports neither of these contentions.

of weaving together in the construction of an argument fragments from all parts of Joyce's text, irrespective of their place in the sequence and the contexts from which they have been prised. To give one small example, in a chapter entitled 'The Identity of the Dreamer' we learn that '**H**owth **C**astle and **E**nvirons' designates, 'in Joycean terms, Dublin as it has been swallowed "schlook, schlice and goodridhirring" (7.18–19 ["hook, line, and sinker"]), interior to a body that has "disselv[ed]" under "the **H**elpless **C**orpses **E**nactment" of sleep into the elements of "**h**allucination, **c**auchman, **e**ctoplasm" (*FW* 423.31, *FW* 133.24)' (*Joyce's Book of the Dark*, 142). Bishop has thus assembled into a sentence of his own phrases from page 3, page 7, page 608 ('disselving'), page 423, and page 133 of *Finnegans Wake*; notice too that the word which knits these diverse elements together – the word 'sleep' – is Bishop's own addition. In this way phrases which belong to quite different sentences serving quite different ends are used to convince the reader that the book concerns the sleeping experience of a single character.

It will immediately be evident that this is a reading technique of enormous power, allowing the interpreter to choose freely from the *Wake*'s vast accumulation of words and phrases; and if it can be used to substantiate the idea of the *Wake* as 'night language' it could be made to work equally well for many other competing interpretative frames.[26] The technique is not, however, entirely new, since uncertainties about the function of context and sequence in the *Wake* have always allowed interpreters some freedom in constructing arguments on the basis of selective quotation. The tradition of reading *Finnegans Wake* as a dream has, as I have tried to show, always necessitated playing rather fast and loose with the text that Joyce published. We might say that what Bishop has done is to challenge those who are dubious about such methods to demonstrate that context and sequence matter at all in the *Wake*.[27] Is Joyce's text simply a kaleidoscope, which the reader can shake into any

[26] If Bishop is to convince his readers that the particular network that he has woven out of the *Wake*'s words is superior to any other that might be created, he has to show that it is in some way more salient in the text than all the others. This he attempts, once more, by exaggeration; he thus keeps informing his reader that a certain theme occurs on 'virtually every page' of the book. According to Bishop, it would be hard to find a page that did not contain references to all of the following ideas (I am following his example in bringing together statements made in different places of his book): bed or night (28–9), the body of the sleeper as a landscape (37), blindness, deafness, dumbness or numbness, or the objects of such imperception (49), death or burial (73), alcohol (137), a dark visual image (if I understand a rather obscure paragraph) (222–3), hearing (273), children's affairs (322), Swift's 'little language' (322), and eggs (375). Are these really more common than words having to do with sex, or water, or crime, or history, or war, or writing, or buildings, or Irish place names, or Scandinavia, or a host of other repeated topics?

[27] Somewhat inconsistently, Bishop retains the idea that the *Wake* has a plot lasting the duration of one night, which means that sequence is, at some level, important to him.

pattern he or she finds pleasant, or is a rigorous reading possible, and if so, by what canons would it be assessed?

Another example of the dangerous power of the interpretative methods seemingly allowed by the *Wake* is to be found in Bishop's handling of portmanteaux. Like all interpreters, he gives many examples of the multiple meanings, all of them relevant, contained within a single portmanteau, but he also frequently uses a strategy of negation to rule out certain legitimate possibilities. Thus we learn that "'recoil" is *not* "recall" (quite the contrary); "Headmound" is *not* "Edmond" (quite the contrary); and "Taciturn" (*FW* 17.13), whose mouth is firmly shut throughout the length of sleep, is *not* "Tacitus'" (*Joyce's Book of the Dark*, 51); or on another page "'tautaulogically" (not "tautologically")' (158); or on another "'gaylabouring" (*FW* 6.23 (*not* "daylabouring"))' (172). In other words, Bishop assumes the hermeneutic right to decide for each portmanteau whether it works by fusing different meanings together as equals or by privileging a single one over the others. On the same page as the second example just given, he quotes Joyce's 'recorporated' and adds '(and "recuperated")', which must provoke us to ask why he does not add '(*not* "recuperated")'. Again, this is an interpretative technique which could be used to justify a number of readings of the *Wake*, and it is not so different from the way in which Joyce's portmanteaux have often been selectively treated in the service of particular interpretations.[28] And again we are forced to ask how we might introduce greater rigour into our interpretative practice, a goal which we will not achieve until we recognize the degree to which that practice is determined (inevitably) by factors outside the text we are reading.

Gordon's and Bishop's books dramatize the problem of *Wake* interpretation (and of all literary interpretation) by taking to an extreme methods which have traditionally been used to reduce the recalcitrant heterogeneity of the text. If they do not convince as readings which should displace all other readings, it is because the very intensiveness of their interpretative activity reveals the massive capacity of the *Wake* to

[28] In discussing the passage from the quiz show earlier I indicated how the passage might be skewed in different directions by such selectivity. Bishop would find much grist to his mill in this passage: as well as the obvious references to sleep and dreams, we could note the frequent suggestions of a state of negativity or non-being: 'vacants', 'hapless', 'dinmurk', 'unstant', 'redissolusingness', 'mindmouldered', 'nihilant', 'dimm'. But this would have overriding significance only if there were not a greater number of references to life, growth, change, colour, smell, and other phenomena suggesting the opposite of unconsciousness. Passages less obviously concerned with sleep and night than this one, though no doubt they would yield some of the themes Bishop focuses on, would provide far fewer examples.

be interpreted, which in turn raises the spectre of a host of interpretations, each as minutely justified as the last. But this is not just a problem of *Wake* interpretation, it is (one aspect of) an interpretation of the *Wake*: for among the many kinds of dream which the *Wake* is about is the dream of interpretation (or, we might say, the dream of accuracy), the dream that we will be able to find in a text a structure of pure meanings that has its own separate being, and that can be contemplated apart from the letters through which we reach it and the contexts we provide to make those letters meaningful. The *Wake thematizes* this dream again and again: it is full of searches for significance, origins, sources, truth, none of which reaches its goal, because these things exist in and not beyond the symbols by means of which they are represented. The *Wake* also *enacts* this dream, by inducing its readers to carry out the same search, over and over. We never give up, and should never give up, the pursuit of pure meaning, even while we know it is a rainbow created by our own perspective on the ceaseless torrent of language. The *Wake* is not a peculiar text in this regard; it is a text which brings home to us – in the most pleasurable way imaginable – how important and how impossible is the dream of meaning that runs through both our days and our nights.

CHAPTER 12

The Wake*'s confounded language*

This talk was given at the 1986 James Joyce Symposium in Copenhagen, in a panel entitled '"Finnegans Wake" and the Language of
Babel'.

Not far from the venue of the Tenth International James Joyce Symposium is a church, Vor Frelsers Kirke, with a superb eighteenth-century
spire, so constructed that around the outside of it a stair spirals discon-
certingly to the top. There is no truth, my guidebook reassures me while
inviting me to make the ascent ('in good weather only'), in the legend
that the builder fell to an untimely death from his newly completed but
not entirely stable tower. But if the story is untrue, how has it gained
sufficient currency to merit an official denial in a guidebook? And why,
in any case, should a guidebook, whose function is to enhance my
pleasure by giving me facts about the objects I see, waste its space with a
legend I am told to dismiss as false?

Evidently, the story of the hapless builder, irrespective of its historical
accuracy, has a vivid appeal which strongly colours the sightseer's
experience of the fantastic spire – an appeal that springs no doubt from
its connection with the wide-ranging family of mythic and literary texts
that work and rework the motif of the building of the tower and the
consequent fall. (Leaving James Joyce out of it for the moment, three
texts we might think of are the eleventh chapter of Genesis, Ibsen's play
The Master Builder, and the ballad of Tim Finnegan.) One way of
representing the force of this motif is to see it as a parable which teaches
the virtue of humility: to build a tower, or to climb a ladder, is to attempt
to rise above one's proper station, and the dizziness that seizes the
mortal who ascends to such heights is the voice of a god – a jealous god,
no doubt – who feels his mastery threatened; or, in more modern terms,
it is the inner voice that whispers to us, just at the fatal moment, that our

technology can never be adequate to our desires.

But we must remind ourselves of the alternative construction which could be placed upon the myth. The tower from which the builder falls is one which has reached the very limits of human capacity; one from which the builder did *not* fall would, by virtue of that fact, be less lofty than it might be. Part of the attractiveness of these stories about builders – the sons of Noah, Tim Finnegan, Solness the Master Builder, the creator of the spire of Vor Frelsers Kirke – is that they invite us to take pleasure in humanity's capacity to arouse the envy of the gods, in the fact that our desires can always outstrip our technology. From this perspective, the Fall is necessarily fortunate, not, as the Christian tradition would have it, because it brings forth otherwise unattested Divine mercy, but because by its own daring it makes manifest the prohibition it transgresses against, and in doing so exposes the hidden power structure – whether we call it the force of God or the force of Nature – within which humanity is obliged to operate.

One of the significant differences between the myth of the first Fall and that of Babel is that the latter is the story of a collective struggle with Divine power, not an individual one. And what the myth identifies as the source of strength of the collective is *language*; it is this that makes possible the development of the technology of brick making, described in some detail in Genesis chapter 11, which leads in turn to the plan to 'build a city and a tower, whose top may reach unto heaven' (AV, 11.4.). But this, interestingly, is not the ultimate aim; we seem to circle back to the power of language, since the purpose of the magnificent city (Hebrew 'Babel' is, of course, Greek 'Babylon') is to 'make us a name, lest we be scattered abroad upon the face of the whole earth' (AV 11.4). The people's fears are, it turns out, quite justified: the Lord reflects on the power which a shared language gives to a community, and is not happy with the prospect. 'Behold, the people is one, and they have all one language; and this they begin to do: and now nothing will be restrained from them, which they have imagined to do' (AV 11.6). He therefore confounds the language of the people, and thus fragments the collective and takes away its power. They do indeed make a name for themselves, but the name is 'Babel', which the Yahwist associates punningly with Hebrew 'balal', or confusion.[1]

The myth of Babel expresses a yearning for a condition of perfect

---

[1] Tim Finnegan's upward mobility is also related to both language and bricks: the ballad informs us that 'He had a tongue both rich and sweet, / An' to rise in the world he carried a hod'.

mutual intelligibility, for a language of total communication shared by all humanity; a utopian community in which no misunderstanding could occur and therefore no strife. Humankind is prevented from attaining such a state not by its own weakness but by a law imposed from outside; to be thus would be to be as gods. Language is therefore our bane when it could be our salvation. Babel signifies both the imaginable possibilities and the actual limitations of collective existence; the word *Babel* in English has come to mean both 'a visionary scheme' and 'a confused medley of sounds'.

It is a commonplace that our post-Babelian condition is more fully evinced in *Finnegans Wake* than in any other linguistic artefact; one of its most notorious features is the cacophony of various languages, sometimes miraculously chiming but more often multiplying dissonant meanings in a confusion of noises. The tireless work of explicators has reduced that dissonance by showing that what at first sight seems an array of discordant meanings is often an elaborate harmony, and one might say that the vision which (consciously or unconsciously) has encouraged *Wake* explication over the years has been the same one that underlies the Babel myth: the dream of achieving a reading in which all the languages of the *Wake* will speak to one another lucidly and comprehensibly, and thus become one language, a new super-language that will unite divided humanity once more, at least in the aesthetic realm. This vision, the explicatory enterprise assumes, was Joyce's vision: *Finnegans Wake* is his tower of anti-Babel, designed and built to counter the destructive act of the jealous god who drove the nations apart, and to bequeath to the world an artefact which, by making out of the kaleidoscope of languages a new tongue and a new name to hold humanity together, will succeed where the sons of Noah failed. If much of the *Wake* sounds to us as Babelian confusion, this must be – so it is assumed – because we are still locked in our monoglot cultural prisons, lacking the energy and enterprise to follow Joyce in his multilingual architectural feat of total unification.

We are not, of course, talking only about the interpretation of *Finnegans Wake*; what is at issue is the hermeneutic drive itself, the urge to translate what is apparently 'confused' into a language which will be entirely transparent, to unweave the polyglot textual fabric into the monoglot thread. The hermeneutic hope is that the Lord will be more lenient this time, and allow the city of mutual intelligibility to be built by means of the new technologies of interpretation and translation (which are, of course, closely related activities). The Babelian texture of the

Wake offers the greatest possible challenge to the interpreter and translator, one fundamental problem being, as Jacques Derrida has pointed
out in discussing Joyce's use of the Babel myth ('Two Words', 155; 'Des
Tours de Babel', 170–1; and 'Table Ronde', 132–3), that the most
successful translation/interpretation of Wakean words will, by definition, be the least successful at relaying a fundamental property of the
text: its being in more than one language at once. But as long as Joyce's
book is seen, like every other book, as intended for, and amenable to,
complete explication, the hermeneutic faith will doubtless survive.

We find, then, that there are two competing uses to which the myth of
the fall from the tower might be put; it could be taken as an encouragement to accept the imperfections that surround us (including the impossibility of perfect communication) as the justly imposed and unavoidable condition of our existence, or a call to regard them as something
unjustly willed upon us (or culpably allowed by us to come into being)
which it is our prime duty as a human collective to overcome. I could
respond to my guidebook entry by lamenting the sad tale of architectural ambition outstripping technical capability or by admiring the
sacrifice that taught others the way forward to more solidly constructed
towers. (Among the larger systems of belief that would tend, respective-
ly, in these directions would be some kinds of Christianity and some
kinds of Marxism.) From the first perspective, the language of *Finnegans
Wake* produces an ironic comedy inviting laughter at our shared ridicu-
lousness and mutual incomprehension (if not an unreadable tragedy
reflecting despair at our hopeless condition); from the second, it constitutes a celebratory comedy demonstrating our potential for imaginative
fertility and mutual understanding.

Faced with these two opposing views, we might, in good Hegelian
fashion, look for a more comprehensive perspective which will at once
explain the contradicting positions and, without rejecting them, move
beyond them. They both, it seems to me, arise from the same conception of language, a conception which cannot be made to cohere with the
way language works in practice. Language is widely seen, in both
popular and scientific understanding, as fundamentally and constitut-
ively a matter of intersubjective communication: a procedure of coding
and decoding pre-existing mental contents, which, if the linguistic
machine is working properly, remain unchanged by the passage from
one mind to another. The efficiency of the procedure depends on the
arbitrariness of the relation between signifier and signified: what matters
is that the code is sufficiently complex and subtle to encapsulate all the

details of the mental contents, and iconic or symbolic relationships would only interfere with this. It is arbitrariness which makes possible the existence of more than one language (since there is no signifier more or less appropriate for any given signified), but it is also arbitrariness that makes possible all types of translation (including interpretation, which translates one text into another more readable text), since the mental contents are assumed to remain constant, and only the way they are encoded varies.

To hold this view of the nature of language is, of course, to be puzzled and disappointed by the empirical evidence, which suggests that the communicative procedure fails more often than it succeeds; there always seems to be some contingent reason why a given utterance is unable to yield wholly and truly its burden of meaning. (I leave aside the vexed problem of how one would ascertain that anything which could be called a completely successful act of communication had in fact occurred.) Particularly unsatisfactory in its failure to communicate a stable pre-existing meaning is the written utterance, and most of all what is called the 'literary text' – with *Finnegans Wake* as the worst offender of all. Hence the two attitudes I have sketched: resignation at the necessary imperfections of a non-ideal world, or hope that technological improvements (better languages, more efficient channels of communication) or sociopolitical advances (increased human solidarity, perhaps) might eventually reveal to us language in its true form, as it should always have been.

A different view of language, however, would not produce this disparity between the idea and the experience; a view that I shall not expatiate on now since it has become familiar, in various versions, in the writing of a number of philosophers and literary theorists, but could be broadly described in terms of its rejection of the communication model and its emphasis instead on language's constituting and conditioning force. Not just an instrument neutrally serving objects and intentions, language operates in and upon the world in a host of different ways, and is already implied in any possible mental content. The literary text, far from being the most aberrant instance of language, is the instance that reveals its nature most clearly, as an endlessly retranslatable complex of signifiers, existing as part of a set of public, and political, institutions, themselves caught in a process of constant transformation. And, in this respect, as in many others, *Finnegans Wake* is the most typical and the most revealing of all literary texts.

The myth of Babel, from this wider perspective, is a story Western culture tells itself to account for the failure of its own model of language to match up to the reality it experiences; language has to be judged as fallen from its true self, whether necessarily or unnecessarily, if the belief in this model is to be sustained. (The difference between intralingual and interlingual failure of comprehension is not a significant one; we can take the story of Babel as referring to the institution of several languages or to the making imperfect of the communicative processes within any single language.) But *Finnegans Wake* retells the myth, a number of times, from a different perspective: neither lamenting language's fall nor trying to secure its recovery, it finds its pleasures in the knowledge that language, by its very nature, is unstable and ambiguous.[2] (The irreverent treatment of artificial world languages like Esperanto and Volapük in the *Wake* functions in a similar way.) Once the belief in a pure communicative language has been abandoned, the sharp difference between monoglot and polyglot discourse disappears; any language is many languages – a Babel of registers, dialects, older and newer forms, slang and borrowed items, accents and idiosyncrasies – and all that the *Wake* does is to extend this logic to its comic extreme. True, no single reader could assimilate all the *Wake*'s languages; but no single hearer could assimilate all the languages – no doubt confused and contradictory languages – that I give utterance to, knowingly or unknowingly, each time I produce an everyday statement.

As Laurent Milesi points out in an informative article entitled 'L'Idiome babélien de *Finnegans Wake*' ('The Babelian Idiom of *Finnegans Wake*'), there is a reference early in the *Wake* to the traditional number of nations – and hence languages – on earth, a reference which reminds us that a linguistic item will have as many meanings as there exist codes in which to place it:

So you need hardly spell me how every word will be bound over to carry three score and ten toptypsical readings throughout the book of Doublends Jined. (*FW* 20.13–18)

But this, of course, is true of every word of every book, not just of our circular story of Dublin's giant. Babel is a condition of all language, not

---

[2] One of Budgen's anecdotes is worth quoting in full:

Joyce once told me (it was during the composition of *Finnegans Wake*) that he thought he had found the meaning of the Tower of Babel story. If I had done my bounden duty I should have been ready with 'what?' and 'how?' and 'tell', but, slow of wit and more apt to ruminate than to ask, I let the occasion slide, so that what Joyce thought was the true inwardness of the Biblical story is anybody's guess. ('Resurrection', 12)

It is perhaps just as well that Budgen's inquisitiveness failed him at this point, since *Finnegans Wake* itself stands as a much richer exegesis of the story of Babel than could have been communicated by even the most meticulous biographer.

just that of the *Wake*, and it is this that provides language with its power to give pleasure and to change the world (by no means incompatible functions). In Joyce's text, the myth of the fall from the shaky tower of Babel may be read, like all the many falls in the book, not as a moral lesson in humility, not as a symbol of defeated human aspiration, but as an instance – comically transformed – of the way we represent to ourselves in language language's refusal to be a mere instrument of transcendent intentions or desires.

CHAPTER 13

Envoi: judging Joyce

A COMMITMENT TO JOYCE

Looking back over these various attempts during the past fifteen years to register the effect, or rather effects, of Joyce on my own thinking and on literary theory and literary culture in the latter part of the twentieth century, I am struck by the unfailing basis on which they all rest: the unquestioned assumption that Joyce's writing is to be enjoyed, admired, and learned from rather than weighed in evaluative scales and pronounced good, bad, or a mixture of the two. This is in part no doubt a matter of personality: a tendency, which I have been aware of in other areas of my experience, to plump for something (a poem, a book, an author, an institution, a country) – often after an extended process of examination and appraisal – in such a way as to give it the benefit of the doubt in further judgements, and to interpret uncertain evidence in its favour at least until negative indications accumulate beyond any denying.[1] (I should make it clear that, one's judgements of people resting on another basis than one's judgements of books, my predilection in favour of Joyce's writing does not extend to his character as we receive in it biographical commentary, a character in which there is clearly much to dislike – though I see little point in spending one's time finding fault with Joyce's behaviour or his attitudes. It will be evident, too, from the foregoing chapters that I also feel no particular allegiance to the critical traditions which have given us the 'Joyce' we read.) This general

---

[1] I am sure I am not alone in this tendency; indeed, it corresponds quite closely to the cultural mechanism producing both stability and change that Thomas Kuhn describes under the name 'paradigm shift' – evidence is interpreted as far as possible in favour of the existing paradigm, but the amount of accumulating negative evidence eventually reaches a point at which this process is no longer possible, and rather rapidly a new paradigm is established that accounts better for the totality of the known facts. Of course my tendency to avoid evaluative criticism could also be partly explained as an aspect of the rejection, discussed in the introduction, of my early Leavisian training.

predisposition in favour of Joyce does not mean, of course, a uniformity of enthusiasm; I have my favourite passages and my less well-liked ones, and at different times I would rather reread this book or chapter than that one.

It is not just a matter of personality, though. Or to put it more cautiously, I am able to produce arguments of a more theoretical nature in favour of this way of treating the complex artefacts and institutions we encounter in our daily experience, and I would like to think that all these are not just rationalizations of a wholly untheoretical character trait. I am, after all, not unusual in my lack of negative criticism: almost everything that has been published on Joyce during the same period has proceeded on its business of interpretative exegesis, historical mapping, biographical exploration, pre-textual investigation, political commentary, or whatever it might be, without seeing any reason for questioning the fundamental proposition that Joyce's work is a fully achieved artistic success and a highly valuable contribution to our cultural life, and often our moral and political life as well.[2] (Later in this chapter I shall consider some exceptions to this generalization.) The philosophical argument in favour of this consistency would run something like this: all judgements are necessarily coloured by prior, often unacknowledged, assumptions, so the idea of a programme of constant objective assessment is an illusion, often a dangerous illusion. Of the various kinds of prejudice, a prejudice in favour of something is most likely to contribute to a realization of its potential value. Different people find themselves drawn to different things, and since we commit ourselves to one entity at the expense of all the others we fail to commit ourselves to,[3] this diversity of commitment ensures the maximization of potential value in a variety of entities. The fact that any object to which I am positively drawn is likely to provoke a negative response from someone else acts as a check on excessive attachments, and provides reassurance that the critical spirit will remain alive in the intellectual community.

There is also an argument for this kind of approach that could be called ethical, especially if we think of ethics as a domain distinct from the codes and norms of morality.[4] This argument might be sketched in

---

[2] One reason for the relative absence of negative criticism of Joyce may be the sheer difficulty of his work, which has made exegesis a dominant, and lasting, critical mode. Richard Poirier notes that 'there have been far fewer persuasively critical than doggedly interpretive readers of twentieth-century or modernist classics', and relates this to the promotion of difficulty as a virtue in modernist writing (*The Renewal of Literature*, 98).

[3] For a forceful account of this 'logic of sacrifice' see Derrida, *The Gift of Death*, 68–71.

[4] In many works, most famously in *Totality and Infinity* and *Otherwise than Being*, Emmanuel Levinas

terms of *alterity* and *trust*. If to act ethically is to respond with justice to the other, this must involve *both* a careful weighing up of the evidence *and* an acknowledgement that the evidence is always inadequate, necessitating what we might term, to rephrase Kierkegaard, a leap of trust in the other.[5] Many of the unfailingly positive responses to Joyce's work arise not from a belief that it is without faults or potentially dangerous effects but from an initial, and continually sustained, *commitment*, which exceeds any objective assessment of aesthetic, moral, or political worth. The parallels with the kinds of commitment we make to other persons, or, sometimes, institutions or communities, will be evident. Normally, there is a built-in safeguard in the knowledge that others have made and will make different commitments, and will remain critically alert to all the possible failings in the object of *my* commitment; so that, looking at the wider picture, the judgements we all make ensure that both the potential value and the inevitable limitations of a wide variety of judgeable entities is registered. We can only, of course, make this leap of trust if we find ourselves in some way summoned by the other, called to respond to it, and much therefore remains beyond our conscious control in this process; but it is possible to prepare the ground, to develop one's receptivity to what might come (though it will still take us by surprise if it is genuinely other) – and equally possible to close oneself in advance to the chance of the other's arrival. If someone tells me, 'I've never been able to appreciate Joyce', I am ready to believe that for solid reasons of individual character, taste, cultural background, and so on, Joyce's writing is simply unavailable to that person; but it is always possible that part of this response is a failure of openness to an alterity that would challenge cherished habits or assumptions.

Of course there are dangers in such a procedure. The attempt to do justice to any person or to any human product always involves risk, because judging, if it is not to be a mere calculation, is a decision made without firm and conclusive grounds. Judging negatively carries the same risk as judging positively; I have no doubt that my dislike of a number of books and authors has robbed me of potential rewards (that I might have both benefited from and passed on to others), just as my enthusiasm about Joyce has blinded me to certain failings in his work. There is an asymmetry, though, between these two kinds of response: a

presents such a notion of ethics. I have discussed the distinction between ethics (in this sense) and morality, as well as the relevance of a Levinasian ethics to the reading of literature, in 'Innovation, Literature, Ethics'.

[5] See Derrida, 'Force of Law', and Attridge, 'Trusting the Other', for elaborations of this sentence.

positive judgement is much more likely to result in careful and extended reading and rereading, and perhaps written commentary, whereas a negative judgement is likely to result in dismissal. What is more, once a critic or a culture has made a large investment in an author, he, she or it is likely to continue to produce positive judgements in a variety of forms and forums. This self-propelling engine produces the familiar disproportions of canonization: the disparity between the attention lavished on certain authors and the lack of attention given to others bears little relation to what might be thought of as their 'actual' merit, though this would be more accurately conceived of as their *potential* merit – value being precisely what is conferred by the processes of canonization.[6] Joyce's work, it seems reasonable to say, has had more of its potential value realized than a great number of other bodies of writing.

What I have outlined above, and attempted to defend, is a particular kind of responsibility to Joyce, or more accurately to Joyce's work, the demands of which I have experienced for many years, and some of the results of which are collected in this volume. But as we pass beyond the year 2000, and we find it possible to say with the likelihood of a fair measure of agreement from readers in many parts of the globe, 'James Joyce was the most important writer of the twentieth century', I am forced to wonder if the safeguards I've described still operate in this case. Saying good things about Joyce (or working on Joyce with the implication that he is worth a great deal of time and effort) has become such a profitable pastime that it seems to have made it all but impossible for counter-voices to emerge, or to be heard if they do emerge. When a body of work has gained such massive international endorsement, when a single artist is the subject of such an extensive and meticulous critical enterprise, is it not time for critics to direct their energies elsewhere, to look for other writers who teach and entertain us in different ways, ways perhaps more appropriate to the needs of the twenty-first century? If, as I argued in the introduction, the best readings of a work or *œuvre* are those that are as responsive to the particularities of their own time and place as they are to the work itself, it may well be that our new millennium, and our increasingly globalized culture, demand that we at least raise some questions about the critical attention we continue to give to Joyce.

There is, it won't be difficult to see, a personal dimension to this sense that it is time to scrutinize the point which has been reached by Joyce

---

[6] I have discussed these processes of canonization in 'Oppressive Silence'.

criticism (and I shall be using the word to cover all types of critical and scholarly activity, including textual scholarship, biographical investigation, and the production of reference books and guides as well as studies of the published works and their cultural and historical contexts). When I started reading Joyce in the 1960s, his reputation, though solidly established in North America (thanks partly to the successes of the New Criticism in schools and colleges), was by no means assured in Britain or in Ireland, and part of the motivation for teaching and writing about him was the sense that his achievements deserved more recognition than they were getting. Now that his face appears on Irish currency and his books on syllabi all over the world, this incentive no longer exists. What is more, when I first wrote and spoke publicly about Joyce I was conscious of a certain insularity in the bulk of Joyce criticism, an unwillingness to take account of important developments in literary theory and philosophy that were making their mark on other regions of the intellectual world. But for some time now, new theoretical initiatives have been quickly registered in Joyce criticism – perhaps sometimes too quickly, before they have been fully understood and worked through.[7] So that motivation has gone too. In asking about our responsibility in the face of Joyce's fame as the millennium begins, then, I am asking, first of all, about my own responsibility.

In taking up these questions, I don't intend to embark on a sociological or literary-historical account of the rise of Joyce's reputation, the early founding and huge success of the 'Joyce industry', the proliferation of Joyce's texts on syllabi and reading lists, and so on. Much interesting work on these topics has been done, and a great deal more waits to be done. We don't have an answer to the question 'Why Joyce?', and perhaps we won't have an answer until he loses the special position in our culture and in many of our personal histories that makes detachment so difficult. The answer that would be most illuminating would be one that is disengaged from the issue of *desert*: a dispassionate account of the features of Joyce's writing and the twentieth-century cultural history within which it found a place (and upon which it had such an effect) that has no stake in arguing whether or not he deserved his triumph. And the issue of desert is closely linked to the issue of *pleasure*: those who enjoy Joyce's writing are thereby disqualified from making, or being seen as making, a neutral investigation – but so are those who don't enjoy it, in

---

[7] In the autobiographical part of the introduction I decribed the easy absorption by the Joyce critical establishment of the post-structuralist innovations I was championing in the early 1980s, and the successive waves of theoretical approaches that followed.

defiance of the massive cultural pressure to do so.

My aim, rather, is to take Joyce's status as a given, and to ask about the demands (aesthetic, ethical, and political) this status makes upon readers and commentators. I speak as an unashamed admirer and enjoyer of Joyce's work; if there has to be a big name in twentieth-century literature, I'm quite happy that it should be Joyce, and that so many people should have read his work as a result. Of course, the corollary that Joyce's works are huge money-spinners has had unfortunate effects, such as the distortion of the editorial endeavours that ought to represent a disinterested zone of careful scholarship – but that's another story.

AN INDUSTRY WITHOUT LIMITS

One view that is heard from time to time is that Joyce criticism has reached the point of exhaustion; so much has now been written about him that the returns are getting smaller and smaller. Consequently, the argument goes, there is no need to make any special effort to counter the critical domination which Joyce exerts; it will fade of its own accord when there is nothing left to say.

This view depends on a particular understanding of the critical and scholarly enterprise, which I have already touched on in chapter 1. When one is starting on a career as a scholar and critic, it's a common, and perhaps even a necessary, mistake to think of one's work as leading, together with the work of one's colleagues, to a solid edifice which will stand as a firm and unchanging basis for further building projects. Each stage in this process, one assumes, will lead the scholarly community closer to the goal of full and final exegesis together with textual stability and historico-biographical certainty. From this perspective on critical practice, the massive accumulation of commentary on Joyce can only be dispiriting: after the deployment of so much skill and the expenditure of so much effort, surely we should be approaching something like a full understanding and appreciation of his work. As unexplored areas become fewer, explications more accurate, and critical judgements sounder, the avalanche of books and articles should be slowing down. But the very opposite seems to be happening.

There are several reasons for this. One is the fact that, although the number of different commentaries on Joyce seems bewilderingly large, it is only a tiny proportion of the *potential* number. Even works significantly less complex than Joyce's – in terms of linguistic elaboration as well as historical and cultural allusiveness – allow of a huge variety of critical responses. We like to think that, because there are so many books on Joyce on our library shelves, there has been a logical progression whereby important topics have been systematically covered and gaps gradually filled; but in fact authors' choices of subject and editors' and publishers' decisions about publication are in large measure the product of pressures and contingencies that have nothing to do with intellectual or cultural need. Think how many biographies of Joyce *could* be written, each quite different from the last; how many editions of each of his books could be produced; how many textual details could be explored, how many critical approaches employed, how many intertextual and historical connections drawn. The graduate student embarking on a dissertation on Joyce is likely to survey the array of secondary literature and feel despairingly that there is virtually nothing left to be done. What we actually have, however, is a small, and rather random, selection of what is possible according to current canons of critical activity.

A second reason why the model of a closer and closer approach to full understanding is not appropriate is that it fails to take the essentially temporal and spatial nature of the cultural field, a topic I discussed in the introduction, into account. That is, the meaning and value of a cultural object – such as *Ulysses* – is a product of that object's interaction with a specific cultural matrix, and cultural matrices vary across time and space. Of course, the temporal and spatial continuities involved here can be extensive – there are some respects in which the original cultural contexts in which Aristotle's or Tagore's work became known are, because of historical connections that span centuries and miles, the 'same' cultural context within which I am speaking today – but they can also be very limited. Next-door neighbours can, quite legitimately, respond to a single text as a wholly different entity, because they receive it within very different cultural matrices, despite their temporal and geographical closeness. The cultural artefact as it is most generally understood – the *Ulysses* that we can discuss and argue over – is constituted somewhere between the extremes of the adjacent-simultaneous and the global-millennial. We are able to treat the object in this way because we come at it at a spatial-temporal level which allows for a fair degree of agreement while leaving open possibilities for disagreement – disagreements which are often not about the object as such but about the appropriate set of determinants within which to read it. At this level the work is relatively stable, and it is easy to forget how much of its meaning and its value depends on where and when we find ourselves at the time of reading. The consequence of the temporality of the cultural object is that Joyce's works, like any artefacts sufficiently rich in their relations to their constituting context, can never be exhausted: after a certain measure of time (in a given place) the object is no longer the same object, and commentary has a new task. In fulfilling its new task, commentary also helps to constitute the object anew. The humanist *Ulysses* is partly displaced by the formalist *Ulysses*, the post-structuralist *Ulysses*, the historicist *Ulysses*, the postcolonial *Ulysses*.

I say 'partly displaced' because we are not dealing with a succession of quite differently constituted works; the sedimented history of readings often persists in its effects, complicating and sometimes enriching current readings. An interpretation of *Ulysses* that can be said to do justice to it in the specific context of the late twentieth century will be alert to its engagement with Ireland's history as a metropolitan colony, but will also take account of its destabilization of the norms of Enlightenment thinking, its formal intricacy, and its convincing representation of the inner lives of human characters. However, working against this survival of past modes of commentary is a third factor that prolongs the critical endeavour: the ease with which we forget what has been written, and write it over and over again, using a newer vocabulary to articulate the same insights. Because the library of Joyce criticism is so vast, there is very little chance that a critic writing today will track down *everything* that has been said on his or her chosen topic; and as the critical history grows longer and longer, the opportunities for recycling increase.

The fourth and final factor behind the increasing productivity of Joyce criticism that I want to mention is a simple but often overlooked truth: the more that is written about a topic, the more there is to write. Every fact invites a further exploration, every judgement a counter-judgement. Not long after Joyce has become a topic for critical writing, Joyce criticism becomes a topic. If the avalanche ever subsides, it will not happen because there is less to say about Joyce and what has been made of Joyce. On the contrary, there is more and more to say about Joyce every year because more has been said – more to build on, more to disagree with. This is part of the explanation for the exponential growth in secondary material that occurs when an author reaches a certain level of canonical prominence, Shakespeare being the most obvious instance. The 'Shakespeare' who is the subject of Stephen's disquisition in the National Library is neither the historical individual nor the sum of his texts; he, or it, is a compound and hardly homogeneous figure produced to a large degree by a series of biographical studies – Brandes, Harris, Lee, and so on – which Stephen (and Joyce) have read, and which provide raw material for further speculation and embroidery.

The new millennium is not likely to bring a diminishment in the quantity of books and articles on Joyce, then.[8] Much of the huge potential for commentary will remain to be tapped; cultural and historical shifts will permit hitherto unforeseen ways of reading; older readings will be forgotten and repeated in new guises; and the mass of existing texts about Joyce, in conjunction with the increasing availability of original documents, will provoke further texts, which in their turn will provoke yet more. There is not much substance to the argument that Joyce criticism has virtually exhausted its topic, and that it is time to turn to other things. If it is true that downsizing would be appropriate in the Joyce industry, it is not because of an imminent drying up of supply or of demand.

A JOYCE COME TO JUDGEMENT

Let us turn, instead, to a different question. My suggestion is that those of us who feel committed to Joyce in the way I have described should attempt to stand back from him, to bracket as far as we can our admiration and enjoyment, and to ask what possible negative consequences follow from the pre-eminence of this particular author within the cultural arena. We might, for instance, ask how the current cultural hegemony exerted by his work matches up to the values embodied in his writing, as we now perceive them. Don't the comic deflations of *Ulysses* and *Finnegans Wake* have a bearing on the eminently serious endeavours of Joyce scholars and editors around the world? How does Joyce's domination of twentieth-century reading lists square with the sympathy for the underdog and the suspicion of authority manifested in his writing? Although it's hard to imagine Joyce himself ever being pleased by a move to dislodge his name from the pinnacle it currently occupies, it could be argued that his global prominence, and the consequent demotion of a number of other writers equally worth our attention, constitute a large-scale instance of the kind of closing off of opportunities that a number of his works dramatize and derogate. (Think of all the lives in *Dubliners* that are confined and limited by those in the social sphere who wield influence and authority.) This is one of the oldest

---

[8] This conclusion could be rephrased in personal terms: my past experience leads me to believe that as long as I am prepared to write on Joyce there will be things I want to say, things that, as far as I know, have not already been said. Hence the need to ask different kinds of questions about the value of continuing to make Joyce a critical focus.

games in the critical book, of course, and one that I have often played: using the values embodied in Joyce's work (as perceived by the critic) as a means to expose weaknesses in the approaches of others, including approaches that, it is claimed, praise Joyce for the wrong reasons.

But such a strategy of displacement, while it would use Joyce's warrant in order to turn away from Joyce and devote one's energies to other writers, would still in a sense leave him unchallenged as the pre-eminent figure, proved yet again to be ahead of his time, foreseeing all our critical and ethical needs. What is more, the general point that the dominance of one author results in the occlusion of a number of others tells us nothing specific about Joyce. Should we not, in assessing Joyce at the millennium's end, aspire to something more nuanced by way of critical judgement than the simple cry of *Basta!*?

Another responsibility, I would suggest, is laid upon us: we have to try to distance ourselves further from our enjoyment of Joyce's work and our involvement in the seductive Joycean milieu in order to ask: are there aspects of Joyce's work that deserve a negative response? Should the conversation about Joyce in the twenty-first century be a debate about strengths and weaknesses, benefits and dangers, as are the conversations about T. S. Eliot, Virginia Woolf, Ezra Pound, Wyndham Lewis, and many other modernist writers? In raising these questions, it is *Ulysses* we need to focus on, since it is above all on *Ulysses* that Joyce's reputation rests. Had he written only the earlier works, he would remain an important twentieth-century figure, but he would not have become the giant we now know. And negative judgements of *Finnegans Wake* are not rare; even if there is seldom a word said against it in the public halls of Joyce symposia these days, there are many complaints in the corridors. It is, I suspect, largely on the strength of *Ulysses'* huge success that the *Wake* has, at least in the past two decades, escaped significant onslaughts in print.

As a way of initiating the process of judgement, let us ask what have been the most persistent and telling critiques of *Ulysses* since its publication, not in order to parry them but in order to assess their merit today. (In doing so, we need to set aside at the outset the numerous objections that have been made on the basis of prudishness, anti-intellectualism, class bias, religious dogmatism, and other prejudices or proclivities which limit the value of the response.) We might think of all evaluations of artistic productions as falling roughly into two categories, though any final separation between them would be impossible: we can call them the *extra-cultural* and the *intra-cultural*. An extra-cultural evaluation judges a work by its likely effects on some domain beyond that of the culture to which it belongs. Intra-cultural evaluations, by contrast, operate in terms of a standard internal to the cultural field in which the work is produced and received; insofar as they are concerned with effects, it is with the effects on the reader in his or her capacity as reader (rather than as religious believer, artist, moral or political agent, and so on), and more particularly as literary reader. (It will no doubt be obvious that I'm putting a lot of weight on a notoriously murky word, *culture*, and that I'm doing this in part, at least, to avoid another murky word, *aesthetic*. This is not the place to defend my practice; suffice it to say that by culture I mean the ensemble of social practices, productions, and knowledges within which what has traditionally been called the aesthetic finds its place, but which embraces much that would be judged unaesthetic, or anti-aesthetic, by traditional norms.)

In defining extra-cultural critiques in terms of the *likely* effects predicated of the artwork, I seek to emphasize that it's only rarely that works are judged by their *actual* effects. One example would be the praising – or blaming – of *Ulysses* for its influence on later writers. Such judgements are more in the nature of sociological than literary judgements; the repercussions that works have on the world happen for a host of reasons, which may or may not have anything to do with features of interest to literary critics or readers.[9] (Many of the events that followed the publication of Rushdie's *Satanic Verses*, for example, failed to throw any light on the text as a literary artefact.) But judging a text in terms of its potential effects (and this often means the effects it would supposedly have if (a) the text itself were widely enough read and (b) the reading proposed by the critic in question were widely adopted) has been a common practice in certain historical periods. There is a long tradition of extra-cultural critiques of Joyce's work, beginning with those early responses which saw it as corrupting and debasing, whether because of its sexual explicitness or its perceived nihilism, or both. An extra-cultural critique is based, of course, on the prior acceptance of certain goals, whether they be religious, moral, or political, which it is felt any work of art should serve.

One strand of such critiques derives its general standards from some variety of Marxism: *Ulysses* has often been pronounced too subjectivist

---

[9] Eliot made the same point in his early essay on *Ulysses*: 'Of course, the influence which Mr Joyce's book may have is from my point of view an irrelevance. A very great book may have a very bad influence indeed; and a mediocre book may be in the event most salutary' ('*Ulysses*, Order, and Myth', *Critical Heritage* I, 269).

and too bourgeois (two related sins) to further the revolution.[10] The names of Karl Radek and Georg Lukács come to mind;[11] less well known (and more balanced) are the critiques of Alick West in 1937 and Arnold Kettle in 1953.[12] 'Second-wave' feminism, especially in the late 1970s and early 1980s, judging Joyce in terms of his representation of women, sometimes found that his writing served to retard progress towards gender equality. Kate Millett, Florence Howe, Carolyn Heilbrun, Sandra Gilbert and Susan Gubar, and others criticized Joyce for his conventional sexist attitudes.[13] Such critiques don't, I feel, carry enough weight at our present moment to contribute towards an argument about the value of *Ulysses*. The hostile Marxists have been countered by other left-wing critics who regard *Ulysses* as a valuable reflection of a certain stage of capitalism (one could cite Franco Moretti's 'The Long Goodbye' and Fredric Jameson's '*Ulysses* in History') or who are unapologetic about their admiration and enjoyment of the book (Raymond Williams would be one example[14]); and the critical feminists have been answered by a large number of others who find in Joyce more to admire than to castigate. There is little evidence that, on the whole, Joyce's work has had a harmful effect upon the societies in which it has been widely read, nor that it has much potential for harm. Whether the claims made for the potential *benefits* a careful reading of Joyce can bring are all justified – and there have been many, humanist, socialist, feminist, post-structuralist, postcolonial – is a different question, which I shall touch on briefly in the last section of this chapter.

AN EXCESS OF TECHNIQUE

To find a way of judging Joyce that has more bite today, we need to turn to intra-cultural critiques. An intra-cultural critique, as I have suggested, attempts to assess the success or failure of the work by measuring it against some standard internal to the cultural field in which it occurs,

[10] A useful survey of Marxist and other left-wing responses to Joyce is given in chapter 2, 'Joyce from the Left: A Brief History', of Trevor Williams's *Reading Joyce Politically*.

[11] For an extract from Radek's paper, see *Critical Heritage* II, 624–6. For other Marxist critiques in the 1930s, see also 'Mirsky on Bourgeois Decadence', 589–92; 'A Communist on Joyce' (Gertsfelde), 616–18, and 'A Marxian View of *Ulysses*' (Miller-Budnitskaya), 654–8. As late as 1957, Lukács attacked *Ulysses* in 'The Ideology of Modernism'.

[12] See Williams, *Reading Joyce Politically*, 18–24.

[13] Bonnie Kime Scott surveys many of these critiques in *Joyce and Feminism*, ch. 6; for Gilbert and Gubar, see 'Sexual Linguistics' and *The War of the Words*, ch. 5 (and my chapter 8 above).

[14] In *Politics and Letters*, Williams asserts the importance of *Ulysses* and *Finnegans Wake* to him and his friends in the Communist Party Writers' Group at Cambridge after 1939 (45), and he continued to admire Joyce's writing – see, for instance, *The English Novel*, 164–8.

most commonly an aesthetic standard (in earlier periods often labelled *taste*) but sometimes a broader one, including – if the cultural field is defined in moral or religious terms – a moral or religious one. Such standards are, of course, culturally produced and hence variable (although this fact is not always appreciated by those who apply them); and a successful work like *Ulysses* to some degree (as Wordsworth put it) creates the taste – or perhaps the moral sense – by which it is judged. I would also argue, along with Derrida, that the 'it' that is being assessed is not a permanently self-identical entity but something more like a repeated event or performance, always changing as the conditions in which it takes place change.[15] Most intra-cultural judgements of Joyce, like most extra-cultural judgements, have been, explicitly or implicitly, positive, whether the standard applied has been that of truth to a certain notion of the historical condition or of human experience,[16] subtlety and complexity of aesthetic ordering, comic effectiveness, or some other measure.

Among the negative evaluations of Joyce on an intra-cultural basis, the most tenacious and widespread (particularly in relation to the later works) has been that there is an excess of technique over content, intellect over feeling, and will over spontaneity. These are closely enough related to be considered a single objection, responding to a single tendency in Joyce's text (though manifested in a variety of ways), and it is this recurrent objection on which I want to focus. Many of those who find today that they cannot read *Ulysses* with any real pleasure experience some version of this unease; and many who do enjoy *Ulysses* can get nowhere with *Finnegans Wake* for the same reason. (There are also those who find most of the later chapters of *Ulysses* – except perhaps 'Penelope' – a disappointment after the earlier ones, because Joyce's technical display becomes harder and harder to ignore or justify in traditional terms.) Some of us relish untangling the delicate threads Joyce has woven together in the later books, while to others it is an excruciatingly tedious business, compared with the insistent onward impulsion in a writer like – to take a name often proposed in opposition to Joyce – D. H. Lawrence. To some degree this must be a matter of individual preferences, the product of familial and social conditioning and perhaps even genetic make-up: sometimes it seems, to parody W. S.

[15] See Derrida, *Limited Inc* and 'Aphorism Countertime'.
[16] Notions of truthfulness or accuracy of representation characterize the entire spectrum of critical/political positions; thus Marxists like Jameson or Moretti value *Ulysses* for its reflection of a crisis of capitalism (although Jameson had earlier found in Wyndham Lewis a more objective image of his time than in Joyce; see *Fables of Aggression*, 57–8 *et passim*), Leavisians like Goldberg value it for its complex instantiation of human experience.

Gilbert, that everyone who's born into the world alive is either a little Joycean or else a little Lawrentian. (As I've already noted, when I was an undergraduate in a fiercely Leavisite English Department in South Africa, I quickly learned to stifle my Joycean tendencies and to pay homage to Lawrence; but the experience didn't turn me into a Leavisian or a Lawrentian. Although both Leavis and Lawrence have lost the central position they held in the schools and colleges of the British Commonwealth for several decades, present-day equivalents are not hard to find.) If it is the case that some such deeply rooted personal predisposition is the real impetus behind a number of elaborate critical arguments, both negative and positive, there is little we can do to allow for it, and we have no option but to weigh up those arguments on their intellectual merits.

The first extended critique of *Ulysses* along these lines is Wyndham Lewis's, in the chapter entitled 'An Analysis of the Mind of James Joyce' in *Time and Western Man*, published in 1927. Although Lewis's overarching argument is that *Ulysses*, like *A la recherche du temps perdu*, is, to its great disadvantage, a Bergsonian 'time-book', much of his criticism is directed at the disparity between elaborate technique and what Lewis sees as banal content. For instance:

What stimulates him is *ways of doing things*, and technical processes, and not *things to be done*. Between the various things to be done he shows a true craftsman's impartiality. He is become so much a writing-specialist that it matters very little to him *what* he writes, or what idea or world-view he expresses, so long as he is trying his hand at this manner and that, and displaying his enjoyable virtuosity. Strictly speaking, he has none at all, no special point of view, or none worth mentioning. (106–7)

Lewis finds Joyce's characters lacking in all interest:

In *Ulysses*, if you strip away the technical complexities that envelop it, the surprises of style and unconventional attitudes that prevail in it, the figures underneath are of a remarkable simplicity, and of the most orthodoxly comic outline. Indeed, it is not too much to say that they are, most of them, walking clichés. (112)

'This conventionality', says Lewis, '(which leaves, as it were, lay-figures underneath, upon which the technical trappings can be accumulated at leisure with complete disregard for the laws of life) is the sign that we are in the presence of a craftsman rather than a creator' (119).[17]

---

[17] Pound, interestingly, appears in 1933 to have agreed with Lewis's complaint that the content of *Ulysses* is conventional (though he finds the technique sufficiently valuable in itself): 'Mr Wyndham Lewis' specific criticism of *Ulysses* can now be published. It was made in 1922 or '23. "Ungh!" he grunted, "He [Joyce] don't seem to have any very new point of view about

Lifeless technique and sterile complexity are also what Leavis finds objectionable in *Ulysses*:

It seems plain to me that there is no organic principle determining, informing, and controlling into a vital whole, the elaborate analogical structure, the extraordinary variety of technical devices, the attempts at an exhaustive rendering of consciousness, for which *Ulysses* is remarkable, and which got it accepted by a cosmopolitan literary world as a new start. It is rather, I think, a dead end. (*The Great Tradition*, 36)

The Great Tradition was published in 1948; fifteen years earlier Leavis had published the review of *Work in Progress* mentioned in the introduction, using terms very similar to Lewis's. For instance, Leavis objected to a comparison that had been made between Joyce's and Shakespeare's liberties with the English language: '[Shakespeare's] miraculous intricacies of expression could have come only to one whose medium was for him strictly a medium; an object of interest only as something that, under the creative compulsion, identified itself with what insisted on being expressed: the linguistic audacities are derivative' ('Joyce and the "Revolution of the Word"', 317). Behind Leavis we may hear his lodestar, Lawrence, whose 1928 comment I cited in the introduction: 'James Joyce bores me stiff – too terribly would-be and done-on-purpose, utterly without spontaneity or real life'.[18]

Boredom, in fact, is the typical experience of those readers who find the technical display oppressive: Leavis finds Joyce's 'subconscious' as exhibited in *Finnegans Wake* 'sadly boring' (319); George Moore is reported as saying of *Ulysses* in 1922, 'I read a little here and there, but, oh my God, how bored I got!' (*JJ* 529); and Jung in 1932 managed to wax lyrical over the apocalyptic boredom produced by the book:

Joyce bores me to tears, but it is a vicious dangerous boredom such as not even the worst banality could induce. It is the boredom of nature, the bleak whistling of the wind over the crags of the Hebrides, sunrise and sunset over the wastes of the Sahara, the roar of the sea. ('*Ulysses*: A Monologue', 114)[19]

anything". Such things are a matter of degree. There is a time for a man to experiment with his medium. When he has a mastery of it; or when he has developed it, and extended it, he or a successor can apply it' (*Critical Heritage* II, 596; from the *English Journal*).

[18] *Selected Literary Criticism*, 149. Underlying Leavis's and Lawrence's intra-cultural judgements is a strongly extra-cultural sense of the importance of literature, of course; writing that is truly alive is also writing that has the power to revitalize what they see as a dying social body.

[19] When the bored critic looks for an adjective to describe the book, it is often 'dull': thus Edmund Wilson, for all his admiration, comments in 1922: 'There must be something wrong with a design which involves so much that is dull – and I doubt whether anyone will defend parts of *Ulysses* against the charge of extreme dullness' (*Critical Heritage* I, 228; from the *New Republic*). Harold Nicolson, in 1931, states: 'At moments Joyce becomes almost overpoweringly difficult to read and, as such, almost overpoweringly dull' (*Critical Heritage* II, 562; from the *Listener*, 1931).

Jung is, however, willing to justify this boredom extra-culturally: for him, *Ulysses* acts as a necessary counter to the sentimentality he feels is rampant everywhere, opposing excess of feeling with complete absence of feeling. Indeed, those who are *not* bored by the book are misreading it, and the fact that it has gone through ten editions in so many years proves that such misreading has been very common:

The book must mean something to them, must even reveal something that they did not know or feel before. They are not infernally bored by it, but are helped, refreshed, instructed, converted, 'restratified'. Obviously, they are thrown into a desirable state of some sort, for otherwise only the blackest hatred could enable the reader to go through the book from page 1 to page 735 with attention and without fatal attacks of drowsiness. (120)[20]

Another early critic of *Ulysses* who, like Jung, balances blame with praise is Rebecca West.[21] She begins the long title essay of *The Strange Necessity*, published in 1928, with an anecdote. Reading a transparently bad poem of Joyce's one day in Paris, she has her earlier suspicions confirmed: 'Mr James Joyce is a great man who is entirely without taste' (15). She goes on to discuss what for her is a consequence of this lack of taste: what she calls 'the gross sentimentality which is his most fundamental error' (15). This may sound like the exact opposite of Jung's complaint; but this is not sentimentality in the usual sense. West describes it in terms that by now sound familiar: instead of 'real creative writing' (17), Joyce's work is willed and calculated. It is governed by narcissism, 'which inevitably deforms all its products with sentimentality, since the self-image which it is the aim of narcissism to create is made not out of material that has been imaginatively experienced but out of material that has been selected as likely to please others' (22).[22]

Complaints about excessive technical complexity in *Ulysses* seem less prevalent in critical studies of Joyce after the 1930s, perhaps in part because 'Work in Progress' and then *Finnegans Wake* made the earlier book seem transparent by comparison, but largely because in the USA –

---

[20] Jameson, in an odd echo of Jung, finds the boredom induced by 'Eumaeus' and 'Ithaca' not a failure on Joyce's part, but a success: 'It is as though Joyce meant here to force us to work through in detail everything that is intolerable about this opposition' – that is, the opposition, hardened under capitalism, between the subject and the object ('*Ulysses* in History', 139).

[21] Austin Briggs provides a corrective to the prevalent idea that West was unremittingly hostile to Joyce; see 'Rebecca West vs. James Joyce, Samuel Beckett, and William Carlos Williams'. He also quotes her statement, appropriate for this chapter, that we have a 'duty of listening to our geniuses in a disrespectful manner' (83).

[22] After this bad start, it doesn't seem likely that Joyce will emerge with much credit; but in fact by the end of the essay West has tipped the scales a long way in the other direction, and *Ulysses* is serving as one of her examples of what she calls 'the necessity of art'.

by this time the source of most serious criticism as it has been ever since
– Joyce's reputation was established and the long project of elucidation
and exegesis (which simply took Joyce's merits for granted) had begun.[23]
The Leavisian inheritance remained powerful in the UK and its colonies, though the effect of this was mostly to inhibit any extended
discussion of Joyce. One exception was the Australian critic Samuel
Goldberg, who attempted a balanced, largely Leavisian, evaluation of
Ulysses in *The Classical Temper* in 1961. Goldberg's admiration is moder-
ated by a distaste for what he calls Joyce's 'busy ant-like industry' (300)
and his 'unintelligent intellectuality' (311); he also cites Lawrence's
complaints (including 'wilfulness' and 'lack of emotional spontaneity')
with approval (309).[24] One of Joyce's limitations as a novelist is 'the
tendency to intellectualize his vital intuitions' (314). Not surprisingly, it is
the later chapters such as 'Oxen of the Sun' and 'Eumaeus' that he finds
most limited (the latter is 'too boring a way of expressing boredom'
(257).[25] Even if we do not find these – or any – chapters of *Ulysses* boring,
technically excessive, over-intellectualized, or too much the product of
the will, critical responsibility demands that we make an effort to
understand these charges, repeated as they have been over several
decades.

A FUTURE FOR *ULYSSES*?

The final intra-cultural critique of *Ulysses* on which I want to focus, and
which will help us to assess the relevance of these charges today, is one of
the few published in the last two decades, and probably the most
significant of them.[26] Leo Bersani published 'Against *Ulysses*' in *Raritan* in
1988 and included it as a chapter of his book *The Culture of Redemption* in
1990. One might have expected an essay by a leading cultural critic of
our time that takes issue with the reputation of Joyce's most highly

---

[23] One exception is Lukács, whose objections in 1957 arose from what he saw as technique for its
own sake in the interior monologue of *Ulysses*, by contrast with Thomas Mann's use of a similar
method in *Lotte in Weimar*, where its purpose is to allow the author 'to explore aspects of Goethe's
world which would not have been otherwise available' ('The Ideology of Modernism', 18).

[24] Goldberg is more outspokenly critical in his volume on Joyce in the 'Writers and Critics' series:
'He was still dogged by the self-image of the "fabulous artificer", the technical virtuoso. And the
result lies visible in the more superficial, mechanical, merely cerebral aspects of *Ulysses*, in the
obvious, laborious "brilliance" that he over-valued – and that led many critics into over-valuing
as well' (94).

[25] Raymond Williams, who writes of *Ulysses*' 'greatness' in *The English Novel*, is probably reacting
similarly when he relates his reservations about *Finnegans Wake* to 'the strains already evident in
the later sections of *Ulysses* (before the last monologue)' (168).

[26] For another example, see Clive Hart, 'Against Joyceanism'.

acclaimed work to have initiated an extended discussion in the many organs of Joyce criticism, and in books and symposia dedicated to Joyce, but there has in fact been very little by way of response: no ripples have appeared in the uniformly positive surface of commentary on Joyce.[27]

Although Bersani's essay is essentially intra-cultural in its arguments, it has an interesting relation to extra-cultural criticism in that it is part of an argument *against* the notion that art has the power to improve the world. Bersani argues that *Ulysses'* failure lies in its very claim to authority, its confidence – shared by most Joyce critics – in its own power to promote the cause of Western culture, the vast intertext in which it situates itself.[28] So Bersani judges that *Ulysses* (like every other work of art) has *no* significant potential to heal the world's wounds, and that its own faith in the potency of literature is a mark against it.

I partly share Bersani's scepticism about the redemptive power of art. I would not wish to deny that works of art can have powerful effects on the cultural/ethical/political world, but I would insist on two qualifications which bring me closer to his position: these potential effects are always unpredictable (potentiality, in other words, does not imply a latent instrumentality waiting to be released), and they are always dependent on readings of the work in question, readings which are themselves – if they do justice to the work – unpredictable. (Once again let me stress that works of art can have, and have had, a host of effects that do not spring from their status as works of art but from other aspects of their make-up.) This effective unpredictability, as I mentioned in the introduction, I see as constitutive of art in the Western cultural tradition; it is closely related to the demand for innovation which is inseparable from artistic creation and to the alterity of the new artwork, or the artwork re-experienced as new. If a work of art *does* have a restorative effect on an individual or a culture, it is not an effect that could have been deduced or foretold with any certainty by a critic, although a critic's work may have been crucial to the particular acts of reading

---

[27] In 'Is There a Case Against *Ulysses*?' Denis Donoghue defends the book against two critics, Bersani and Jameson. He conflates their two very different responses (Jameson, as we have seen, in fact offers a positive assessment in his only extended discussion of *Ulysses*), and reads them as if they were echoes of early Stalinist objections to the book's preoccupation with its characters' subjective experiences. If this were the case being made against *Ulysses* by either Bersani or Jameson, there would be simpler rejoinders than Donoghue's trawl through Saussure, Deleuze and Guattari, Levinas, Derrida, Barthes, Benveniste and Marcuse to find an account of language that does not assume a punctual origin in the subject.

[28] Interestingly, Franco Moretti makes the opposite argument: that the author of *Ulysses* 'considers the aesthetic sphere incapable of being either an example to, or a compensation for, the state of the world' ('The Long Goodbye', 208).

which produced it. The important question, then, is not whether *Ulysses* has had or is likely to have certain consequences in the world, but whether Bersani's description of it as a work which implies certain claims about those consequences is accurate, and if it is, whether the making of those claims constitutes a flaw. ('Accuracy' here, I should add, is not a matter of objective measurement, but of the degree of conviction that the critic's reading can carry among other attentive readers of Joyce at this moment in cultural history.)

Some of Bersani's difficulties with *Ulysses* echo the complaints we have already heard from Lewis, West, Lawrence, Leavis, and Goldberg. His depiction of *Ulysses* as a conventional novel of character psychology disguised as an avant-garde experiment sounds like Lewis. When he calls it 'a text to be deciphered but not read' (175) he sounds like Lawrence and Leavis.[29] And when he speaks of the 'technical machinery' that 'frequently obscures our view of what is happening' (156), he himself acknowledges Goldberg's study of *Ulysses* as a 'notable expression of this complaint' (226 n2). As with many of the readers who find the excess of technique a problem, Bersani fails to acknowledge the degree to which the book demands a way of reading different from that required by most novels, and therefore finds his expectations disagreeably thwarted. For instance, he stresses – quite rightly, I believe – that part of *Ulysses*' lasting popularity rests on the intimacy with which readers feel they come to know Stephen, Molly, and Leopold, but he assumes that this must mean that stylistic features serve as reflexes of character in an entirely conventional manner. The deformed names in 'Scylla and Charybdis', he suggests, arise because Stephen is playing with them in his mind; the style of 'Eumaeus' is how Bloom would write the chapter, and provides us with a fuller picture of his personality. Whatever credence one might give to these examples (I'm not at all convinced by them), they imply a way of reading the stylistic peculiarities of *Ulysses* that is bound to produce confusion and frustration. What the best readings of the book over the past twenty years have taught us is that it is perfectly possible to enjoy the credible minutiae of individual personality and the sense of intimacy they produce without assuming an organic relation between style and character. Joyce's technical extravagances, and the pleasures they offer the reader, are not wholly con-

---

[29] Morris Beja pointed this out in 'Approaching Joyce with an Attitude', his introduction to a panel on 'Hostile Responses to Joyce' at the 1992 Dublin Symposium – one of the rare instances of counter-voices being given a space within the Joyce establishment, even if Joyce tended to emerge triumphant as usual.

cerned with accurate portrayals of people we might meet; without compromising that accuracy, they provide insights – very often comic insights – into the very processes of linguistic representation, historical reporting, psychological theorizing, political programming, and so on.

A related issue is that of the phenomenology of the reading experience: critics like Lawrence, Leavis, Goldberg, and Bersani like to be carried forward in a minute-by-minute flow by the novel they are reading, the elements of their intellectual and emotional apprehension working together in an illusion of continuity and wholeness. *Ulysses* holds up this preference for inspection, as only one of a number of ways of reading; and those who are able to take pleasure in tracking back and forth, skipping and rereading, moving from text to reference book and back to text, sharing partial insights with a group and having them disconfirmed or extended, and simultaneously registering the vividness of the reality represented *and* the comic exposure of the subterfuges of representation, are bound to derive a great deal more from Joyce's writing. Not surprisingly, Bersani finds parts of 'Ithaca' barely readable (as well as being 'relentlessly tedious' (177)) – and it *is* barely readable by the mode of verbal ingestion he prefers.[30]

Notwithstanding these limitations in his approach, I believe that Bersani's critique points us towards an aspect of *Ulysses* that should at least make us hesitate before we triumphantly carry it into the third millennium as the supreme literary text of our time. Particularly useful is his recognition – implicit if not explicit – that it is not *Ulysses* as such (if there were such a thing) to which he is saying a regretful farewell but *Ulysses* as it has been produced by its readers and their changing cultural matrix over the past seventy-seven years. As I have been arguing, the *Ulysses* which we are trying to evaluate in this way is not the book that appeared in 1922, or the book that upset Lewis in 1927 and appalled Jung in 1932, or even the book Goldberg tried to evaluate in 1961. Thanks to the amassed achievements of Joyce critics over several decades, partly in response to the features that disturbed these critics, the *Ulysses* of 2000 is something different: a dense encyclopedic hypertextual web of internal cross-references, historical and cultural allusions, and authorial emendations and accretions, existing not as an isolated linguistic and material entity but as a borderless presence within a continuous expanse of signifiers, visual and aural, textual and graphic, substantial and electronic. Before very long, we (or our wealthier libraries) will be

[30] Curiously, Bersani argues that *Ulysses* teaches us how to read it (163–4) – but he means by the expenditure of effort on exegesis, not by discarding old habits of linear consumption.

able to purchase a magnificent embodiment of this evolved entity (no longer a 'book', let alone a 'novel'): a hypermedia *Ulysses* which, it is promised, will include 'several versions' of the text, definitions, annotations, source works ('such as *The Odyssey* and *Hamlet*'), Joyce's schemas, an archive of critical books and articles linked to specific textual sites, maps, photographs, film clips, songs and sound effects, and a complete audio performance.[31] To read *Ulysses* today as primarily a novel of character and event is to read it against its history, against what it has become. Although Bersani begins his essay by proposing to approach *Ulysses* 'naïvely', he quickly, and correctly, adds that 'this decision can be little more than a ruse' (155). And at the end of the essay he ascribes the erroneous ascription to art of redemptive power not to Joyce's book on its own but to 'the community of *Ulysses* and its exegetes' (178).

Although for many of us this historical transformation of *Ulysses* into a richly varied, unlimited, unboundaried, intertextual fabric has enhanced, rather than diminished, its enjoyability, it may be just this that has rendered Joyce's work less worth our attention as critics. This is not, as I pointed out earlier, because we are left with less to do than earlier critics, but because the hypertextualizing of *Ulysses* has diminished the force of the book that exploded upon the cultural stage in 1922, and made our task a very different one. What those earlier hostile critics were reporting on was *Ulysses'* otherness, its refusal to be assimilated to existing cultural norms, its powerful resistance to the most strenuous interpretative efforts. Many readers quickly gave up; some, like Lewis, West, and Jung, worried away at it even though they had at best very mixed views of what it was doing; and some glimpsed through the intensity of their engagement a new future for literature. Joyce's unprecedented freedom of technique, his unashamed appeal to the intellect, his elaborate and unorganic construction demanded new modes of reading and new ways of understanding the processes on which reading depends.

What Bersani is registering in his essay, on the other hand, for all its echoing of earlier comments, is a problem that exists in the present, thanks to the highly successful labours of the Joyce industry: an excessively cosy relation between Joyce's text and the cultural envelope within which it finds its meanings. Western culture, he comments, 'dies in the Joycean parody and pastiche, but, once removed from historical time, it

---

[31] I am quoting from the advance description of *James Joyce's 'Ulysses' in Hypermedia*, directed by Michael Groden, announced by the University of Pennsylvania Press for publication in 2000. Reports have appeared of a similar project being supervised by John Kidd at Boston University.

is resurrected as a timeless design. Far from contesting the authority of culture, *Ulysses* reinvents our relation to Western culture in terms of exegetical devotion, that is, as the exegesis of *Ulysses* itself' (170). In elaborating his case, Bersani contrasts *Ulysses* with Flaubert's *Bouvard et Pécuchet* and with the writing of Samuel Beckett. Flaubert, he writes (and the comment seems equally apt for Beckett), 'erases our cultural memory at the very moment he awakens it' (163). For these writers, 'the textual act of quotation is simultaneously a disqualification of the citational process'. The work of art 'can only exist in a continuous anxiety about its capacity to sustain itself, perhaps even to begin itself'. For Joyce, however, 'art is by definition the transcendence of any such anxiety' (163); Joyce's intertextuality functions not as an erasure of cultural memory but as a principle of cultural continuity.[32]

I am not convinced that the *Ulysses* of 1922 *did* function as a principle of cultural continuity; it was certainly not received as such.[33] But it may be that the *Ulysses* of 2000 does, that the work of exegesis and commentary, allusion-hunting and cross-referencing, theoretical and cultural placing, though it has inevitably failed to exhaust the text's difficulties, has succeeded only too well in disarming it of its alterity and finding a snug cultural home for it. No longer a challenge to the way we read and think, it has become a triumphal assertion of the scope and integrity of the culture of which it is one of the finest monuments. Where earlier readers grappled with page after dense page, a great deal of it incomprehensible, we turn to Thornton or Gifford, the *Bloomsday Book* or *The Chronicle of Leopold and Molly Bloom*, to ease our passage.[34] It might be

---

[32] In *The Renewal of Literature*, Poirier argues, like Bersani, against a notion that the reading of literature can be a source of cultural renovation; but he adopts a very different attitude to the technical feats of modernist writers, including Joyce. Of the latter he writes, 'No one more brazenly celebrates his own sheer capacity for what James called "doing"' (110); but this is in the context of a claim that the reading of such works is 'an activity by which with great difficulty we can become conscious that any structure, technique, code, or system of signs is likely to prove no more than extemporized and transient' (113). Poirier is surely correct to insist that 'it is not the substance but rather the act of allusiveness or of schematization which should occupy the reader' (107), but it may be that the act of reading *Ulysses*, at least as an advanced student or professional scholar, is no longer the vigorous, demanding, chancy business that Poirier celebrates.

[33] Eliot was a notable exception, but there is every indication that he was responding to the *idea* of *Ulysses* (or his idea of *Ulysses*), and not to the text, and that few others shared his sense of the book's culturally wholesome character.

[34] It is evident, I trust, that I am not finding fault with these and other guides and reference books; my concern is only with their unintended effects. Most of them represent meticulous labours that have been of inestimable help to me and to innumerable other readers, and they are an entirely necessary department of the Joyce industry. And perhaps one should note that it only takes a group of astute readers, armed with all the reference books, to tackle a few paragraphs of *Ulysses* to discover how much remains speculative and challenging.

objected that we do not have to read *Ulysses* in this way, through the lens of reference books and exegetical texts, but there is certainly great pressure to do so; and there would be something disingenuous, as Bersani notes, about pretending they didn't exist. It might also be said, and this would be a fair comment, that the book as Joyce wrote it must have contained the potential for such a fate (as perhaps *Bouvard and Pécuchet* did not); I would add, however, that this was not a necessary destiny, but depended on unforeseeable cultural changes – for which it was partly responsible. Nor is this just a matter of the fate of one book. Culture thrives on constant innovation, on the unpredictable, unprogrammable coming of the other, the original artwork, critical study or philosophical argument, which changes all the rules, again and again. Culture in turn is imbricated with the political, ethical, and social domains, and so – even if we refrain from judging the individual artwork in terms of its effects on the wider society – these *are* ultimately questions of human good.

If this account of what I have called the hypertextualized *Ulysses* is accurate, there may be sufficient reason to turn our attention elsewhere – not merely because it is grabbing the limelight and casting other worthy books into darkness, but because its cultural supremacy, and the scholarly efforts which reflect and promote that supremacy, have turned it into a text that confirms us in our satisfied certainties instead of one that startles and defies us and thus opens new avenues for thought and pleasure. It now reassures us of our place in what might otherwise seem a chaotic universe, or it provides a model of coherence to take refuge in, a satisfying structure where the details all make sense – or if they do not, we can be confident that one day they will, thanks to the tireless efforts of a world-wide band of scholars. In so doing, *Ulysses* works in concert with the globalizing tendencies of international capital, which create a spurious sense of rich complexity by reducing differences and distinctions. Even readers who are out of sympathy with its non-linear, highly mediated narrative and stylistic procedures, such as Bersani, respond to it not as a profound challenge to their assumptions and beliefs but, thanks to the availability of a mass of helpful criticism, as a dismissable intellectual exercise, smugly sure of its honoured place in the world.[35]

---

[35] One might, however, set against Bersani's response Derrida's rather similar account of the encyclopedic ambitions of *Ulysses*, which – for Derrida – are not productive of self-satisfaction but of the profoundest anxiety, no less profound for its inseparability from the laughter which the book generates and which Bersani, surprisingly, makes little of; see 'Two Words for Joyce' and 'Ulysses Gramophone'.

To take up the specific charge made by Bersani: does *Ulysses* make an implicit claim about the redemptive power of art? Of *Ulysses* in 1922 (and I hope it's clear by now that I'm not talking about different editions) the answer seems to be clearly 'no': in the very excesses of its cultural ambition, its gargantuan appetite for the fragmented output of Western cultural production at every level, its playful disregard of deep-seated assumptions about narrative, representation, and truth, it overwhelmed and intimidated the reader. Of *Ulysses* in 2000 I'm not so sure: I'm not certain that it offers to redeem the failings in our culture, but it may be all too easy to read it as offering a reassurance that those failings are of no great concern. If the intra-cultural standards by which we judge a work include an openness to the future that registers as unassimilable otherness, an alterity that demands change on our part – and I would argue that they must – then *Ulysses* no longer deserves the centrality which it rightly achieved when it first made its astonishing appearance.

Of course this is only one possible outlook for *Ulysses*. In my own writing on Joyce's work I have tried to preserve, or rather find new ways of producing, its difficulty and strangeness, its resistance to what is habitual and shallow in our cultural practices, and a number of others are continuing to work valuably in this vein – though it must be said that there are now other texts and other writers who lend themselves more fully to this project (one of whom, as Bersani appreciates, is Beckett). The future may hold new modes of response to Joyce which will transform his works into challenges once more. [36] Criticism and literary history that, rather than focusing on Joyce, examines his work in the context of its time (including the context of Ireland's colonial subjection) may continue to throw up fresh and provocative insights. [37] The very magnitude of the encyclopedic Joycean hypertext can itself be unsettling, as Derrida has remarked, [38] and it may be possible to produce a hypermedia version of *Ulysses* that is anything but reassuring – one that revives, in new ways, the provocations and disturbances of the original publication. That there are two such projects in progress is all to the

[36] Although most of the work being done on Joyce's notebooks and other draft material is continuous with the grand exegetical project that dominated Joyce criticism in the twentieth century, some of it has had the very different aim of defamiliarizing the published text and raising fresh questions about what it means to 'read Joyce' – notably the ITEM group in Paris.

[37] See my comments at the end of the introduction.

[38] In 'Two Words for Joyce', Derrida describes the discomfort of inhabiting Joyce's memory, 'which is henceforth greater than all your finite memory can, in a single instant or a single vocable, gather up of cultures, languages, mythologies, religions, philosophies, sciences, history of mind and of literatures' (147). He continues: 'I don't know if you can like that, without resentment and jealousy.'

good, in reducing the risk of monumentality and in demonstrating, by the inevitable differences between the two productions, the contingency and incompleteness at work in even the most ambitious critical projects. There is also a growing hyperspatial Joyce presence on the World Wide Web, made up of a number of institutional and personal websites, each with links to other sites and to an array of Joycean and non-Joycean material. This network, in its lack of a single directorial will, its constant-ly evolving content and reach, the potential unreliability or irrelevance of its information, the absence of a centre or boundary, and in the consequent demands it makes upon the user as a creative, ingenious, energetic participant is perhaps more likely to keep the Joycean spirit alive in the third millennium than the CD-ROMs or DVDs issued by university presses.

And we still have the challenge of *Finnegans Wake* – one can imagine Joyce, having just completed *Ulysses*, foreseeing the day when it would no longer make almost impossible demands on the reader, and immedi-ately setting to work on the book that would, without question, keep us baffled into the next millennium. We have no shortage of reference texts and guides to help us with the *Wake*, but as anyone who has wrestled with a single page knows, these leave unaddressed more problems than they solve. This is not to deny the extremely valuable work of exegesis that has helped to make Joyce's last book more readable than could have been imagined fifty years ago, nor the effects of cultural develop-ments – the tangle of aesthetic, critical, and political conditions that we term 'postmodernism' – that have rendered it less freakishly isolated. The fact remains that the *Wake* is largely unassimilated, and the day when our exegetical and theoretical efforts are equal to its demands will not dawn soon. If such a consummation ever were to be achieved, our cultural map, as I have argued elsewhere, would have to have been completely redrawn.[39]

It is important to note, too, that what I am saying in no way implies that the reading or teaching of *Ulysses* should abate: new readers, in or out of school, are much more likely to experience a text akin to the one that was read in 1922 or 1961, in spite of the fact that many of Joyce's technical innovations have now found their way into the aesthetic practices of popular culture. It does imply, however, that the best teachers (like the best critics) are those who find ways to sustain the

[39] See chapter 7 ('Unpacking the Portmanteau, or, Who's Afraid of *Finnegans Wake?*') and chapter 8 ('Deconstructing Digression: The Backbone of *Finnegans Wake* and the Margins of Culture') of *Peculiar Language*.

disruptive force of *Ulysses* even while they do their necessary work of explaining and demystifying.

In the end, of course, the decision to stop writing about a particular author can only be an individual one, and it is made for a host of reasons, many of which have little to do with the perceived quality or importance of the writer in question or the contemporary state of culture. I may absent myself from the next wave of Joyce criticism, but I have no expectation that the flood will abate in the near future, and I am confident that outstanding books and articles will continue to appear within it, perhaps even some that address the questions raised in this chapter. If the new millennium brings more serious critiques of *Ulysses*, and they are taken more seriously, that will be all to the good; if the Joyce industry finds itself growing leaner (if not meaner), there will be some worthwhile beneficiaries; but whatever changes we see, it is hard to imagine that Joyce won't, once again, have the last laugh.

Works cited

Aarsleff, Hans. *The Study of Language in England, 1780–1860*. Minneapolis: University of Minnesota Press, 1983.

Atherton, James S. *The Books at the Wake: A Study of Literary Allusions in James Joyce's 'Finnegans Wake'*. New York: Viking Press, 1959.

Attridge, Derek. 'Countlessness of Livestories: Narrativity in *Finnegans Wake*'. Beja and Norris, eds., *Joyce in the Hibernian Metropolis*, 290–6.

'Criticism's Wake'. Benstock, ed., *James Joyce: The Augmented Ninth*, 80–7.

'Finnegans Awake, or the Dream of Interpretation'. *James Joyce Quarterly* 27 (1989): 11–29.

'Innovation, Literature, Ethics: Relating to the Other'. *PMLA* 114 (1999): 20–31.

'Joyce and the Ideology of Character'. Benstock, ed., *James Joyce: The Augmented Ninth*, 152–7.

'Joyce, Jameson, and the Text of History'. *Scribble 1: genèse des textes* (La Revue des Lettres Modernes, Série James Joyce, 1), ed. Claude Jacquet. Paris: Minard, 1988. 185–93.

'Joyce's "Other."' *James Joyce Literary Supplement* 2.2 (fall 1988): 7–8.

'Molly's Flow: The Writing of "Penelope" and the Question of Women's Language'. *Feminist Readings of Joyce*, ed. Ellen Carol Jones, Special issue of *Modern Fiction Studies* 35 (1989): 543–65.

'Oppressive Silence: J. M. Coetzee's *Foe* and the Politics of the Canon'. *Decolonizing Tradition: New Views of 20th-Century 'British' Literature*. Ed. Karen Lawrence. Urbana: University of Illinois Press, 1991. 212–38.

Peculiar Language: Literature as Difference from the Renaissance to James Joyce. Ithaca: Cornell University Press, 1988.

'The Postmodernity of Joyce: Chance, Coincidence, and the Reader'. *Joyce Studies Annual* (1995): 10–18.

'Remembering Berni Benstock'. *Hypermedia Joyce Studies* 1.1 (summer 1995).

The Rhythms of English Poetry. Harlow: Longman, 1982.

'Singularities, Responsibilities: Derrida, Deconstruction, and Literary Criticism'. *Critical Encounters: Reference and Responsibility in Deconstructive Writing*. Ed. Cathy Caruth and Deborah Esch. New Brunswick: Rutgers University Press, 1994. 106–26.

'Theories of Popular Culture'. Kershner, ed., *Joyce and Popular Culture*, 23–6.

'Trusting the Other: Ethics and Politics in J. M. Coetzee's *Age of Iron*'. *The Writings of J. M. Coetzee*, ed. Michael Valdez Moses. Special issue of *South Atlantic Quarterly* 93 (1994): 59–82.

'The *Wake*'s Confounded Language'. *Coping with Joyce: Essays from the Copenhagen Symposium*. Ed. Morris Beja and Shari Benstock. Columbus: Ohio State University Press, 1989. 2628.

Attridge, Derek, ed. *The Cambridge Companion to James Joyce*. Cambridge: Cambridge University Press, 1990.

Attridge, Derek, and Daniel Ferrer, eds. *Post-structuralist Joyce: Essays from the French*. Cambridge: Cambridge University Press, 1984.

Attridge, Derek, and Rosemary Jolly, eds. *Writing South Africa: Literature, Apartheid, and Democracy, 1970–1995*. Cambridge: Cambridge University Press, 1998.

Aubert, Jacques, and Maria Jolas. *Joyce & Paris 1902 . . . 1920–1940 . . . 1975: Papers from the Fifth International James Joyce Symposium*. Paris: Editions du CNRS/Villeneuve-d'Asq; Publications de l'Université de Lille 3, 1979.

Ayto, John, and John Simpson. *The Oxford Dictionary of Modern Slang*. Oxford: Oxford University Press, 1992.

Baldick, Chris. *The Social Mission of English Criticism, 1848–1932*. Oxford: Oxford University Press, 1983.

Barthes, Roland. 'Introduction to the Structural Analysis of Narratives'. *The Semiotic Challenge*. Trans. Richard Howard. New York: Hill & Wang, 1988.

Beck, Warren. *Joyce's 'Dubliners': Substance, Vision, and Art*. Durham, NC: Duke University Press, 1969.

Beckett, Samuel, *et al. Our Exagmination Round His Factification for Incamination of Work in Progress*. Paris: Shakespeare & Co., 1929.

Begnal, Michael H. *Dreamscheme: Narrative and Voice in 'Finnegans Wake'*. Syracuse: Syracuse University Press, 1988.

'The Language of *Finnegans Wake*'. Bowen and Carens, eds., *A Companion to Joyce Studies*, 633–46.

Beja, Morris. 'Approaching Joyce with an Attitude'. Beja and Norris, eds., *Joyce in the Hibernian Metropolis*, 71–5.

Beja, Morris, *et al. James Joyce: The Centennial Symposium*. Urbana: University of Illinois Press, 1986.

Beja, Morris, and David Norris, eds. *Joyce in the Hibernian Metropolis: Essays*. Columbus: Ohio State University Press, 1996.

Bennington, Geoffrey. *Lyotard: Writing the Event*. New York: Columbia University Press, 1988.

Benstock, Bernard. *James Joyce*. New York: Frederick Ungar, 1985.

Joyce-Again's Wake: An Analysis of 'Finnegans Wake'. Seattle: University of Washington Press, 1965.

Narrative Con/Texts in 'Ulysses'. London: Macmillan, 1991.

Benstock, Bernard, ed. *James Joyce: The Augmented Ninth*. Proceedings of the Ninth International James Joyce Symposium, Frankfurt 1984. Syracuse: Syracuse University Press, 1988.

Benstock, Bernard, and Shari Benstock. *Who's He When He's at Home: A James Joyce Directory*. Urbana: University of Illinois Press, 1980.

Bersani, Leo. *The Culture of Redemption*. Cambridge, MA: Harvard University Press, 1990.

Bishop, John. *Joyce's Book of the Dark: 'Finnegans Wake'*. Madison: University of Wisconsin Press, 1986.

'Reading *Finnegans Wake* "in Context": 23.16–24.30'. *A Collideorscape of Joyce: Festchrift for Fritz Senn*. Ed. Ruth Frehner and Ursula Zeller. Dublin: Lilliput Press, 1998. 231–58.

Blamires, Harry. *The Bloomsday Book: A Guide Through Joyce's 'Ulysses'*. London: Methuen, 1966.

Studying James Joyce. Harlow/Beirut: Longman/York Press, 1987.

Boheemen, Christine van. *The Novel as Family Romance: Language, Gender, and Authority from Fielding to Joyce*. Ithaca: Cornell University Press, 1987.

Bolt, Sydney. *A Preface to James Joyce*. Harlow: Longman, 1981.

Bowen, Zack, and James F. Carens, eds. *A Companion to Joyce Studies*. Westport, CT: Greenwood Press, 1984.

Briggs, Austin. 'Rebecca West vs. James Joyce, Samuel Beckett, and William Carlos Williams'. Beja and Norris, eds., *Joyce in the Hibernian Metropolis*. 83–102.

Brockman, William S. 'Composite Portraits'. *James Joyce Quarterly* 43 (1997): 365–80.

Brown, Richard. *James Joyce and Sexuality*. Cambridge: Cambridge University Press, 1985.

Budgen, Frank. *James Joyce and the Making of 'Ulysses'*. 1934. London: Oxford University Press, 1972.

'Resurrection'. *Twelve and a Tilly: Essays on the Twenty-Fifth Anniversary of 'Finnegans Wake'*. Ed. Jack P. Dalton and Clive Hart. London: Faber & Faber, 1966. 11–15.

Burgess, Anthony. *Here Comes Everybody: An Introduction to James Joyce for the Ordinary Reader*. London: Faber & Faber, 1965.

Joysprick: An Introduction to the Language of James Joyce. London: André Deutsch, 1973.

Cameron, Deborah. *Feminism and Linguistic Theory*. London: Macmillan, 1985.

Campbell, Joseph and Henry Morton Robinson. *A Skeleton Key to 'Finnegans Wake'*. New York: Harcourt, Brace & Co., 1944.

Card, James Van Dyck. *An Anatomy of 'Penelope'*. Rutherford, NJ: Fairleigh Dickinson University Press, 1984.

Carens, James F. '*A Portrait of the Artist as a Young Man*'. Bowen and Carens, eds., *A Companion to Joyce Studies*, 255–359.

Cheng, Vincent J. *Joyce, Race, and Empire*. Cambridge: Cambridge University Press, 1995.

Cixous, Hélène. 'The Character of "Character"'. *New Literary History* 5 (1974): 383–402.

'The Laugh of the Medusa'. *New French Feminisms: An Anthology*. Ed. Elaine

Marks and Isabelle de Courtivron. Brighton: Harvester Press, 1981. 245–64.

Prénoms de personne. Paris: Editions du Seuil, 1974.

Coates, Jennifer. *Women, Men, and Language: A Sociolinguistic Account of Sex Differences in Language.* Harlow: Longman, 1986.

Colum, Padraic. Preface to James Joyce, *Anna Livia Plurabelle.* New York: Crosby Gaige, 1928.

Connor, Steven. *Theory and Cultural Value.* Oxford: Blackwell, 1992.

Deane, Seamus. *Celtic Revivals.* London: Faber & Faber, 1985.

Strange Country: Modernity and Nationhood in Irish Writing Since 1790. Oxford: Clarendon Press, 1997.

Deane, Seamus, ed. *Nationalism, Colonialism, and Literature.* Minneapolis: University of Minnesota Press, 1990.

Deming, Robert H., ed. *James Joyce: The Critical Heritage.* 2 vols. London: Routledge & Kegan Paul, 1970.

Derrida, Jacques. *Acts of Literature.* Ed. Derek Attridge. New York: Routledge, 1992.

'Aphorism Countertime'. Derrida, *Acts of Literature*, 414–33.

Dissemination. Trans. Barbara Johnson. Chicago: University of Chicago Press, 1981.

'Force of Law: The "Mystical Foundation of Authority"'. *Deconstruction and the Possibility of Justice.* Ed. Drucilla Cornell, Michel Rosenfeld, and David Gray Carlson. London: Routledge, 1992. 3–67.

The Gift of Death. Trans. David Wills. Chicago: University of Chicago Press, 1995.

Glas. Trans. John P. Leavey, Jr., and Richard Rand. Lincoln: University of Nebraska Press, 1986.

Limited Inc. Ed. Gerald Graff. Trans. Samuel Weber and Jeffrey Mehlman. Evanston: Northwestern University Press, 1988.

Margins of Philosophy. Trans. Alan Bass. Chicago: University of Chicago Press, 1982.

'My Chances/*Mes Chances*: A Rendezvous with Some Epicurean Stereophonies'. *Taking Chances: Derrida, Psychoanalysis, and Literature.* Ed. Joseph H. Smith and William Kerrigan. Baltimore: Johns Hopkins University Press, 1984. 1–32.

'Psyche: Invention of the Other'. Derrida, *Acts of Literature*, 310–43.

'Telepathy'. *Oxford Literary Review* 10 (1988): 3–41.

'Des Tours de Babel'. *Difference in Translation.* Ed. Joseph F. Graham. Ithaca: Cornell University Press, 1985. 165–207.

'Two Words for Joyce'. Attridge and Ferrer, eds., *Post-structuralist Joyce*, 145–59.

'Ulysses Gramophone: Hear Say Yes in Joyce'. Derrida, *Acts of Literature*, 253–309.

'Women in the Beehive: A Seminar'. *Men in Feminism.* Ed. Alice Jardine and

Paul Smith. New York: Methuen, 1987. 189–203.

Derrida, Jacques, *et al.* 'Table ronde sur la traduction'. *L'oreille de l'autre: otobiographies, transferts, traductions: textes et débats avec Jacques Derrida.* Ed. Claude Lévesque and Christie V. McDonald. Montreal: VLB Editeur, 1982. 123–212.

Derrida, Jacques, and Christie V. McDonald. 'Choreographies' (interview). *Diacritics* 12.2 (summer 1982): 66–76.

Devlin, Kimberly. *Wandering and Return in 'Finnegans Wake': An Integrative Approach to Joyce's Fictions.* Princeton: Princeton University Press, 1991.

DiBernard, Barbara. 'Technique in *Finnegans Wake*'. Bowen and Carens, *A Companion to Joyce Studies*, 647–85.

Donoghue, Denis. 'Is There a Case Against *Ulysses?*' *Joyce in Context.* Ed. Vincent J. Cheng and Timothy Martin. Cambridge: Cambridge University Press, 1992. 19–39.

Dowling, Linda. *Language and Decadence in the Victorian Fin de Siècle.* Princeton: Princeton University Press, 1986.

Downing, Gregory M. 'Richard Chenevix Trench and Joyce's Historical Study of Words'. *Joyce Studies Annual* 9 (1998): 37–68.

Duffy, Enda. *The Subaltern 'Ulysses'.* London: Routledge, 1995.

Eagleton, Terry. *Heathcliff and the Great Hunger: Studies in Irish Culture.* London: Verso, 1995.

Ellmann, Maud. 'Disremembering Dedalus: *A Portrait of the Artist as a Young Man'. Untying the Text: A Post-structuralist Reader.* Ed. Robert Young. London: Routledge, 1981. 189–206.

'Polytropic Man: Paternity, Identity and Naming in *The Odyssey* and *A Portrait of the Artist as a Young Man*'. MacCabe, ed., *James Joyce: New Perspectives*, 73–104.

'To Sing or to Sign'. Beja *et al.*, eds., *James Joyce*, 66–9.

Ellmann, Richard. 'Backgrounds of "The Dead"'. *Kenyon Review* 20 (1958): 507–28.

The Consciousness of Joyce. Oxford and New York: Oxford University Press, 1977.

James Joyce. Revised edition. Oxford and New York: Oxford University Press, 1982.

Ulysses on the Liffey. London: Faber & Faber, 1972.

Fairhall, James. *James Joyce and the Question of History.* Cambridge: Cambridge University Press, 1993.

Ferrer, Daniel. 'Echo or Narcissus?' Beja *et al.*, eds., *James Joyce*, 70–5.

'The Freudful Couchmare of ∧ d: Joyce's Notes on Freud and the Composition of Chapter XVI of *Finnegans Wake*'. *James Joyce Quarterly* 22 (1985): 367–82.

Fish, Stanley. *Is There a Text in This Class? The Authority of Interpretive Communities.* Cambridge, MA: Harvard University Press, 1980.

French, Marilyn. *The Book as World: James Joyce's 'Ulysses'.* Cambridge, MA: Harvard University Press, 1976.

Freud, Sigmund. *The Interpretation of Dreams*. 1900. Trans. James Strachey. Harmondsworth: Penguin, 1976.

    Jokes and Their Relation to the Unconscious. 1901. Trans. James Strachey. Harmondsworth: Penguin, 1976.

    The Psychopathology of Everyday Life. 1905. Trans. James Strachey. Harmondsworth: Penguin, 1975.

Froula, Christine. *Modernism's Body: Sex, Culture, and Joyce*. New York: Columbia University Press, 1996.

Frye, Northrop. *Anatomy of Criticism: Four Essays*. Princeton: Princeton University Press, 1957.

Gabler, Hans Walter. 'Narrative Rereadings: Some Remarks on "Proteus", "Circe" and "Penelope"'. Jacquet, ed., *'Scribble' 1*, 57–68.

    'The Seven Lost Years of *A Portrait of the Artist as a Young Man*'. *Approaches to Joyce's 'Portrait': Ten Essays*. Ed. Thomas F. Staley and Bernard Benstock. Pittsburgh: University of Pittsburgh Press, 1976. 25–60.

Garrett, Peter K., ed. *Twentieth-century Interpretations of 'Dubliners': A Collection of Critical Essays*. Englewood Cliffs, NJ: Prentice-Hall, 1968.

Gibbons, Luke. '"Have You No Homes to Go To?": Joyce and the Politics of Paralysis'. Howes and Attridge, eds., *Semicolonial Joyce*. Cambridge: Cambridge University Press, 2000.

    Transformations in Irish Culture. Cork: Cork University Press, 1996.

Gilbert, Sandra M. and Susan Gubar. 'Sexual Linguistics: Gender, Language, Sexuality'. *New Literary History* 16 (1985): 515–43.

    The War of the Words. Vol. 1 of *No Man's Land: The Place of the Woman Writer in the Twentieth Century*. New Haven: Yale University Press, 1988.

Gilbert, Stuart. *James Joyce's 'Ulysses': A Study*. 1930. New York: Random House, 1955.

Givens, Seon, ed. *James Joyce: Two Decades of Criticism*. New York: Vanguard Press, 1948.

Glasheen, Adaline. *Third Census of Finnegans Wake: An Index of the Characters and Their Roles*. Berkeley: University of California Press, 1977.

Goldberg, S. L. *The Classical Temper: A Study of Joyce's 'Ulysses'*. London: Chatto & Windus, 1961.

    Joyce. Writers and Critics Series. Edinburgh: Oliver & Boyd, 1962.

Gordon, John. *'Finnegans Wake': A Plot Summary*. Syracuse, NY: Syracuse University Press, 1986.

Gottfried, Roy K. *The Art of Joyce's Syntax in 'Ulysses'*. London: Macmillan, 1980.

Gross, John. *Joyce*. London: Fontana/Collins, 1971.

Grossberg, Lawrence, Cary Nelson, and Paula Treichler, eds. *Cultural Studies*. New York: Routledge, 1992.

Hart, Clive. 'Against Joyceanism'. *James Joyce Broadsheet* (16 February 1985): 1.

Hayman, David. 'The Fractured Portrait'. *Myriadminded Man: Jottings on Joyce*. Ed. Rosa Maria Bosinelli, Paola Pugliatti, and Romana Zacchi. Bologna: Editrice Bologna, 1986. 79–88.

    Joyce et Mallarmé. 2 vols. Paris: Lettres Modernes, 1956.

Ulysses: The Mechanics of Meaning. Revised edition. Madison: University of Wisconsin Press, 1982.

Heath, Stephen. 'Male Feminism'. *Men in Feminism.* Ed. Alice Jardine and Paul Smith. New York: Methuen, 1987. 1–32.

'Modern Literary Theory'. *Critical Quarterly* 31.2 (summer 1989): 35–49.

'Le Père Noël'. *October* 26 (fall 1983): 79–99.

Henke, Suzette A. *Joyce's Moraculous Sindbook: A Study of 'Ulysses'.* Columbus: Ohio State University Press, 1978.

Herr, Cheryl. *Joyce's Anatomy of Culture.* Urbana: University of Illinois Press, 1986.

Hofheinz, Thomas C. *Joyce and the Invention of Irish History: 'Finnegans Wake' in Context.* Cambridge: Cambridge University Press, 1995.

Howes, Marjorie, and Derek Attridge, eds. *Semicolonial Joyce.* Cambridge: Cambridge University Press, 2000.

Horkheimer, Max, and Theodor W. Adorno. *Dialectic of Enlightenment.* Trans. John Cumming. London: Allen Lane, 1973.

Humphrey, Robert. *Stream of Consciousness in the Modern Novel.* Berkeley: University of California Press, 1954.

Hutchinson, Chris. 'The Act of Narration: A Critical Survey of Some Speech-Act Theories of Narrative Discourse'. *Journal of Literary Semantics* 13.1 (1984): 3–34.

Jacquet, Claude, ed. *'Scribble' 1: genèse des textes.* La Revue des Lettres Modernes, Série James Joyce 1. Paris: Minard, 1988.

Jameson, Fredric. *Fables of Aggression: Wyndham Lewis, the Modernist as Fascist.* Berkeley: University of California Press, 1979.

The Political Unconscious: Narrative as a Socially Symbolic Act. Ithaca: Cornell University Press, 1981.

'*Ulysses* in History'. *James Joyce and Modern Literature.* Ed. W. J. McCormack and Alistair Stead. London: Routledge & Kegan Paul, 1982. 126–41.

Joyce, James. *Anna Livia Plurabelle.* Preface by Padraic Colum. New York: Crosby Gaige, 1928.

Dubliners. Ed. Hans Walter Gabler. New York: Garland, 1993.

Dubliners: Text, Criticism, and Notes. Viking Critical Library. Ed. Robert Scholes and A. Walton Litz. New York: Viking Press, 1969.

Finnegans Wake. 1939. London: Faber & Faber, 1975.

Letters. Ed. Stuart Gilbert and Richard Ellmann. 3 vols. New York: Viking Press, 1957–66.

Oeuvres, 1. Ed. Jacques Aubert. Paris: Gallimard, 1982.

Poems and Shorter Writings. Ed. Richard Ellmann, A. Walton Litz, and John Whittier-Ferguson. London: Faber & Faber, 1991.

A Portrait of the Artist as a Young Man. Ed. Hans Walter Gabler with Walter Hettche. New York: Garland, 1993.

A Portrait of the Artist as a Young Man. Case Studies in Contemporary Criticism. Ed. R. B. Kershner. Boston: Bedford Books, 1993.

Stephen Hero. Ed. Theodore Spencer, revised John J. Slocum and Herbert Cahoon. London: Jonathan Cape, 1956.

Tales Told of Shem and Shaun. Preface by C. K. Ogden. Paris: Black Sun Press, 1929.

Ulysses. Ed. Danis Rose. London: Picador, 1997.

Ulysses: A Critical and Synoptic Edition. Ed. Hans Walter Gabler with Wolfhard Steppe and Claus Melchior. 3 vols. 1984. 2nd impression. New York: Garland, 1986.

Ulysses: The Corrected Text. Ed. Hans Walter Gabler with Wolfhard Steppe and Claus Melchior. London: Bodley Head and Penguin, 1986.

Jung, Carl Gustav. '*Ulysses*: A Monologue'. *The Spirit in Man, Art, and Literature*. Trans. R. F. C. Hall. *Collected Works*, vol. 15. Princeton: Princeton University Press, 1953. 109–34.

Kenner, Hugh. *A Colder Eye: The Modern Irish Writers*. London: Allen Lane, 1983.

Dublin's Joyce. Chatto & Windus, 1955.

Joyce's Voices. London: Faber & Faber, 1978.

The Mechanic Muse. Oxford and New York: Oxford University Press, 1987.

'The *Portrait* in Perspective'. *Two Decades of Joyce Criticism*. Ed. Seon Givens. 2nd edn. New York: Vanguard Press, 1963. 132–74.

Ulysses. London: Allen & Unwin, 1980.

Kershner, R. B. *Joyce, Bakhtin, and Popular Culture: Chronicles of Disorder*. Chapel Hill: University of North Carolina Press, 1989.

Kershner, R. B., ed. *Joyce and Popular Culture*. Gainesville: University of Florida Press, 1996.

Kiberd, Declan. *Inventing Ireland: The Literature of the Modern Nation*. London: Jonathan Cape, 1995.

Kuhn, Thomas S. *The Structure of Scientific Revolutions*. Chicago: University of Chicago Press, 1962.

Lakoff, Robin. *Language and Woman's Place*. New York: Harper & Row, 1975.

Lamos, Colleen. 'James Joyce and the English Vice'. *Novel* 29 (1995): 19–31.

Laroque, François. 'Hallowe'en Customs in "Clay" – A Study of James Joyce's Use of Folklore in *Dubliners*'. *Cahiers victoriens & édouardiens* 14 (October 1981): 47–56.

Lawrence, D. H. *Selected Literary Criticism*, ed. Anthony Beal. London: Heinemann, 1955.

Lawrence, Karen. 'Joyce and Feminism'. Attridge, ed., *The Cambridge Companion to James Joyce*, 237–58.

The Odyssey of Style in 'Ulysses'. Princeton: Princeton University Press, 1981.

Leavis, F. R. *The Great Tradition: George Eliot, Henry James, Joseph Conrad*. London: Chatto & Windus, 1948.

'James Joyce and the "Revolution of the Word"'. *Scrutiny* 2 (1933): 193–201.

New Bearings on English Poetry. London: Chatto & Windus, 1932.

Revaluation: Tradition and Development in English Poetry. London: Chatto & Windus, 1936.

Philosophy Through the Looking-Glass: Language, Nonsense, Desire. London: Hutchinson, 1985.

Lecercle, Jean-Jacques. *Philosophy of Nonsense: The Intuitions of Victorian Nonsense Literature*. London: Routledge, 1994.

The Violence of Language. London: Routledge, 1990.

Leerssen, Joep. *Remembrance and Imagination: Patterns in the Historical and Literary Representation of Ireland in the Nineteenth Century*. Cork: Cork University Press, 1996.

Leonard, Garry, and Jennifer Wicke, eds. 'Joyce and Advertising'. Special issue of *James Joyce Quarterly* 30.2/31.1 (1993).

Levinas, Emmanuel. *Otherwise Than Being or Beyond Essence*. Trans. Alphonso Lingis. Pittsburgh: Duquesne University Press, 1998.

Totality and Infinity. Trans. Alphonso Lingis. Pittsburgh: Duquesne University Press, 1969.

Lewis, Percy Wyndham. *Time and Western Man*. London: Chatto, 1927.

Lloyd, David. *Anomalous States: Irish Writing and the Post-Colonial Moment*. Dublin: Lilliput Press, 1993.

Lukács, Georg. 'The Ideology of Modernism'. *The Meaning of Contemporary Realism*. Trans. John and Necker Mander. London: Merlin Press, 1963.

Lyotard, Jean-François. *The Postmodern Condition: A Report on Knowledge*. Trans. Geoff Bennington and Brian Massumi. Minneapolis: University of Minnesota Press, 1984.

MacCabe, Colin. *James Joyce and the Revolution of the Word*. London: Macmillan, 1979.

MacCabe, Colin, ed. *James Joyce: New Perspectives*. Brighton: Harvester, 1982.

McCarthy, Patrick. 'Structure and Meanings of *Finnegans Wake*'. Bowen and Carens, eds., *A Companion to Joyce Studies*, 559–632.

McConnell-Ginet, Sally, *et al.*, eds. *Women and Language in Literature and Society*. New York: Praeger, 1980.

McHale, Brian. *Constructing Postmodernism*. London: Routledge, 1992.

Postmodernist Fiction. London: Methuen, 1987.

McHugh, Roland. *The Sigla of 'Finnegans Wake'*. London: Edward Arnold, 1976.

Maddox, Brenda. *Nora: A Biography of Nora Joyce*. London: Hamish Hamilton, 1988.

Mahaffey, Vicki. 'Père-version and Im-mère-sion: Idealized Corruption in *A Portrait of the Artist as a Young Man* and *The Picture of Dorian Gray*'. *James Joyce Quarterly* 31 (1994): 189–206.

Manganiello, Dominic. *Joyce's Politics*. London: Routledge & Kegan Paul, 1980.

Milesi, Laurent. 'L'Idiome babélien de *Finnegans Wake*'. *Genèse de Babel: Joyce et la création*. Ed. Claude Jacquet. Paris: Editions du CNRS, 1985. 155–215.

Miller, J. Hillis. 'Ariachne's Broken Woof'. *Georgia Review* 31 (1977): 44–60.

Monk, Leland. *Standard Deviations: Chance and the Modern British Novel*. Stanford: Stanford University Press, 1993.

Moretti, Franco. 'The Long Goodbye: *Ulysses* and the End of Liberal Capitalism'. *Signs Taken for Wonders*. Revised edn. London: Verso, 1988. 182–208.

Mulhern, Francis. *The Moment of 'Scrutiny'*. London: New Left Books, 1979.

Nolan, Emer. *James Joyce and Nationalism*. London: Routledge, 1995.

Noon, S. J., William T. 'Joyce's "Clay": An Interpretation'. *College English* 17 (November 1955): 93–5.

Norris, Margot. 'The Critical History of *Finnegans Wake* and the *Finnegans Wake* of Historical Criticism'. *Joyce and the Subject of History*. Ed. Mark A. Wollaeger, Victor Luftig, and Robert Spoo. Ann Arbor: University of Michigan Press, 1996. 177–93.

    The Decentered Universe of 'Finnegans Wake'. Baltimore: Johns Hopkins University Press, 1976.

    Joyce's Web: The Social Unraveling of Modernism. Austin: University of Texas Press, 1992.

O'Connor, Frank. 'Work in Progress'. James Joyce, *Dubliners*. Ed. Robert Scholes and A. Walton Litz. Viking Critical Library. Harmondsworth: Penguin, 1976. 304–15.

Ogden, C. K. Preface to James Joyce, *Tales Told of Shem and Shaun: Three Fragments from Work in Progress*. Paris: Black Sun Press, 1929.

Ong, Walter J. *Fighting for Life: Contest, Sexuality, and Consciousness*. Ithaca: Cornell University Press, 1981.

Onions, C. T. *The Oxford Dictionary of English Etymology*. London: Oxford University Press, 1966.

Owens, Cóilín. '"Clay" (1): Irish Folklore'. *James Joyce Quarterly* 27 (1990): 337–52.

Paris, Jean. 'L'agonie du signe'. *Change* 11 (1972): 133–72.

Parrinder, Patrick. *James Joyce*. Cambridge: Cambridge University Press, 1984.

Partridge, Eric. *A Dictionary of Slang and Unconventional English*. 8th edition. Ed. Paul Beale. London: Routledge & Kegan Paul, 1984.

Peake, C. H. *James Joyce: The Citizen and the Artist*. London: Edward Arnold, 1977.

Pearce, Richard, ed. *Molly Blooms: A Polylogue on 'Penelope' and Cultural Studies*. Madison: University of Wisconsin Press, 1994.

Poirier, Richard. *The Renewal of Literature*. New York: Random House, 1987.

Polti, Georges. *The Thirty-Six Dramatic Situations*. Trans. Lucille Ray. Ridgewood: Editor Company, 1917.

Pope, Alexander. *The Poems*. Ed. John Butt. London: Routledge & Kegan Paul, 1965.

Potts, Willard, ed. *Portraits of the Artist in Exile: Recollections of James Joyce by Europeans*. Seattle: University of Washington Press, 1979.

Prince, Gerald. *A Dictionary of Narratology*. Lincoln: University of Nebraska Press, 1987.

Rabaté, Jean-Michel. *James Joyce, Authorized Reader*. Baltimore: Johns Hopkins University Press, 1991.

    'Lapsus ex machina'. Attridge and Ferrer, eds., *Post-structuralist Joyce*, 79–101.

    'Le nœud gordien de "Pénélope"'. Jacquet, ed., *'Scribble' 1*, 121–41.

Rasula, Jed. '*Finnegans Wake* and the Character of the Letter'. *James Joyce Quarterly* 34 (1997): 517–30.

Readings, Bill. *Introducing Lyotard: Art and Politics*. London: Routledge, 1991.

Rice, Thomas Jackson. *Joyce, Chaos and Complexity*. Urbana: University of Illinois Press, 1997.

Riquelme, John Paul. '*Stephen Hero, Dubliners,* and *A Portrait of the Artist as a Young Man*: Styles of Realism and Fantasy'. Attridge, ed., *The Cambridge Companion to James Joyce*, 103–30.

Royle, Nicholas. *Telepathy and Literature: Essays on the Reading Mind.* Oxford: Blackwell, 1991.

Saussure, Ferdinand de. *Course in General Linguistics.* Trans. Wade Baskin. Glasgow: Collins, 1959.

Scholes, Robert. '"Counterparts" and the Method of *Dubliners*'. James Joyce, *Dubliners.* Ed. Robert Scholes and A. Walton Litz. Viking Critical Library. Harmondsworth: Penguin, 1976. 379–87.

Scott, Bonnie Kime. *Joyce and Feminism.* Bloomington: University of Indiana Press, 1984.

Segall, Jeffrey. *Joyce in America: Cultural Politics and the Trials of 'Ulysses'.* Berkeley: University of California Press, 1993.

Senn, Fritz. 'Foreign Readings'. Senn, *Joyce's Dislocutions*, 41–4.

Joyce's Dislocutions: Essays on Reading as Translation. Ed. John Paul Riquelme. Baltimore: Johns Hopkins University Press, 1984.

'Righting *Ulysses*'. MacCabe, ed., *James Joyce: New Perspectives*, 3–28.

Shechner, Mark. *Joyce in Nighttown: A Psychoanalytic Inquiry into 'Ulysses'.* Berkeley: University of California Press, 1974.

Showalter, Elaine. *Sexual Anarchy: Gender and Culture at the 'Fin de Siècle'.* New York: Viking Press, 1990.

Spoo, Robert. *James Joyce and the Language of History: Dedalus's Nightmare.* Oxford and New York: Oxford University Press, 1994.

Steinberg, Erwin R. *The Stream of Consciousness and Beyond in 'Ulysses'.* Pittsburgh: University of Pittsburgh Press, 1973.

Taylor, Dennis. *Hardy's Literary Language and Victorian Philology.* Oxford: Oxford University Press, 1993.

Tennyson, Alfred, Lord. *Poems.* Ed. Christopher Ricks. Harlow: Longman, 1969.

Thorne, Tony. *Bloomsbury Dictionary of Contemporary Slang.* London: Bloomsbury, 1990.

Tindall, William York. *James Joyce, His Way of Interpreting the World.* New York: Scribner's Sons, 1950.

A Reader's Guide to James Joyce. London: Thames & Hudson, 1959.

Todorov, Tzvetan. *The Poetics of Prose.* Trans. Richard Howard. Ithaca: Cornell University Press, 1977.

Toynbee, Philip. 'A Study of James Joyce's *Ulysses*'. Givens, ed., *James Joyce: Two Decades of Criticism*, 243–84.

Unkeless, Elaine. 'The Conventional Molly Bloom'. *Women in Joyce.* Ed. Suzette Henke and Elaine Unkeless. Brighton: Harvester, 1982. 150–68.

Valente, Joseph. *James Joyce and the Problem of Justice: Negotiating Sexual and Colonial Difference.* Cambridge: Cambridge University Press, 1995.

'Thrilled by His Touch: Homosexual Panic and the Will to Artistry in *A Portrait of the Artist as a Young Man*'. Valente, ed., *Quare Joyce*, 47–75.

Valente, Joseph, ed. *Quare Joyce*. Ann Arbor: University of Michigan Press. 1998.

Vandevelde, Arthur W. 'De dromers en de Wake'. *Kruispunt* 85 (December 1982): 108–13.

Veeder, William. 'Children of the Night: Stevenson and Patriarchy'. *Dr Jekyll and Mr Hyde after One Hundred Years*. Ed. William Veeder and Gordon Hirsch. Chicago: University of Chicago Press, 1988. 107–60.

West, Rebecca. 'The Strange Case of James Joyce'. *The Bookman* 68.1 (September 1928): 9–23.

The Strange Necessity. London: Jonathan Cape, 1931.

Whittaker, Stephen. 'Joyce and Skeat'. *James Joyce Quarterly* 24 (1987): 177–92.

Williams, Raymond. *The English Novel from Dickens to Lawrence*. London: Chatto & Windus, 1970.

Politics and Letters: Interviews with New Left Review. London: New Left Books, 1979.

Williams, Trevor L. *Reading Joyce Politically*. Gainesville: University of Florida Press, 1997.

Wilson, Edmund. *Axel's Castle: A Study in the Imaginative Literature of 1870–1930*. 1931. Glasgow: Collins Fontana, 1961.

'The Dream of H. C. Earwicker'. *The New Republic* 91 (12 July 1939): 270–4.

'The Dream of H. C. Earwicker'. *The Wound and the Bow: Seven Studies in Literature*. Boston: Houghton Mifflin, 1941.

'H. C. Earwicker and Family'. *The New Republic* 91 (28 June 1939): 203–6.

'James Joyce'. *The New Republic* 61 (18 December 1929): 84–93.

'James Joyce'. *Axel's Castle*. New York: Scribner's Sons, 1931.

Letters on Literature and Politics, 1912–1972. Ed. Elena Wilson. New York: Farrar, Straus & Giroux, 1977.

Wirth-Nesher, Hana. 'Reading Joyce's City: Public Space, Self, and Gender in *Dubliners*'. Benstock, ed., *James Joyce: The Augmented Ninth*, 282–92.

Wollaeger, Mark, Victor Luftig, and Robert Spoo, eds. *Joyce and the Subject of History*. Ann Arbor: University of Michigan Press, 1996.

Young, Robert. 'The Language of Flow'. Beja *et al.*, eds., *James Joyce*, 89–92.

White Mythologies: Writing History and the West. London: Routledge, 1990.

Index